Katherine Kastler Young
(NOW)

The Clover Collection of Verse
FIRST EDITION – VOLUME TWO

EVELYN PETRY
Editor

The Clover Publishing Company, Washington, D. C. 20008
PRINTED IN THE UNITED STATES
OF AMERICA

Copyright 1969, C.P.Co.

LIBRARY OF CONGRESS CARD CATALOG NO. 68-59291

INTRODUCTION

In this Second Volume of Clover, we find nearly two-and-a-half times the number of new poems as in the First Volume, published November 25, 1968.

The interest of poetry buffs has bolstered our spirits while burning the midnight oil trying to keep abreast of the tide that never seems to ebb.

No one was more surprised (and pleased!) than we were to discover that word of the Clover Poetry Contest had somehow spread from the U.S.A. to places as far away as Australia—and not just an isolated instance.

A proposal to include the list of winners in a special section of this book seemed impossible at first, but the dedication of our staff to deliver the goods to the printer in time has paid off—especially well for the First Prize Winners who ended in a tie!

Volume III will be a book filled with prize-winning work!

A LETTER FROM THE EDITOR:

There is a never-ending source of amazement that pours out of our mail-bags. I shall forever be amazed at the number and diversity of people who are *really hooked* on poetry—both readin' and writin'.

Another amazing thing is the length of time it takes to put such a collection together into a book—the Living Showcase, we call it. Details involved go so far afield from usual thinking that the mind boggles when we see these pages and reflect on the incredible things that had to go on before!

With few exceptions, the poets in this beautiful volume have never been in print until now. And all but a few returned their proofs properly marked. Every now and then some tyro would decide to practically re-write the whole business. They could do themselves a real favor by looking up "editor" and "emend" in a good dictionary. Remember, the editing here is to help a poem get *in*, not stay *out*...

So ends the lesson for today. Oh, one more thing: a pen name sounds like a big deal when it's your own private property—but you're the only one who knows, unless you're already famous. Be careful how you hide your talent!

Evelyn Petry

Dedication

CONTENTS

TO A CURTIS NAMED GEORGE

To our
Associate Editor,
In Appreciation:

We know a young man with a good steady hand,
And a talent for setting up verses.
How for months he's been poring over work that is boring!
(With rare and inaudible curses).

He never complains and he never exclaims,
With his temperment under a cover;
But he recently stated (somewhat elated):
"I'm a father—and MarJo's a mother!"

So a Curtis named George made a future to forge,
With necessities somewhat pecunier;
And a verse in his name—and he'll like it the same
('Tho the verses were written for Jun-i-or!)

Ye Editor & Ye Publisher
(with no apologies to anyone)

POEMS

TO MY LADY EVELYN

I've never seen the meadow so green,
Or the golden sun so bright.

I never knew, before I had you,
How the stars *do* glisten at night.

I've never played such a lovely charade,
Where the heart and the soul make the rules—

And if I should lose, because of a ruse—
I'll know why we lovers are fools.

Cy (with all my love)

ROYAL WARRANT

My prince rides in on charger white
To tryst with me 'most every night.

He tells me of his deeds that day:
The dragons he set out to slay,
And vows undying love for me
And I vow back my loyalty.

I know he'll never let me down—
(we serve the *biggest* drinks in town!)

Betty Middledorf

5

AND IN THE BEGINNING

Down in the mud and slime of desolation
Mankind flounders and wallows about
Bound about with fogs of indecision
Clouds of unrest, disaster and doubt.

So has it been since time beginning
So will it always be
But through the fog a light shines briefly
And changes destiny.

Out of the mud and slime a man emerges
Tall and strong as a gnarled tree
He stands on his hind legs and shouts to the Heavens
Defying all of the powers that be.

And so as it was in the beginning
Life continues according to plan.
When everything else was finished
Out of the mud God made a man.

Martha H. Daniel

UNATTAINABLE SOUL

There's a depth in thee I cannot find
That stretches outward in your mind.
Your powers of will and strength of soul
Go down and down. And far below
That flimsy covering of yourself
There lies, an iron, soul-encasing shell
I cannot break; nor find the key
That would unlock your mind to me.

If a blazing summer-fire
Can light in you a fair desire,
Then I can melt the ice, in part,
The ice imprisoning your heart.
The depths I'll find and so shall reach
And nevermore will have to seek.

Barbara Jo Noyes

THE SINGLE STATE

Happy and carefree is the single state.
    Its rewards . . . its fulfillments are large and great.
With much to look forward . . . little to care
    makes this walk in life unfit for a pair.

With no one to ask or compromise with
    lends bachelorhood with an air of myth.
One dish to wash . . . one meal to cook
    allows girlie time for the fashion book.

Each apartment is furnished in excellent decor;
    rich taste radiates from the ceiling to floor.
When money runs short, and ends don't meet
    the substitute for caviar is a loaf of whole wheat.

Then suddenly one day you wake up to fact
    that in this life there's a definite lack.
You can't quite place it . . . it's all so vague.
    It haunts you over your toast and poached egg.

When all at once there's a chill in the air . . .
    these rewards—these fulfillments are so solitaire.
The conscious wakes up, and finally comes through
    it's time, and you're ready, to whisper "I do."

                                  Kathi Frank

ON OUR ANNIVERSARY

May the mood of flowers
in early spring, at dawn
repeat to you this day
the love which I have sworn

        G. Robert Crawford

                Stay together young lover
                Always have faith in each other
                There is always someone
                Who will try to break your heart
                But don't let that get you down
                Just remember I'm always around

                                  Curtis Douglas

TO MARY RUTH RZESZUT

When our Jeannie married Raymond,
Not a soul could have denounced it:
No one in town could recognize
The way the priest pronounced it!

And since that time came Anne,
With Andy close behind,
Plus Mary Ruth—a team that suits
Pawpaw and Nana fine.

J. Frank Schairer

ICE-WHITE SOUNDS THE WINTER

Listen!
Night-cold winter air,
    clear and ice thin
Shattered to pieces by sound
Like a crystal goblet breaking.
Heavy thick-ice trees
    crackle sharp and glassy
Echoing up and down the street.

Listen!
Winter-warm snowflakes
    soft and gentle
Drifting lazily to earth
Like white stars falling.
Big-flake muffled snow
    piling up all around
And covering the world in cotton-stuffed silence.

Cynthia L. Williams

CROCUS

The verses I read seem to me all the same—
God, Spring or Sex is the name of the game.

I guess in a way they're all the same thing—
So I'll stop writing verses and go for a fling
                    —Next Spring.

Sarah Ann Rapped

8

BOYS TODAY, MEN TOMORROW

I got you, you're dead, bang, bang
From backyards childish voices rang.
Imaginary game of war and soldier
Neighborhood pals played, in the sun of summer.
Twentyish, some younger, today their ages,
And a controversial war abroad rages.
To stop the aggression from the foe
These boys today, men tomorrow must go.
And be among the wounded, the counted dead
In the name of our country's pledge.

Little boys, in backyards of today,
Who imaginary war and soldier play:
When you reach your military age,
On what continent and what history page
Will record your destiny and fate—
Peace! —or nations in war and hate?

Mary M. VonFarra

THE GIFT OF HOPE

A temporary relief from despair
Hope . . .
A temporary feeling we share
Hope . . .
A temporary secureness based on belief
A temporary feeling often ending in grief
Hope . . .

Shirleen Thompson

YOUNG LOVE

It was a sparkling jewel
Without a collector's price
Whose value grew with each new day
And whose story it told
With glittering gems of wisdom—
Forgetting all the ugliness of the world
And shimmering with grandeur
Until it was dropped and shattered...
It was only glass.
Mary Etcheverry

9

JUST SUPPOSE

If you were a crow,
And I, a piece of corn;
No seeds would you sow;
No young would be born.

If you were a rat,
And I was the cheese;
You'd get big and fat,
From eating all you please.

Since you are a mouse,
And I am a cat;
You came in my house,
And that's the end of that.

Lulu McCallum

OF POETS

There are those
Who should write prose.

Florence Beck Unangst

THE CALL OF YORK HARBOR

To glimpse a lonely Sea Gull
Spread winged, motionless in flight,
To smell the briny ocean's salt
In swirling fog held tight.
To live but for a moment in
That silent world of white,
And hear again the fog horn's
Mournful warning through the night.
Grant me this poignant longing
Locked in memory's sweet sight.

Priscilla Wieland

SNOWFLAKES

The first few
were shy—
just hints of a grin.
Their fragile
frames danced lithely
about.
Then—becoming more
brave
they burst into laughter
pealing from hill to hill.
Their supple
bodies whirled round
and round
till slightly ashamed
they left
leaving their echo
to envelop all.

Deborah Rung

BEACON

Moon.
Weave me
a thread
so fine
and string
your silken net
through clouds
reflecting that
subtle glow
for wayward stars
and my dying
dreams.

Donald Foscue Modrall

BEHAVIOUR

We behave in society
With great propriety
Practise sobriety
To avoid notoriety
Speak with brevity
Absence of levity
State with clarity
Avoid hilarity
In matters of gravity

Joe Farber

POMEGRANATES

I opened summer's door
Silky and gentle;

I stepped through the doorway
Into her room . . .

I sat beneath her tree
And ate her fruit—

Winey and red . . .

Olga Wahlsten

SOMEWHERE, SOMEDAY, SOMEWAY

Somewhere in this world is the boy I will marry
Someday there will be a baby I will carry
Someway we will find our happiness
Somewhere there's a world for me with no sadness
Someday I'll have a home of my own
Someway I'll be a person well known
Someday to my children I will say
Somewhere, Someday, Someway

Marlene J. Hulmes

FRIENDSHIP

One day
sitting on the
metal blocks
in the schoolyard
a sandy-faced boy
with a colored bandaid
on his mercurochromed knee
held out his hand
to offer me
half a sticky dripping
peanut butter and marshmallow sandwich
in return for half
a freshly mayonnaised tuna.

Amy Klainer

ACCEPTANCE

If I were a bird
   Instead of a tree
I'd fly through the air
   Or go to the sea
But since I'm a tree
   And have to stand still
I'll just hold a nest
   For the whippoorwill

Roberta Ramsey

11

AUCTION

I recollect Samantha Jane
She left no will, poor thing.
In April damp with sobbin' rain
They held the auctioning.

First bids were on the ol' wood stove
That's where she baked them pies,
While Bill was pickin' half the grove
To fill the bin with spies.

The dishes went to ol' Maude Shad
I never liked Maude much.
That teapot I want mighty bad
To put on top my hutch.

Crocheted by hand, Jane's Sunday rug
I bought and glad I did.
When kinfolk git the callin' bug,
I may jest keep it hid.

Four-poster, solid oak, the bed
That welcomed bride and groom,
Went fer cents to the pedlar's shed
Fer his ol' dirty room.

She slaved too hard, Samantha Jane,
At makin' folks content,
But farmers biddin' in the rain
Fergit all sentiment.

Regina E. Gier

COOL IT

Remember, young ladies, when you wish
For a bird-in-the-hand 'stead of two in the bush—
With a bird in the hand you sometimes lose:
'Cause a bird in the hand can *ruin* your shoes!

Louise Swett

12

THE CLOAK THAT HIDES OUR HEAVEN

The weight of the world . . . its fullest scope, its
    slightest minutae,
Bears down heavily on restless shoulders.
To have glimpsed joy and freedom, dominion
    and peace,
Is now like the scent of fruits denied . . .
The more alluring for this awareness.

To run, to hide, to forget, to deny . . .
These are choices that do not exist, that are
    unreal.
So it is that we can only work to understand,
    to perceive,
And allow the rest to be revealed.

It is as always . . . one step at a time . . .
And no less so when the last step seems wrong,
    or even backward.
We can only love, only prove, in the way we
    know how, at this moment,
Hoping that all else is ripening within us for
    tomorrow's need.

For today, this is all;
But to know that the cloak that hides our
    heaven has no fibre,
And the dreams which really bind us, too,
Will have their day.

Bonnie B. Gibbs

SLAVERY

A brave little maid in her deep grave laid,
For her mean master made her work *Faster!*
On her head was a price, in her bed there were lice.

She had stood so fine on the platform line—
Now, a brave little maid in her deep grave laid.

Margaret Wiggins
Age 9

13

NEVER END MY WAY WITH YOU

Never end my way with you.
It cannot be too soon,
Nor can it be too late.
I have seen your face before
In every countless day I've lived.
I know the sound of all the words
That you will ever speak—
For I have said them all
And will surely say them all again.

Never end my way with you;
For I must have your breath in me.
And I must know your tears in my eyes,
Your heartbeat in my chest
Your song on my lips.
I must feel your sadness
And know your joy.

Never end my way with you—
For ever if there was today
Tomorrow must be, then.

Christopher Hobbs

OF CROCUS AND MEN

Oh, vanity, your heathen quest
For Easter finery be dressed . . .
Thusly, praise the golden calf
With beauty sought in your behalf.

Yet look upon the barren ground
With winter's blustery chill still found;
The crocus interrupts the sod,
Beautied by the hand of God.

Weep not that vanity be crushed . . .
And egotistic echoes hushed.
For finery can not disguise
Hypocrisy from Jesus' eyes.

JoAnne Jurich

14

PHILOSOPHY

Believe instead of doubting; smile, do not frown,
Put trust in your brother
    And "love one another"
For "love makes the world go round."

Give friendship instead of hatred;
Put joy where sorrow once reigned,
Give all of yourself and take not from another,
Give pleasure but never give pain.

Why fight when you can be peaceful?
Why condemn when you can forgive?
    When our paths drift astray, God shows us the way,
That our lives we may happier live.

Laurie Dykstra

A LOSS

I lost a part of my world today.
A love of mine is turning away.
For a few short years he needed me;
But it's fading now, I'll set him free.
Moments of pleasure, a little pain;
Days were of sunshine, a few of rain.
With prayers I'll wait to help should he fall,
He knows he need only turn and call.
Each way he turns, he'll find new faces.
Wealth he'll search for in far strange places.
Yes, part of my world drifted away;
My small son started to school today.

Loralee

TO SUSAN LYNN KENNON—

We know a lovely little girl
Now honest, and no foolin'
Her Mother is a red-head
And her Great Grandpa is Dulin—

I wonder, when she's big enough
To make her own appraisal—
If she will mark the prices up
(just like her Grandma Hazel)?

Lyn Petry

15

A SUNSET

As I look at the glorious sunset,
    Brightening the western sky,
I think no more beautiful colors
    Are seen by the human eye.

I watch as the sun slowly sinks now,
    And the beauty will soon fade away.
A hush and quiet is settling down,
    For this is the end of the day.

I see the shadows falling fast,
    And the locust is adding his song.
In the distance, a train is whistling low.
    It too will be gone 'ere long.

The voices of children are silent.
    They soon will be going to bed.
Lights are appearing in windows,
    Quietly now, their prayers are said.

And as I gaze in wonder
    At the sky so dark and bare.
I think it but a miracle
    That those colors once shone there.

Marie Gustafson

SEA SHELLS LOST

We wept for all the sea shells lost . . .
Picked broken fragments from the sand
And rued the carelessness of all
Who failed to cling to beauty's hand.

A few steps closer to the sea
We found a perfect blue-green shell,
Then as I bent to pick it up
The waves reclaimed it . . . just as well.

Roberta Mathis

16

THE OCEAN'S UNSEEN BEAUTY

I walk along the beach at night
As waves caress the shore
I feel a lift from daily care
For I have strength no more

I find a world of peace within
The scourge of the sea
But there is vigor in the skies
A challenge just for me

What makes me want to wander
In the magic trance of night
Why is there unseen beauty
In the midst of the ocean's fight

The ocean is relentless
It's a quiet world of peace
It has no sense of guidance
It knows not when to cease

The waves call out like a lonely soul
Denied its chance to live
Calling, calling, perhaps to me?
But what comfort can *I* give?

I'm an intruder, I guess I'll leave
The sea can be alone
I'll not return for now I know
It is happy in its home

So the ocean goes on laughing
As skies above behold
For the ocean's unseen beauty
Is a treasure more pure than gold

Linda S. Hauff

We cannot escape the summer sun.
And so,
    we must be caught up by it,
and relent to its intoxication,
Saving the burdens of our minds for the
    drearier
    days,
Letting our spirits run free
on the barefoot sands of summer.

Mary Osmond

UNSPOKEN

The moon through skeleton trees
Sifts cold silver on crystal snow
And night congeals winter's tears
That glitter on sloping eaves.
The wind strides from the north
Swirling a sequined cape
That outshines the stars;
Boisterous, bold, prying at our doors,
Puffing in loud, rude gusts
Down the smoky flues
And wailing in the inglenook.
Old winter tugs at the heart
With many unspoken things—
Long winters ago return in ancient rune,
In blackened glyphs on the chimney stones
To bring back forgotten dreams,
Lost loves and faded memories.
Outside, trees stand forlorn,
Bereft, lifting tremulous hands
In their wordless plea
To the cold white moon
And wind slinks away,
Stirring infinitesmal notes
From quivering prisms on kneeling shrubs.
Within, the heart surrenders to
Something not written in music,
Not sung in words.

Ruth B. Field

THE GARDENER POET

Jasmine by my window sill,
Mimosa by my gate,
Roses all around the rill,
Of my small estate.

Can my book of verse fulfill,
All I contemplate?
In search of beauty, will a quill,
Or trowel, be my fate?

Sophie Isabelle Michel

18

EARTHLY RHYTHMS

The earthly rhythms that bind us to
this world are so much that even a beggar
walks away, head low, not seeking to be
part of such, but rather like a scrap of
paper in the wind, blowing freely.

The leaf swings away from the wind
for the branch refuses to spring from the
root, clinging, clinging.

Last night the stars shone in their
normal splendor except for the falling
one which wanted to be free.

Why have these things happened?
You start to analyze—don't!

The earthly rhythm is ours; we have
finally unbound ourselves and flow freely
as the element of time; and time, too,
shall stop.

Lorraine H. Prehart Fourcaud

YOU ARE WHAT I GIVE

You are what I will give to this world, so please be
    good, for there is bad enough,
You are what I shall leave behind, and I shall be
    remembered through you
Good or bad it remains in your hands

You are the better part of myself, for I have
    nurtured, loved you, and given you the wisdom
    to choose right from wrong
You have come this far with my help, now you
    must help yourself and go the rest of the way
    alone,
And whatever you become is up to you,
For you are what I leave this world, you are my
    child

19   *Evea Vedder*

LINCOLN

Son of the South you were—
Tall moulded in Kentucky.
Now you are stepson of the North . . .
Become a prairie lawyer
With mind and body moulded by books and by the axe.
Now you are part of Illinois.
Here, in Illinois, lies your heart
Held, in death, by Nancy Hanks,
And, in life, by words.
Freedom, Charity and Love . . .
These are new words, or so they seem to some,
But they are not new, for you have always known them
As have other men before you.
Yet, there are some who will never know these words,
And, because of this tall man, your destiny is clear.
You will be Chief of State
And save this Union precious to your heart.
You will become immortal at far flung Gettysburg
Uttering words which men will carve in stone.

But there is one—
Now in his brief hour upon the stage—
Whose path will cross with yours;
And, when these paths cross, you then will die
And belong to the ages.
But the words will never die—
Even when all the Blue and Gray clad men are dead—
The words will live
And your name will come to be the meaning of the words.

Daniel A. Dugan

BIRTH

A delicate
fern slowly
pushed its
way through
the deep
dark soil
to the
tranquil
silence
of
the
dawning
day.

Wanda L. Dickson

AUTUMN

Autumn's crispness in the air,
A new season to behold,
Tumbling leaves fall everywhere,
Colors bright of red and gold.

Pumpkins, turkeys, cornstalks too,
Harvest time is here,
Beautiful Indian summer glow,
I love this time of year.

Anne Craig McLaughlin

20

MISSOURI

Scent of dogwood and sycamore trees;
Perfume of mimosa on the evening breeze.

Crickets chirping in the warm, still night;
Fireflies busy in their summer flight,

Heat of the day, then warmth of the eve
Beneath the stars—oh, the spell they weave!

Song of an op'ra, sung to be heard
By the heavens, the trees, an occasional bird.

'Squitoes a-lightin' as summer sun dims;
Squirrels cease their chattering romp
    through oak limbs.

Katydids singing, without them no sleep;
Such peace and serenity—mem'ries to keep.

The Big Dome faced on streets not too wide,
And watching the river, it guards it with pride.

And up on a hill, city lights down below,
Lovers might walk (they'd be whispering low)

For too many thoughts uttered, too many
    dreams spoken,
The night might awaken, the spell might be
    broken.

Patricia Laatsch

BEFORE AND AFTER

Time like the sluggish tortoise creeps
On feet uncertain of each step
But leaves behind upon its path
Bold certainties too quickly fled.

Norma Nance

THE TREE HOUSE

There's a sand-colored box in our crabapple tree.
It's taller than you and it's taller than me.
It's sand-colored because all its boards are not new.
It's higher than me and it's higher than you.

It's not finished yet—this retreat of our son's.
We wonder, sometimes: will it ever be done?

From here on the ground it looks strong, does not bend.
Someday he may just invite us to ascend—
In the dignified way—via ladder, like "kids"—
Not by bo'sun's chair method: his friends' way, and his.

But, until that time comes, we'll admire and respect
Independence, creativeness, need to reflect,
Which, undoubtedly, started his charged urge to build;
Making noise, using tools, tearing clothes, never still.

Harriet C. Meyerink

THE ATTIC

Hanging on by gossamer threads
The precarious threads of a cobweb;
Teetering there on the brink of a storm cloud,
Memories not quite forgotten.

The fog of a memory
Old and musty with the age of a lifetime;
Hoping to break through the opaque window
Of unconsciousness, trying to wake the sleeper
Within.

Linda Riggins

SPRING'S OFFERING

Musty smells, and damp, dank, rotted leaves
   Heaped against yet drowsy forest trees,
Make spongy cushions for chipmunks, squirrels and beetles
   And super-tones from forest breezes
Defrosts the groundhog's icy shadow,
   All, much a part of Spring's own lavish ransom
Should Winter's furry coat of snow,
   Remain no more!

Beatrice Rogers Papa

A FRIEND

If you could be a friend to all
While others turn away,
If you could wear a happy smile
While sad or feeling gay,
If you could be a cheerful soul
When everything goes wrong,
And help all others in despair
And always sing a song.

And take the blame for lots of things
You know you never did,
While others whisper of the things
You know you never said.
If you could shed a ray of hope
To those who need it so;
And set the streams of happiness
In other hearts to flow.

And yet to no one would complain
Or add on to their woe,
But pray to God to bless them all,
And feel secure also.
And while your friends speak ill of you
And hold themselves above
If only you could just return
Their evil with your love.

If you could only share your things
And ask nought in return,
If you could ever be like that
You've nothing else to learn,
For you would be a friend worthwhile
To seek, to win, to hold;
And now whoever reads these lines
Begin your life to mold.

Elsie Martin

Like Adam and Eve tasting the tree of
      knowledge,
Too much learning can weigh on the brain
      and force the physical man out of the
      garden,
Those whose eyes have been opened too
      far through the efforts of their minds
      will seek blindness again.

Susan Ralston

THE WONDERS OF HIS LOVE

When I look upon the meadow, and the
    mountain peak so high,
I think about the wonders of my Lord
    up in the sky;
I think about the flowers, and the love
    he gives to me,
Of the rainbow after showers and of
    life enternally.
    Though all the while I'm thinking of
      the blood He shed for me;
    Then I feel the love surrounding the
      dark shadows of the tree.

When I look upon the sparrows, while
    they fly around so free,
I think about the angels and the Lord
    I'm going to see;
I think about the sunshine, and the dew
    drops of the morn',
Of the stars up in the heavens, and the
    love for God I've sworn.
    But all the while I'm thinking of my
      sins as on I live;
    Then I feel the love surrounding, and
      I know He will forgive.

Then I think about my Savior, of my God
    up in the sky;
And I know that He'll be with me, as
    through my life I try.
He'll comfort me in trouble, He'll ease the
    ugly pain;
And He'll give me all the sunshine, to
    cover up the rain.
    If you don't know the comfort of my
      Lord and God above,
    Then give yourself this moment to
      the wonders of His love.

Linda G. Pyle

TRUE DEATH

We do not die
    when our hearts cease to beat,
'Tis when our dreams
    lie broken at our feet.

We do not die
    when eyelids close at last,
'Tis when our hope
    and faith and love are past.

Wilma Marshall

A TEXAS LAMENT

The Texas wild clover is blooming again
    With lavender blossoms fragrant and sweet;
Mesquites, lacy and silver, are around me
    And a carpet of green grass under my feet.

It dots the prairie with eye-filling beauty,
    That brings back a sad memory . . .
Of that lovely Spring in the long ago past,
    When you said farewell to me.

We stood together on a high rocky crag
    O'erhanging a deep ravine,
Gazing at the far horizon so blue . . .
    That danced with a shimmering sheen.

With cool Texas winds caressing our face,
    And cattle grazing silently near . . .
It seemed that with so much to live for
    Fate was proving too severe.

Out of my dreams you went faraway . . .
    Leaving me here so alone,
And now as I stand on the rocky crag
    The Texas wind seems to moan . . .

Helen M. Bell

DUSK

All lies in darkness
As the last sunbeam
Slowly stoops from age
Behind a fading
Mountain that has increased
In height since morning.

With the passing of the day,
Dusk has acquired wisdom,
A hint of pessimism,
Plus a trace of hesitation.

Marca Jean Campbell

THE DAWN

A breathless darkness reigns supreme;
A pensive quietness hovers round;
All nature slumbers peacefully;
Not ev'n the nightbirds make a sound.

The powers of night begin to wane;
Fair day is standing at the door
To seize the scepter which the night
Has oft' accorded her before.

A slight breeze begins to stir;
Caressingly it wakes the earth,
And whispers of the coming day—
The light with hope and joy and mirth.

From out the wide expanse of night,
The timid day appears in view,
So faint at first, then hastens in
A dazzling splendor to accrue.

And so the night has passed away,
Gone with its shadows, doubts and fears;
The dim uncertainties have fled
Into the peaceful bygone years.

Mamie Brown

TO CYNTHIA MAO

Cynthia is here at last—
Lots of future, but no past
(Unless you count the waiting time);
Now she and Agnes both are fine.

David Mao

A PSALM OF LIFE

Stalking there, the lurid figure,
Lurid, yet so ghastly bright.
Moving slowly in upon me,
In the bleak, dark, dead of night.

Moving slowly, ever slowly,
Till his gruesome form of dread
Hung in insolence above me
While he gazed upon my bed.

While he gazed with glaring glances,
Down upon me in my bed,
Cringing there beneath the covers,
Filling heart and soul with dread.

Never had I seen this person,
If a person he be called.
For his figure shown in lucents.
Spectors danced upon each wall.

As he stood and gazed upon me,
And I watched with fainting breath,
Slowly rose his bony finger,
This, thought I, is surely death.

Soon this mortal leaves forever,
Earth behind with no return.
With no monument for memory
Etched upon a Grecian urn.

Who will grieve now at my parting?
Only she who held me near.
Who alone will mark my passing?
Life! Whom I have held most dear.

Reginald Kirkland Smith

FOR WHOM TO MOURN?

Why should I weep for mankind,
When a tear shed
For a fallen bloom
Might moisten a seed,
Sprout a flower,
A fresh one—
To feed my hungry eyes,
And soothe an ailing heart.

Thomas Jay Tozer

A great weariness is come upon me.
A despair of all things futile in this world.
Society dictates and we must do those
    things that day by day inflict themselves
    upon our true desires.

I would break free
But I am weighted by the needs for
    standards that are not mine.
The years that pass, mark milestones on
    the path of forced conforming.
I would not . . . . . yet I do.
Weak will that hides itself in reason.

Broken bonds are yet my dream.
My dream is yet to live as I desire.
There is futility in reaching for these
    senseless goals when goals ought not to be.
Each day is day enough.
Each day is wasted in a life that sees no way
    that differs from another.

The worldly levels and insistence on a code
    for life are foreign to the one who lives
    for life alone.
My inward self rebels in vain
The circle tightens rein
And thoughts of wheeling free alone,
Fall withered to the ground.

Colleen Johnson

HEAVENLY FATHER

Heavenly Father, up above,
Please protect the land I love.
Watch over the grass, the trees, and
   the hills.
Watch over the farmer and the soil
   that he tills.
Watch over our leaders, the rich ,
   and the poor.
Help us help ourselves a little bit more.
But most of all, I pray, Lord please,
Watch over our boys as they fight
   overseas.
They're fighting for us that we may
   be free.
Watch over them all, I pray Lord
   to Thee.
Amen

Dawn Timmons

'Tis time to shed a tear
The birds are bidding a
   fond adieu
And traveling on to summers
   hiding place
With time and strength for
   shadows,
A tiny sparrow will greet
   its destination
The sunlight warms his tired
   wings
And sends a bit of rain to
   cool him
He travels swiftly through
   tiny drops of ice,
And shivers as he exits
   quickly.

Susan A. Rizzo

HARBINGER OF DAWN

There never is a better fling
Than meeting robyn in the spring . . .
   (Although we sometimes are distressed
   By robyn ruining our bed-rest.)

Steve Haggerty

AWAKENING

In blissful innocence I went when
But a child, from dawn 'til dark,
From hour to hour, from day to year,
Without the stark
Realities of life, I had no fear.

Then like Eve I ate the fruit one day
That taught me right from wrong,
O' Fateful day, O' Hateful day,
'Tis nothing more than growing up,
But such a plaintive song.

Temptation! Oh temptation! I fought
But then succumbed in weaker moments.
Until at last I ceased to fight,
And in my mind there was no doubt
But right was wrong and wrong was right.

Wrong won so many times on this battlefield
Of life, that for a while
I prayed to God that I might die,
But He was unaware, for He hears not
The voice of the Unborn Child.

Oh reckless youth! Where Sin is King
You fight for power and heights.
But you need not doom your soul.
No sin is unforgivable, if by
God's rules you make things right.

Now old am I with fevered brow
I know the bitter truth
O life, I realize that sinful Age
Is farther yet from heaven
Than was foolish Youth.

Mary Watson Lee

A FIREPLACE

What is a fireplace, you may ask
   A chore to do, a dirty task?
Wood to chop and carry in
   Logs to bring, or coal from a bin?
What is a fireplace, please ask me
   A place to dream, strange lands to see.
The Orient—a paradise isle
   Japanese blossoms, or Egypt's Nile—
The past, the present, the future too
   Dancing shadows of golden hue—
Laughter, tears, and memories dear
   Children, loved ones, seem so near.
Mountain streams and moonlight too
   Shimmering stars from out of the blue.
Raindrops glistening on the ground
   Ships at sea—then homeward bound.
Every time a different scene
   Every time a different dream—
So sit with me and we will trace
   The magic of—a fireplace.

'Ollie' Erdman

A QUESTION OF TIME

Tomorrow is now—and now is
Yesterday.
And tonight when I sleep,
It shall be a hundred
Yesterdays—now.
And when I wake,
It shall be tomorrow,
And maybe—yesterday.

Robin Stelzenmuller

SUMMER STORM ALLURE

A panorama Nature sends
She on the world unlashes,
Melodramatic comedy,
These stimulating splashes!

She growls and rocks and shakes the earth,
She crashes through taut silence
With loud, vibrating chords, with mirth
She pelts the earth with violence.

The lightning zigzags through the air,
Mad torrents hide sky's ceiling,
The wind is whistling with a blare,
Sends trees and plants all reeling.

And then as quickly does she cease,
This sly, wise-weathered Mother,
The world she ventures to appease
By changing to another.

The sun comes forth from 'hind the clouds,
For now the whimsy's o'er.
The summery world's again alight,
All Nature comes ashore.

The tonic air is bracing clear,
The birds their notes procure,
Sun-baked ground has rain-soaked tang,
Of summer storm allure.

Blanche Bowman

Crushes.
Silly, serious.
Bewildering, confusing, hurting.
Part of growing up.
Crushes.

Dee Dee Ferguson

MESSAGE FROM THE DOOMED

Looking out on my vast domain,
I wonder if things will ever be the same.
Will I ever, again, be happy,
As in my little shack I used to be.
If I had seeked joy instead of fortune,
Would my life be this miserable doom.
Oh, to the Lord, I do pray,
Each and every despicable day—
To make things as they used to be,
But in this place—God cannot hear me.
Back to my shack I would gladly go,
And my little garden, I'd gladly sow.
But, I know this cannot be,
This strife was brought on by only me.
To this world, I am doomed,
And by my evil have been consumed.
Now I wish I had followed God,
And down the devil's path had not trod.
Fortune and fame were my search,
And for them I did not wish to work.
So—I turned to that evil way,
And to all living, these words I say.
I plea with each one of you,
To be careful in what you do.
Be careful in what you wish for,
Upon that bright and shining star.
Be not selfish in any way,
And do not play all the day.
I leave you with one last thought,
Which I, regretfully, was not taught.
Work for your needs honestly,
Let happiness and peace, your motives be.
Do not seek self-glory, fortune, and fame,
And one day eternal life with God, you'll gain.
I say this to you from the depths of my heart,
As I wish my life over, I could start.
Torture is mine because God, I did fail,
And I am forever—doomed to hell.

Janet Laurie Hamm

Careless dumb cricket
fiddling to the marigolds —
ah, fat cat smiling!

Joline Standish

DEATH OF A VIRGIN

Two maiden ladies sat rocking, rocking
   Watching the traffic whizz by
'Round the house came a little hen running, running
   Wings spread and tail feathers high
A rooster sped after her panting, panting
   With a wicked gleam in his eye
Their course the maidens glance followed, followed
   From each breast rose a tremulous sigh
Around and around he chased her, chased her
   As the traffic kept whizzing by
Exhausted and frantic she paced him, paced him
   The maidens' fond hopes stood high
Then she broke to the traffic still running, running
   A flutter of feathers, a sigh
The watchers clasped hands so proudly, proudly
   You see? She would rather die!

Jane M. Haney

A WONDER

It came from heaven,
So precious and fair,
But it wasn't a stone,
Though glowing and rare,
It's eyes were like stars,
Twinkling in the night,
And it looked like an angel,
Who was tired from his flight.

It's hands were like roses,
Soft from the dew,
From the moment I saw it,
I guess that I knew,
This was a gift from God alone,
From the womb of a mother,
A *baby* had grown.

Carol Bergeron

THE STAR OF HOPE

Star of Hope and heavenly light,
Shining in the sky so bright,
While rejoicing angels sing,
Praises to our Lord and king.

While the shepherds watch their sheep,
And their lonely vigil keep,
Heavenly hosts all gathered around,
Fill the air with joyful sound.

Holy infant in the hay,
Sent to us on Christmas Day,
When the cattle standing near,
Wonder at the joy and cheer.

Shepherds come and humbly kneel,
Worship Him in happy zeal.
Wise men bring their presents rare,
Gladly then their gifts to share.

Come all people world around,
Worship with a joyful sound,
To the Saviour long foretold,
By the holy men of old.

W. M. Marquam

TIME OF THANKSGIVING

When glory of autumn fades away
And trees drop their mantles of red and gold,
Reaching their branches to skies so gray,
Sheltering their buds from winter's cold,
When fruits have ripened and grains gathered in,
And stored for our future need,
This is the time for our thanks to begin
To God who gave us the plentiful seed,
For friends and homes, the joy of living
But most of all for sharing and giving.

M. Elizabeth Crooker

41

EVENING THOUGHTS

When another busy day is done,
Do you look at what you've done?
Do you ever sit and ponder,
While you stare out yonder,
Did I really do my best today?

Did I wear a great big smile,
As I traveled many a mile?
Or did I hastily judge another,
When I could have been a brother?
Did I really do my best today?

Did I give my family all they need,
As all their cares I tried to heed?
Or did I someone's feelings hurt,
Just by being much too curt?
Did I really do my best today?

Lord, may I have another chance,
So when you cast your glance,
And when another day has passed,
I can with honesty say at last,
I really did my best today!

Grace C. Nolan

DON'T THINK OF BAD THINGS

Don't think of death when there is life.
Don't think of sorrow when there is joy.
Don't think of weeping when you can laugh.
Don't think of war when there is peace.
Don't think of hell when there is heaven.
But pray to God you know the difference
    between them.

Melodie Rissler

LET US SING

Let us sing said the brook as it babbled along
Through woodland and fields to the sea.

Let us sing said a bird as it warbled
From branches high in a tree.

Let us sing said the wind as it whistled its song,
Yet, let us not forget, there are those
Who are sad along life's way,
Who we must help to be happy and gay.

Let us help them forget the sad things in their life,
Look for a future more bright,
Look for a rainbow and end of the strife,
A bright day that follows the night.

Bessie W. Dunham

AUTUMN MOOD

Against the bright October sky
Bright, twirling leaves go twirling by,
Apples cluster on the ground,
The partridge drums a hollow sound.

Bittersweet clings to walls of stone
Where chipmunks hurry-scurry home,
Shadow and sunlight play a game,
Scarlet of maples turns to flame.

Valleys are misty shafts of gold,
Outline of mountains blue and bold,
Song of cricket echoes shrill,
The edge of night is hushed and still.

Betty Hunter

THE FORTUNE TELLER

Edge silently through the worn velvet
parting in the middle,
and see the fortune teller.

Musty old woman smell mixed with the
dust on the table and the chairs and the
rust on the pipes and the spots on the floor
meets you, and you sit near the cards
while the Jacks and the Queens wait their turn.

And she means
to tell you your fortune in cards
and in tea leaves, as the opiate of tea scent
erases the hulabaloo of outside away.

Close comes her wrinkled hand, a mummy claw
pulling you back centuries
to witches' covens and black sabboths
and musty old woman smell mixed with the
dust on the alter in black and the
crust on the skulls and the
rust of the blood-red blade in the cracked alter board...
...and Madame Defarge knits the tea leaves
into the hideous pattern of you...
and the queen is dragged into the tumbril
and over the cobblestones, onto the guillotine

and the next queen is black.

"Are you Leo?" asks the mummy hand.

And you answer the red fingertips and
the penetrating stare of the blue bandana
as she tells you of yourself...
...under a minute tea leaf lurks the Lion,
and it pounces from the cup onto the table
and up,
over the crystal ball, and snaps at the mummy
hand reeking of crusty, musty horrid old woman
            smell...
and you give her a dollar and the table
has change on it,
so you leave and buy the Lion a cotton candy.

44   *J. P. Rosenfeld*

TO AN ASTRONAUT

Youth, polish up your armor
And bear that standard high,
And ride your fiery charger
Right up into the sky.
With new frontiers to conquer,
New mysteries to explore,
New wonders to discover
No one has seen before.
You are a chosen hero,
Just like a knight of old,
So ride your swift horse Pegasus
And be as brave and bold.
The red blood courses through your veins,
The glint is in your eye—
So gallop on those heavenly lanes
And let those steel hooves fly.
Time, distance, space, you'll conquer all,
E'en Mercury and Mars;
First reach the moon and win this race,
And catch a falling star.
So gallop on brave astronaut
And keep that banner flying;
The world has need for such as you,
Who are not afraid of dying.

Louise Frick

A WHIPPOORWILL CALLS

The swallows dart about the lake
Where shadows softly drape the hill
With now and then a silence break
Of wistful calling whippoorwill.

A sudden splash of feeding bass
With ripple wave is quickly still
And quiet is broken once again
By haunting cry of whippoorwill.

Jean Capps Owenby

IMPRESSIONS OF MARCH IN NEW YORK

March, month of rebirth and Spring,
Comes in slowly, stumbling,
                And shriveled;
                Trying to hide
                Her nakedness.

Sobs of stilted, sad robots,
Moving in futile search of Spring.
                Car horns, factory smog;
                Rush to work.

Children crying as they play in alleys,
Lovers walking and gazing sadly at
                Trees gnarled,
                Cancerous and stunted;
                Brown crab grass;

Cement covering dead flowers.
And somewhere, faraway, a
Quiet stream breaks the silence
                In a green valley
                Dotted with flowers;

Marred not yet by man.

Carol Lee Corbett

WHEN YOU FEEL LOW

When you feel low and beaten down,
Just go outside and walk around.
Listen to the wind as it blows through the trees,
And listen to the birds sing sweet melodies.
Lie down by the brook and watch the water flow,
And think of the days of long, long ago.
Think of your dreams and the future to come.
Think of God and your eternal home.
Then when you think of the bad day you've had,
You'll feel much better and not so sad.

Gwyn Vaughn

WANDERERS

Wanderers? Yes, two restless souls
Always moving to seek our goals.
Here awhile, then some place new;
Only remembered by very few.
But there it stands for all to see,
Our traditional weeping willow tree.
Each new place that we choose to live,
It's the one lasting gift that we always give.
And when once again we wave our good-byes
We can always tell by the way it sighs;
A symbol of friendship we've left standing there
For all of our recent neighbors to share.
Now if all of God's children could only see
The joy that's gained by planting a tree.
Peace, like the leaves, could bud and grow strong,
And the sigh in the willow become a great song!

Laura Rishling

WHAT IS LOVE?

What is love?
Is it a flying dove
Finding peace
Where you expect it the least?

Is it knowing someone cares;
Or having a friend with whom to share?

Is it having a neighbor
Who does you a favor?

Is it feeling afraid
Then being saved?

Where is love
In this world of war?
Look carefully now,
It may be at your own door.

Kathy Callaway

47

COME, ENTER MY MIND

Come, enter my mind.
Walk softly on the words of my
    mouth,
Tread gently on the feelings of my
    heart,
Stand still and listen.

For to enter my mind is to know
The thoughts that are hidden deep,
Waiting for you to unlock them.

Enter quietly and leave as you
    have come,
Knowing that you, and only you
Have journeyed the path with me.

Come, enter my mind.

Joy Grey

VOICE OF LOVE

How could you who were lyrical
suddenly go mute?
You who taught me the miracle
of love's lovely lute.

Can you really think possessing
replaces spoken word?
Is love's speech so embarrassing,
speech that once we shared and heard?

From you I shall hide my sadness
that your song is still,
and try for proof in love's madness
that silence need not kill.

Natalie Harris

48

FLYING

To be carefree as the bird on the wing,
To fly so high — from my heart to sing.
To be so gay, as a day in May,
And to ride on the wings of time far away.
To see the heavens up above
And look down, upon the earth with love.
To ride the clouds by night and day,
And see the wonders far away.
All of this, I could do and see
If the art of flying was given to me.

To float o'er mountains and distant hills,
And forget the earth and its fancy frills.
To see the sights of places afar,
Where nothing could ever my spirits mar.
Where nothing could hinder or block my way —
To seeing a new and brighter day.
To hide from earth's entangling snares;
Forget my worries; forget my cares.
All of this I could do and see;
If the art of flying was given to me.

Joanne Saxon

DREAMS

I dream, I dream, so far away.
  My thoughts seem to have nothing to say.
The episodes are so exciting and real.
  The life-like figures send me chills.
I wish this dream to live until,
  Forever, forever . . .

Is this dream a reality,
  Does this dream involve me?
Yes, I am dreaming this dream.
  I live this dream against my will
Yet, I wish this dream to live until,
  Forever, forever . . .

Maria Triva Elmo

GOING HOME

With my heart full of hope I look for the day
    when contentment comes to me.
To return to the place I loved in my youth
    and set my spirit free.
For I've traveled so far and started anew
    each time that I was asked.
But somewhere on this road of life
    I knew it couldn't last.
There are those who can travel and reap great reward
    starting a home anew.
But after a while it all wears thin and
    feelings start to come through.
So I long for the days of that simple life,
    of friendships deep and strong.
It flows through your blood and the call is there
    and you know it can't be wrong.
The roots of my life are severed by time
    and demand to be resown.
For where in this world can you wander through
    the familiar fields of home.
The days of my life are numbered in time
    and I long to settle down.
And all that I ask, just one last request,
    return to my old home town.

Joan M. Longe

CLOUDS

The clouds are like mountains in the sky,
and I will reach them when I die.
Now I must conform with society,
and do all I can do, see all I can see,
but never, ever be completely free.

Luther Lyn Lutes

50

GOD BLESS HAPPY DOUGHNUTS

God bless happy doughnuts
    floating upon clouds of coffee-colored whipped cream
    to assuage the appetite of those
    exhausted with eating lotus petals.
Make happy sounds and live—the world exists for us!

God bless rainbow-colored ostrich feathers
    tickling, teasing, making playful gestures
    and undulating, tawny flesh, liquid bronze and
    burnished copper, smoldering, burning,
                    teasing, tickling.
Make happy sounds—make haste to live!

God bless work, satisfying, rewarding:
    "Steel girders strong enough to hold up America,"
    Bees' nests filled with office workers,
    Salesmen, admen, hucksters, hustlers,
    Selling, ading, hucksting, hustling.
Make happy, useful sounds and live!

God bless women:
    Having babies, pop, pop, pop.
    Twirling rainbow-colored ostrich feathers.
    Making happy doughnuts upon clouds of coffee-colored
                    whipped cream . . .
Making happy sounds.

Maurice Whitaker

WHEN I THINK OF SPRING

When I think of spring, I think of kites
    in the air and a nice long breeze
    that can almost freeze.
Gay people running around, gay people
    lying on the ground.
Paper airplanes ready to attack,
    knocking down others from the back.
Box kites, plain kites, fun to fly,
    people going on trips and waving goodbye.

David Scott McMahon

PIL-GRIMM'S FAIRY TALE

A pretty Puritan maiden
   Sat astride the Plymouth Rock;
Enticing of demeanor
   She had wandered from the flock.

She saw a Pilgram Father
   With musket—stern and lorn—
Striding martially to church
   That sunny sabbeth morn.

He saw the pretty Puritan
   Astride that Plymouth Rock,
A secular temptation
   In a most provocative frock.

She asked, "Oh, Pilgrim Father,
   Which, sir, which shall it be:
'ONWARD CHRISTIAN SOLDIER'
   Or 'ABIDE WITH ME'?"

Roy Harris Russ

THOUGHT MACHINES

Simple lives for simple people,
Compound hive, and concrete steeple,
Numbered humans marching past,
Thought machines we are at last.
March up to the head computer,
Push a punch card in, and then,
Out there comes a coded message,
Which decides the fates of men.
Are they spared or will they die,
Or will they forever ply,
Through their simple lives; those people,
Compound hive, and concrete steeple.

Lee Ballentine

52

SONNET

wish then, and dream you do not dream,
upon a cloud as old and rare as time;
dream soft of airy silk in ancient hand
held lightly, brushing half a grain of sand
from some old granite peak
but once in floating ages far too vast to seek
the then or there in this night's dream;
dream warm and flowing things of time,
and dreamlike know our love shall sound
the depths of undreamt Kalpas, flesh and color bound;
dream sinking through the mist at edge of dream
into all the lights of every lovefilled time . . .

but watching you, and for your dreaming sake,
I bid you warm and unbelieving, wake

M. G. Jacobs

DESOLATE

Day so gray and gloomy
Lurks as a shadow
Over the deserted town;
Even the smallest of insects
Isn't to be found.
Rough and rowdy winds
Sweep the streets
Of litter,
Leaving the avenue barren.
Trees reach upward,
Praying,
For a miracle
To give them green.
Windblown dust, biting,
Cuts the flesh
Of you,
The lone one,
The only one around.

Dorothy Kirk

SMOKE RINGS

Dear old Dad in his old arm chair
Sending smoke rings in the air
He draws slowly, then puffs fast
Each ring's a porthole to the past.
As barefoot boy he roams once more
Down beneath the sycamore
And in its leafy shade he swims
Diving from its mighty limbs.
Upon its trunk his sweetheart's name
He carves with tender love
Then strolls with her down lover's lane
Where branches meet above.
The call to have a cup of tea
Awakes him from his reverie
He heaves a sigh, sends one more curl
Looks up and smiles at that same sweet girl.

Ethel Huber

DOUBT

The summer time is coming;
   School will soon be out.
The time has come for happiness;
   Of this there is no doubt.

The trees are all beginning
   To spread their magic arms,
And all the cities' children
   Wish they lived on the farms.

For every will of spring
   There is a summer route.
For everything there will be time.
   Of this there is no doubt.

There are so many wonders
   Of life and love to shout
Of summer and its peacefulness;
   Of this there is no doubt.

Anne Hawkins

AWAKE! THERE'S A NEW DAY

Awake! There's a new day on the horizon waiting
    to greet you!
It's creation bursting forth in streams of light,
Bending down to kiss the dew.

Awake! Drink up the blooming freshness instilled
    in its cup of purity.
Toast the day's quiet noiseless serenity,
Knowing alas, that it cannot last.

Awake! Arise and sense the warmth of the day's
    growing essence.
Stretch your being to the fullest and feel the
    circulation rushing,
To alert all points of its presence.

Awake! Hear the bird's song proclaiming the
    day's birth anew.
Each chirp reaffirming the delivery of goodness and
    beauty throughout,
For all, not just a few!

Betty Taylor Louder

HATS EVERYWHERE

Boyish hats, girly hats,
Pink and yellow swirly hats.
Winter hats, spring hats,
Little everything hats.
Light hats, dark hats,
Walking through the park hats.
Ugly hats, nice hats,
All sugar-and-spice hats.
All these hats are very fine,
But yours is yours, and
Mine is mine!

Sharon L. Gregory

THE PATHS OF LIFE

We walk the lonely paths of life
To find, what, we do not know
For in this world of stress and strife
Our fears of life still grow.

The paths of life go many ways
The right one we must seek
And as we travel day by day
The world becomes more bleak.

Once we find our path of life
Our direction, is it clear?
For in this world of stress and strife
What dangers, lurking near?

Our fears of life are sometimes grim
But on we all must go
Our love of God and only Him
Can make our lives aglow.

Maryann Borek Robertson

FACES

Amused, solemn, and quizzical faces,
All are caught in public places.
Whatever the occasion, wherever the land,
At the beach or on the sand,
At the store, at the zoo,
Faces are found and so are you.

Karen Passmore

A MOUNTAIN LAKE

There's nothing like a mountain lake reflecting every hue
Of evergreens and pinacles and vivid skies of blue

The snow-capped peaks which tower above reflected down below
Their jagged spires and glaciers afford a wondrous show

How calm and crystal clear the lake; how mirror-like it seems
Nestled softly neath the hills, its sleek, smooth surface gleams

It seems to have been painted with turquoise and with jade
I do not think that anywhere is found a lovelier shade

A pretty, precious, priceless jewel is the little mountain lake
In a splendid natural setting which only God can make

Annette Marquardt

A RAY OF SUNSHINE

Our ray of sunshine is a joy to see,
It can warm you
Delight you
Or fill you with glee!

Two years old — that's his age
Already, we are his slaves.
His dreams and adventures
    are ours to share
This wonderful ray of sunshine
    is always there!

No, 'tis not the sun I speak of —
But a tiny little boy
A bundle of love
A heap of joy — our grandson!

Suzy Selway

I WANT TO BE ME

Striving for goals I don't care to obtain;
Living the life of a man I don't know.
Pushed into this life which is sapping my brain;
Until the voice there inside me cries halt.

And this voice inside me says don't give a damn
'Bout what others say I should be.
Now go lead the life that I've wanted to lead;
And then I will truly be me.

Searching for answers already found;
Isn't the real way to learn.
And living by standards of "how it will sound,"
Makes my blood come up to a burn.

For I am my conscience, my soul, and my being;
And not some uncaring machine.

Charles H. Fogle

YOUR FUNERAL

Your flesh shall go to the grave some day
When your dead body's laid away.
You'll get a floral tribute too,
The flowers that your friends bring you.
A service shall be held somewhere;
You'll get kind words and then a prayer.
The hearse will then haul you away,
And at your grave someone will pray.

Each one should think while yet alive
That their day, too, shall soon arrive.
How many friends that are your's while here
Forget you once you disappear.
Each life on earth since time began
Must always have a final end.
So give yourself to Christ today
And be prepared to go away.

Robert Gerald Mitchell

NOVEMBER

Frosted nights
And tear gray mornings,
Days when the sun plays hide and seek
Through leaf-bereft trees,
I wish I could have held
Summer captive, locked secure
In gold filled chambers
To be let loose
On days like these.

Vera Koppler

SONG OF MYSELF

My inner self hungers for leadership.
My desire for authority is distinctively present.
But not for greed. No, just for self satisfaction.
I want to accomplish.

I want to be the highest among highest,
And look above to see myself
And look down only to see my reflections;
I want to dine on the 49th floor.

My somewhat empty mind
Searches for necessary nourishment
And the main course must be success
Or I will starve.

I know it will not last forever
And someday I'll put away my knife and fork.
And my silk napkin.
But not until I fatten my conscience.

Irene Young

A DREAM

As I sit by the fire
    on a dark and rainy night,
I dream of faraway places
    and of what it must be like,
To roam the mountain meadows
    and all the valleys too,
To cross the tumbling rivers
    and all the deserts through.
To wake up at dawn
    with the first stroke of light—
And see God display His beauty
    in nature's sunrise bright.
To lie at rest in the night
    and watch the countless stars,
To listen to the singing wind
    as the soft whispers of sleep overtake.
Oh, how I wish I knew
    what it was like!

Wolf-Andre Wanka

GOD'S PROMISE

The air is brisk, the day is bright—
The sky is blue, no clouds in sight.

Why should your heart be heavy and sad?
With God in His heaven, you should be glad!

Why should you let the cares of each day—
Their sadness and sorrow within your heart stay?

"I'll bear all your burdens, I'll carry your load"
This is God's promise as you travel life's road.

What good is this offer, if you heed it not—
And struggle along with the cares that you've got?

Marjorie Steeves

I WANT A HOUSE

I want a house,
A little house will do,
Nestled in the sand hills
Beside the ocean blue.
I want my friends to linger,
To chat and sup with me,
I want to hear the sea gulls cry
Across the open sea.

I want to catch the big blue crabs
And fish along the shore,
Sometimes to swim in the ocean
Just outside my cottage door,
I want to feel as free
As the sea gull in his flight,
I want my house to be
A haven and delight.

Marie Elise Gorse

A TROUT STREAM

Gently the mountain stream flows downward,
Over the falls bubbling deeply into a pool.
Beautiful is the trout dreamland I've found,
With fresh, pure, clean water feeling so cool.
So superbly along the stream trees stand,
Bringing peaceful relaxation which is rejoiced.
Also realizing the value of this precious land,
While love and appreciation should be voiced.
Yearningly my memories desire to see,
Rainbows swimming from underneath a rock.
As nature arouses deep pleasure inspiring me,
And influencing me secretly into thought.

Nola Jean Currence

TREASURES OF LIFE

The really important things in life
    are things that money can't buy.
The sun that rises sleepily
    and slowly warms the sky.

The singing strains of a symphony.
    The murmur of a brook.
The glowing warmth of a fireside,
    accompanied by a book.

The beauty of the first snow fall.
    The promise found in spring.
The gentle breath of the summer's breeze
    that teaches the forest to sing.

The frantic haste of the river
    rushing to its end.
The happy sound of laughter.
    The knowledge of a friend.

The freshness of a fragrant rose,
    bathed in tears of dew.
The gentle touch of a loving hand.
    The moments shared with you.

Margaret Shroll

COMPULSION

As the moth,
Impelled,
Responds to the fire's glitter,
To singe its wings
And woo its ending,
So must I return to you
To hurl my heart
Against
The indifferent flame.

Jean C. Higgins

JUST LIVING

There's something Mother used to say
  That I have found so true,
"You learn a lot from living—for
  Just living teaches you."

And what a teacher "living" is
  You learn the hardest way,
One might have taken good advice
  And spurned the pits of clay.

For others who have walked this path
  And learned a thing or two—
With all sincerity and love
  Would pass them on to you.

But if we do not care to learn
  From others who are kind,
Then "living" teaches us the things
  That they have left behind.

Cammie Anderson

JUST MIGHT BE

"How now Brown Cow?"
"I'm fine Mr. Moose.
How is your goose?"
"Oh! My goose got loose."

"How's your octopus?"
"She is sick Mr. Moose,
after she ate your goose."

So, the moral of this is:
Keep your goose in a pen and
not loose, because your neighbor
just may have an octopus.

Patsy A. Goodman

63

LANTERNS ON THE LEVEE

Stands a secluded old log cabin
   'Neath the levee of ole "Miss"
Where stately magnolia trees reach
   Their blossoms high to kiss
Each stray little moonbeam shining
   Down, softly down, as if to teach
Every petal that grows in every tree.
   The reason: the old Negro dwelling
There, places lanterns on the levee.

It wasn't such a long time ago,
   (At least the story goes that way)
The moon failed for many a night,
   No sun shone throughout the day.
The rains came—the winds came too,
   Yet the barges kept struggling away.
Death was there and Fate dealt a hand
   With the torrent directing o'er all the play,
Surging and routing to claim the land.

Lanterns became a familiar sight
   And welcomed, surely, by many a man
As they burned by day and through the night.
   Who was it come where the need
Was so great? Who was it did fight?
   The lights were seen by those who see.
'Twas saving grace, they did concede,
   Tho' no one knew to whom thanks to
Give for the lanterns on the levee.

The stardust is drying and it glows
   With a clear lustre in the night,
And always one can see, if he but look
   For all of the lanterns burning bright.
They'll never fail, fully all do know,
   There's a tender who keeps 'em in sight.
The stage is the same except for he—
   The old Negro has left, but I'm sure
He watches the lanterns on the levee.

John Porter Duke

SOMEONE

I need someone to love me,
I need someone to care;
I need to know you'll always
    be waiting for me there.
High upon the mountain,
    or far beyond the sea,
I need to know you'll always,
Be waiting just for me.

No matter where you wander,
No matter what you do;
I'll be waiting always,
Be waiting just for you.
Someday I will find you,
Wherever you may be;

    and we will walk together,
    beside the gentle sea.
Then we'll both be happy,
    as happy as two could be;
    because we'll be together,
Beside the gentle sea.

Jeanne C. Lewis

So simple is the care of love
All nature knows its magic.
It cautions us in all it does
That dullness is not tragic.
The grass is greener after rain,
The wind gives gentle buffing—
To see the lustre once again,
Even romance needs a dusting.

Ann Romer

THE BREAK OF DAY

In the cool quiet still of morning all
    wrongs are washed away,
And everyone begins anew with the
    coming of day.

All quarrels seem petty compared
    to the one that is fought between
    the darkness and the rising sun.

Chasing the stars away, the sun comes
    into sight,
A glorious victor emerging from a
    fight.

Victorious, yet wounded, she guards
    the sky she claims,
Until the moon comes up and for the
    night does reign.

Doomed to eternal battle, we are
    luckier by far,
That we were born mere people and
    not a roving star.

Doris Searcy

MY DREAM

I would like to fly into the high blue sky
Look upon the earth as through a giant's eye,
Up, where the clouds are white,
Up, where the sun shines bright;
I would go so high, I'd hear the angels sing
Even go so high, I'd hear God's church bells ring;
Someday I'll make my one dream come true
And go flying high in the blue.

Jeannie Fink

GRANDMA

Today you're something you've never been
And you'll never be the same.
You've joined a special group of people
That isn't known by just one name.

Some are Grandma, some are Nana
To others, Granny will do.
Some will come when called Grandmother
Those that are called Grams will too.

There are many uses for Grandmas
Almost too many to mention.
They are a special type of person
That deserve a lot of attention.

They are called upon to babysit
But sometimes they volunteer.
They accept the challenge willingly
Without the slightest fear.

They boast the ego of Mom and Pop
They spoil the children rotten.
A Grandma's love is something grand
That will never be forgotten.

Earl J. Gosvener

OH! PINWHEELS

Pinwheels, Pinwheels, Oh!
    Pinwheels,
The're fun! Oh yes!
I love pinwheels;
Twirl and twirl,
Oh! Wind blow.

William Dale Graber
Age 7

OUR RECIPES

When first this land was settled,
And the women all did come,
They brought with them the best they had
Of treasures from their home.

Each one had brought her recipes
Across each different sea,
To make this place a home just like
The home that used to be.

Then in the friendship of the land
They traded here and yon,
To learn of others different ways
To put the "kittle" on.

They gave their best to dearest friends
Who in turn gave to them you see.
For 'twas like a visit from a friend
To use her recipe.

Martha Dolin

A STAR YET TO BE BORN

My world is brightened with so many stars;
Each representing some phase of my life,
Some may be as great as the world itself,
Some insignificant as grains of sand;
But as life does not stand silently by
And surely as the mind does dare to dream,
There is enough room in this world of mine,
Yes, for a brighter star yet to be born.

Pauline Long Smith

THINK OF ME

Next year when the stars cover
  a cloudless sky,
And the waves beat on a crystal
  shore,
Think of me.
And when you're walking down a
  woodland path,
And a timid rabbit stops and watches
  in surprise,
Think of me.
And if you're driving down a country
  road,
And the fragrance of honeysuckle seems
  to drift around you,
Think of me,
Because I'll be thinking of you.

Norma Yarbrough

SWEET YOUTH

Children building castles
In the sands along the way;
Working toward perfection
For the waves to wash away.

Children, in their innocence,
Without a worldly care,
Playing in the sunshine
While the breezes stop to stare.

An adult world filled with problems,
But the children will play on;
Tomorrow comes so swiftly,
Too soon their youth is gone.

Cathy Fowler

THE WINDOW

With great force
The wind rushed at the window.

The glass cried in anguish;
The pane prayed for salvation;
The framework shrieked for help;
The wind knew no mercy.

It shattered glass,
   ripped pane,
      corrupted framework.
It knew no love, but hate,
And so it did destroy.

Michael G. Cloutier

The darkness crept silently
   over the shelf
And as I watched the last ray of sunlight leave,
   disappearing as if God were dimming the
   ceiling lights,
I felt deserted. Alone. Lonely.

I see everyone as toys —
   on that same shelf —
That must be put away at exactly five-thirty
   every day.
And every day is the same as last year's days.

When will a brighter sun come and stay —
   Oh, please stay a while.
Stay and keep me company.
But no one listens, no one answers.
   And I am left again —
      Deserted, as in a strange place;
      Alone, as in single;
      Lonely, as in crying.

Martha Jane Phillip

NIGHT INTERLUDE

Cool specks glow silently, listening; still.
A drowsy glimmering sea falls quietly on soft sand.
All is calm.
And I lie inside the night
Wondering . . .
Why a different world is brought with day.

Stephen Shumaker

AUTUMN

It was autumn
For a moment
And the woods
Possessed a song.
The bubbling brook
Played music
As it gaily rushed along.
The scene was bold and vital
As it captured all in sight;
Chestnuts, oaks and maples
Glowed within the golden light.
The wood was etched in splendor
As it rustled in the breeze;
Slanting rays of sunlight
Softly fell between the trees.
The air was fresh and crispy
Like a scented garland wreath;
Merry creatures chattered
As the stubble crunched beneath.
It was autumn
For a moment
Now the darkness falls too soon,
The snow will spread her beauty . . .
There's a ring around the moon.

Lucille Holmes Giles

WHAT A BEAUTIFUL SIGHT!

The endless stretch of sand,
The moon's golden footpath across the water.
The soft rhythm of the waves,
Gently kissing the beach
And then silently receding.
Although he is many miles away,
You can almost feel his presence.
He seems so near.
You hear him softly calling your name,
He sounds so real, so close.
And then you know.
You turn and run to him,
And feel his warm embrace.
He has come to you.

Janet Moore

RAIN

autumn
drowns
in sobs
in torrents:
rain
in the streets
in the streets beneath
my window pane

all
all my hopes
go down the drain

picnic in the park
is
off:

rain.

Carole Ann Edwards

72

TO LOVE

To love is to give,
To give is to live,
To live is to care,
To care is to share,
To share is to feel,
To feel is to desire,
To desire is to need,
To need is to want,
To want is to keep,
To keep is to treasure,
To treasure is to know,
To know is to fulfill,
To fulfill is to complete,
To complete is to finish,
To finish is to end,
And that my good friend,
Is simply the beginning,
Of how to love.

John J. Price Jr.

FRIENDS

We seek a friend
And find a friend
Then take life with a smile
For that's the only way it seems
To make life seem worthwhile

We spread a little sunshine
To take away the rain
Each weary mile we seem to smile
And drive away all pain

But to hold a friend
We must be a friend
And sorrow we must hide
For the pathway of men is narrow
But the gates of Heaven are wide

Horace A. Ferguson

73

LOVELY SNOWFLAKES

Snowflakes kissing each other
Far from the heaven above.
Seeking a happy landing
Flying up and down with love.

While some flakes go drifting,
Others lay with melted tears
Looking back up to heaven
Where there is nothing to fear.

Some of them get together
In bunches just like a hill,
As if to last forever there
Upon the wornout window sill.

But when the sun peeps out
In the morning blue sky,
The fleshy little flakes melt
And lay together to say goodbye.

Wm. Beck

MY PRAYER

Help me to walk the straight and narrow way.
And if from it I should some day stray,
Draw me Dear Lord with cords of love
To think of Thee and heaven above.

When in this world of sin,
Help me some soul to win.
Help me to think of Thee above
And Thine everlasting love.

We know Thou art a God of love,
Who sits enthroned in heaven above.
Help me to think of Thee above
And Thine everlasting love.

Winifred Dykgraaf

SONG OF FAITH

In my back yard I've found a wren
Who has become my friend and joy.
He sings with such a throbbing note
His throat jumps upward to the sky.
Sheer gaiety of lusty song
Escapes his tiny soul, and fills
My patio with trills of merry sound.

His day must be a blessed one
He must be full of great content.
His work to do, his world full blown,
He sees the beauty from his view—
God's kingdom, and he plays a part.
If 'tis only I who learned today
Mister brown wren has done well.

In my green and golden childhood
My grandfather had such a wren
By his back door, amid his beloved garden,
We'd share its cheery caroling while
Flowers were tended and stories told.
Now I know how, in one of many ways,
Loved ones live eternal in God's fold.

Roberta H. Smith

WISDOM

Culture thy mind, where the true beauty is,
Not thine face to deceive with,
Then all that you say, will be carried away,
By others who, someday, will need it.

Sam Simon Apkarian

HONEYSUCKLE

The honeysuckle, mocking God
imitates the lillies of the field;
Holding Solomon's staff and rod
all things to honeysuckle yield.
Its lilly skin (deceptive as such
to those who linger in its touch),
cannot be made to loose its clutch.
The crumbling trees, now turned to dust,
were strangled by its flowered lust;
The helpless trees who cannot pick
up their roots as skirts, must stick
fast to the ground, and prey become:
it must, to the honeysuckle succumb.
The voluptuous vine of surface beauty
kills for pleasure, not for duty.
As it winds its way up the kind tree's trunk
as a painted woman long been drunk,
it leaves the tree for dust and junk.
As its Judas' kiss is tightened by day,
the harder it is to pull away—
'Till the Sampson-like tree with its leafy head
is stripped of its leaves and left for the dead.
Honeysuckle, you are well named.
The honey you suck, or life-blood it be,
illegally: the life-blood you suck from a tree.
For what purpose in life were you put here on earth?
As the lilly, you feign you toil not nor spin,
such is your life: you prey on the birth
of new trees which you know you'll win.
When your flower is withered and your stem faded brown—
Where, oh great honeysuckle are you to be found?
There you serve your purpose well:
Downward you are quickly bound
coiling round bodies deep in hell.

John Mucci

REST, MOTHER!

"Just stay in bed, and get plenty of rest—
Do what the doctor says—he knows best!"
Well, he may know all about health and such,
But of being a mother he doesn't know much!

What's to be done with the children—all five?
They are still healthy, and loud, and alive!
How can you rest when no one is there
To give them their meals, and comb their hair?

Who is to do all the washing—so much!
The cleaning, cooking, and keeping in touch
With car pools, dancing and baton lessons?
Who will attend the P.T.A. sessions?

So drag yourself out of that nice warm bed,
And try to forget the ache in your head.
Say to yourself: "When they're grown and I'm free,
A nice, quiet, nervous breakdown for me!"

Irene Smith

RING THOSE BELLS

Ring the joyous bells then
   For a girl and boy.
Mark a glad beginning
   Of lifelong pain and joy.

End the solemn service,
   Old, yet ever new.
Hearts are full of gladness,
   But eyes are filled with dew.

Final prayer is ended.
   Now the lines reverse.
Joined in holy wedlock,
   For better or for worse.

Gladys Reimer

YOUNG BRIDE

You're intrigued by a new pattern,
A vista of life yet unknown,
Ready to end maiden sojourn
For wifehood and bright marriage throne.
Young bride, with your heart now winging,
Love's light in your life keep singing.
Young bride,
Sweet bride, you're so bubbling with joy,
God bless your marriage to this boy.

You're lighting with hope your threshold,
You're singing a matin of praise
For warm, promised love to enfold,
That will bless and hallow your days.
Young bride, with your heart now winging,
Love's light in your life keep singing.
Young bride,
Sweet bride, you're so bubbling with joy,
God bless your marriage to this boy.

Blanche Bowman

SHIFTED

Treble clef, the flutist plays.
The music leaves; illusion stays.
Backhanded writers changed the score
    of tones so clearly heard before.
Golden myths of ancient years
    are sung by plastic balladeers
    who resurrect the fables three:
    The person I, Myself, and Me.

Carol Dervage

THE HAYBAGGER

Up in the meadow, soft and green
A shelter for horses is plainly seen.
Amid the deep shadows in there
A pair of brown eyes outwardly stare.

As I walked up t'ward the shelter here
A spotted horse is seen quite clear.
The sound of munching, the smell of hay
The soft little nicker that says "Let's stay."

I took up the brush, the cloth and comb,
I brushed and combed and cleaned 'til he shone.
I brought the saddle, the bridle too,
I tacked him and mounted and off we flew.

We cantered the meadow and trotted the stream,
When we took the woodland, we were all out of steam.
We walked up the mountain, a beautiful scene,
Then back to the meadow, soft and green.

Barbara A. Kendig

CONVERSATION

The world stands at an abyss;
Annihilation is just around the corner.
Gray sacks of bones with sunken eyes
Sear into the memory.
Violent death in the streets
Becomes a spectator sport.
The black face pleads
For acceptance as a human being.

Of what shall we talk?

Football! Baseball! Basketball!
They touch not mortality, imagination,
    or responsibility.

Lawrence Aeschlimann

ELEGY IN VIETNAM

Little feet
Are quiet now in Vietnam.
They no longer scamper
Through the narrow streets.

Little feet
Bare in noon-time heat
Toddled about in Vietnam
When life was flower sweet.

Little feet
Were stopped in Vietnam
One sun-filled day
Where two shade paths meet.

Little feet
Running to safety
Stumbled and were still
In rubble of village street.

Little cherub face
Upturned to Vietnam skies—
Foreign planes drone overhead
Unseen by big dark eyes.

Charlotte Townsend Springer

REGRET

When last I looked, the leaves were brown,
    But now they've blown away;
I should have watched them drifting down,
    Regret of yesterday.

The leaves were dry, they could not cling,
    Unfed by branch above;
They fell away, as does a dream,
    Unnurtured by your love.

Joy Butner

80

MURMURINGS

Of all the loveliest words in this land
Murmuring is the most beautiful penned.

That word can express the most beautiful things,
The murmuring of the wind in the spring
As it whispers "welcome" to a new blade of grass
That has burrowed its way through the earth at last.

The lullaby murmurings of the rain as it falls
On all roofs alike, low or tall
Lulling to sleep each one of us
Who cares to listen to this loveliness.

The gurgling of the creek rushing past
Inviting us to sit down on the grass
And listen to its lovely song
As it murmurs to us "dream on, dream on."

The murmurs of all small noises at night
That overflows our souls with delight
And we go to bed, but we cannot sleep
For the murmuring, murmuring, chirps and peeps.

There are many, many lovely things
But the most lovely of all is a murmuring.

Betty McCort Crahan

A hand that refreshes mine when it's tired
   and hot,
A hand that warms mine when it's cold
   and raw,
A hand extended to help me if I fall off
   the beaten path,
A hand so delicate, yet firm and under-
   standing,
A hand so large that it makes me
   feel secure,
A hand that when mine joins his,
   I know I couldn't be happier.

Kathy Kelly

NO PARKING PROBLEM

Many cities have a problem,
Sometimes a smaller town
On where to park the many cars
That come from all around.

But I never have to worry
Tho' traffic comes and goes,
I have a nice old apple tree
That in my yard there grows.

It's there my traffic likes to park
From early morn 'til dark;
Some come for food and some to work
But there's always room to park.

No attendants are ever needed
Or parking meters, too.
I like to watch the birds that park
And greet old friends and new.

Hilda B. Augur

GOLD UPON GOLD

Your smile tendered tenderness and touched to the
depths of my heart,
As in memory the first spring daffodil glowing in
the morning sun.

Gold upon gold
to closely hold
Like the dawn, stealthily as an elf it entered, glorious
in its awakening,
And left me shaken and brooding as the burnished
scarlet autumn leaves.

Scarlet upon scarlet
today I miss you.

Esther Stormy

WHAT IS MAN, O GOD, THAT THOU SHOULDST BE MINDFUL OF HIM?

Who can measure the care, the love, solicitude
and pride God hold for this —
    His masterpiece?
"Though dust thou art to dust returneth" —
    gold dust — in the Hands divine.
An atom radiating splendour from grace,
    the grace of the Sun of God. In radiance
It gleams and glows — and shows
    the handiwork of God.
"Be thou faithful unto death," O tiny microbe —
    and thou shalt reign over the universe
        a tiny part
      of which thou art!

Elizabeth V. Murawski

BEECHES

Once a forest giant was I,
Who spread o'er much the land;
But age and rot have made me lie,
A-bed a cold wet ground.

Now where once I stood, a cedar grows,
So green so fine so proud.
And along a path a hunter goes,
Stalking; not so loud.

Yet all the while my seedlings bud,
In meadow field and row;
To stand again to fire and flood,
And while the cattle low.

And tho' I lie still, my branches bare,
My growth was lo for naught;
For around me grow in grove and pair,
My seed the earth has caught.......

James S. Banta

SOMEONE WE KNOW

Long hair and sandals
And a long, dark beard.
A picture of a rowdy;
A picture that is weird.

He's got some crazy notion
Of peace here on the earth,
Of integrity of human life;
Its value and its worth.

His posters and his leaflets
Speak of crazy things,
Like justice, love, and peace and such,
And he's got some songs he sings.

He's been arrested on the street
And borne away to jail.
He's also been in Monday court,
Only he didn't get out on bail.

He'll give his life for what he thinks,
If that is what it costs.
And anyone can plainly see
This guy is really lost.

Who is this kooky character
Whom it isn't hard to hate?
Look close, his name is Jesus,
Whose birth we celebrate.

Brad Bradshaw

AND ALL'S WELL

I sit and stare at the midnight sky
And watch the heavens moving by.
Each separate star shines all a-glow,
The crescent moon completes the show,
And all and all is calm and bright
This lovely, mystic, well-lit night.

Michael S. Hahn

THE HOBBYISTS

Those folks a hobby does not charm
May often view with some alarm
The actions of those persons who
Collect what's old and shun the new
Who change from normal folks to gluttons
And gather glass, old banks and buttons
Who'd rather have a horsehair chair
Than the finest new things anywhere
Who travel miles until they hear
The strident tones of some auctioneer
Who stand all day in sun and rain
And next day trek right back again
Until some moldy gem they've landed
So that they're not left empty handed
I've seen some folks spend quite a lot
And hurry home with some old pot,
Some creaky, broken, run-down rocker,
Marble-topped stand or brass doorknocker
To normal folks it seems erratic
To yearn to plow through some old attic
But those the hobby bug have bitten
Are proud to say that they're quite smitten
By Wedgwood or by Satin Glass
They form a rabid, frantic class
They look on those with some disdain
Who from the hobby craze refrain
They really think a guy's not sane
Who'd rather a plastic chair than cane
They'd be glad to spend their money galore
For a wooden Indian from an old cigar store
They pity us folks for what we've missed
By not becoming hobbyists
I swear they'd trade a brand new car
For an old cherry table brought from afar
They're a happy, cheerful, friendly crew
Who treasure the old and laugh at the new
You can call them nuts but not me, my son
You see I happen to be married to one!

James F. Dowling

THE GAMING SPOOR IS WIDE

The gaming spoor is wide,
   where hunter fares to tread,
The snowshoe rabbits hide
   in wooded maze, well fed
And found to be a whitened blot
   against the pillowed snow
To be or not, a trophy shot
   that nature might bestow.

Full dress and on parade
   the cocky pheasant wends—
A jaunty-hipped brigade
   in monarchy pretends,
His brassy tone in concert
   near cornstalk or the like
Soon o'er the strait through farmer fence
   on calmer garden hike.

So too, the duck and fatted goose
   give reference to a "blind"
Where frozen-like in cattailed ruse
   the hunter solus, pined.
On beaded wing the turkeys wild
   in flapping format hail
A sunburst necklace grandly styled
   for sky of azure veil.

The gaming spoor is wide
   where hunter fares to tread
The partridge takes a bride
   in glen so nature said.
Red fox in tawny verdant,
   is "bounty" scurrying home
And mink in brindled moor can't
   elude on trapper's loam.

Sassy squirrel with billowed tail
   in sycamore cloaked white,
Whose fur-piece could, for elves avail
   make him a regal sight.
Yes, the gaming spoor is wide
   where hunter fares to tread,
With spirits bonafide
   for sport and body fed.

Ken Haag

IF I CAN HELP

If I can put hope within the heart
    Of some poor hopeless soul;
If I can help someone to start
    On the upward path to stroll;
If I can help him reach the crest
    Of life's steep hill someday;
If I've done that, I've done my best
    To help a traveler on life's way.

I recall how often I have been
    Afraid, almost hopeless, dismayed;
Someone was there on whom to lean,
    To console, to keep me unafraid.
If I can help someone to gain
    His heart's desire and reach his goal;
My life will not have been in vain,
    If I can help one living soul.

Verda Marie Holt

When I was young
The world seemed young,
And yellow roses bloomed.
And it was spring.
The old spoke of winter,
But it was spring.

A lovers' lane
A ring
A vow.
And it was spring.
The old spoke of winter,
But it was spring.

On the side of a hill
A mound of earth,
A tall while stone,
Now I'm alone.
The old spoke of winter.

Loretta Dodson

PRICELESS FRIENDSHIP

The priceless Vessel of Friendship
   Is a Chalice from which we sip.
Each drop a refreshing treasure
   As it passes from lip to lip.

The priceless Plant of Friendship
   Takes Joy and Tears to nourish.
It needs our benevolent Care
   To blossom and to flourish.

The priceless Chain of Friendship
   Joins numerous links of gold.
It takes many rings of memories
   To fashion and to mold.

The blessed Tie of Friendship
   Is a mutual tie that binds
In fellowship, the human spirit
   Of kindred hearts and minds.

The priceless Book of Friendship
   Has pages that unfold
The Caring for each other
   Is the Sweetest Story told.

Signe Wigby

MORNING MIST

An early morning mist upon the landscape lay,
Awaiting breath of breeze to blow it all away.
It filled the air with moisture,
A fragile veil of filmy lace.
It drenched each flower and shrub and tree,
Washing nature's dusty face.
It trimmed each little blade of grass with tiny crystal
   beads.
It reached into the earth and wakened dormant seeds.
Then came a gentle puff of wind, as day succeeded dawn
And suddenly the early morning mist was gone.

Jennie Jenkinson

THIS GREAT WORLD'S GOD

I am this great world's god.
Peoples and nations bow down before me.
I am known by many different names,
Perhaps the best-known is that of "Materialism."

Nations great and small are swayed by my impact.
Through me their power and status are reckoned.
Human lives are dedicated to my increase,
I am the yardstick of their success.

The Church of the Living God has become my prey.
Many of her shepherds, too, are my disciples.
The crying needs of eternal souls no longer their
    objective,
Rather the comforts and prestige I do bestow.

Yes, I am this great world's god.
I hold the souls of peoples and nations firm.
Tomorrow? Ah yes, tomorrow may be this world's
    great reckoning.
But I shall have had my day! I am content!

Deana Lee Wold

LOST LOVE

You poured a life of love into my hands
But like a child, I spread my fingers wide
And let your love slip through, like grains of sand
To drift, defiled, into life's ebbing tide.
Yes, I was young and did not know the cost
A foolish heart must pay for love that's lost
When careless fingers fail and spread apart
An empty spot is left within the heart
Today I search life's barren beach
Still hoping to retrieve one tiny grain
Of love, so swiftly swept beyond my reach
But my frantic search is all in vain
If I could live that moment just once more
I'd be content to cancel all the rest
I'd grasp each grain of love that you would pour
And cup my hand against my aching breast

Henry R. Savastano

89

THE FASHION SHOW

The blessed golden age
   Works hard without wage
In the versatile workshop,
   Where things come out tip top.
Drawing, knitting, painting, sewing
   Until dresses start flowing.
And every lady in the arena
   Looks like a prima ballerina.

Fair Ladies:
   The famous, stylish fashion show
Year by year glows its glow,
   Day after day like a carousel,
A merry-go-round without a bell.
   It is amusing, entertaining, a delight to see,
And brings gaiety to the whole community.
   Keep up! You are queens for the day!
To the end of the show in your finery stay!
   Do not doff your festive gowns,
And proudly wear your gracious crowns!

Noah Pessah

TO A GRADUATING SON

As you leave this goal behind you
And you climb to greater heights
May your pathway be a smooth one
And your future ever bright.

You have the stuff that makes success
So don't you ever shirk
Good fortune comes to those who wait
But while they wait they work.

Now be forever mindful
Of the task that's yet to do
May good luck, health and happiness
Forever follow you.

Daisy Fries

TURMOIL

Riot-torn cities, destruction, despair —
A feeling of hatred all through the air.
The seemingly pointless outbursts of hate;
Who is there among us to open that gate?
We hear of freedom, we hear of peace.
But speech is fruitless if hatred won't cease.
It's up to each person to destroy his own pride —
To walk with a friend, side by side.
We must swallow our selfishness, banish the fear,
Until the bell of freedom we hear.
There are violent battles for equality —
No one will face reality.
So until the world is together again,
A new life for man cannot begin.

Janet Zimmerman

NEUTRALITY

O, haste to find this heavenly place
Where hatred cannot show its face.
Fair circumstance—
A dream come true—
Situate in ocean blue.
O, neutral ship—
O, neutral sea.

Haste to find this heavenly place
Where animosity must cease.
Meet the opponent face to face,
Ye who seek for lasting peace—
No unfair conference could be
In a neutral ship
On a neutral sea.

Frances Macy Decker

MY CLOVER

Where are you, four-leafed clover
Growing by my cabin door
I've searched full half the morning
Aren't you growing here any more?

You used to look up at me
When I came out to play
But now you're hiding from me
I've wasted half the day

Searching and worrying
Because you are not here
You were in abundance
At this time last year

Tell me, is my luck changing,
Will it grow from good to bad?
You used to bring me happiness
Your hiding makes me sad.

Oh, there you are sweet clover
I see your little head
Peering half open at me
From out your little bed.

May Nelson Martt

THE UNIVERSE

A velvet void, swollen with stars,
Clasps veiled Venus, and rusty Mars,
While giant bodies evade its embrace,
And lumber slowly in frigid space.
Crystal caverns on Jupiter and Saturn,
Stone watchers of the endless pattern,
See soaring meteors twist, then turn.
Dripping dipper and dancing light rays,
Freshen for moments the endless haze,
Amid, about, beyond nothing.
Mystery mission on an unchartered sea,
Endless eons, never to be free.

Janet L. Sauerbrey

SERENITY

Day turns to dusk,
The moon comes peeping
Through the silver-coated clouds;
The stars begin to twinkle.
All is still and quiet.
I wander through the lanes
And meadows enjoying this
Beauty and quiet and serenity.
I become quiet and still, too,
Forgetting the cares and troubles of the day
Which have been laid to rest.
Alone with nature, with God, and myself,
I find quiet and peace and strength
To go on and continue with this life.

Lilly Ann Anderson

MAGIC

I'll take a pinch of stardust
A dram of moonbeams too,
I'll make a magic potion
To cast my love on you.

I'll weave my spell around you
Though you will never know
What caused the joy inside you
And why you love me so.

I'll conjure up some magic
Would put a witch to shame
And when you love me madly
Your heart will be to blame.

My spell will last forever
My power will be so strong
My heart is yours my darling,
So my magic can't be wrong.

Bette M. Poorman

93

DESTINY

We are born trying to seek
the reason why.
We can look at the past but
not ahead,
For destiny is there until
we are dead.

Lillian Keeley

EASTER

When spring first awakened
On the farm, long years ago.
Easter was a special day
T'was bunny time, you know.

We fashioned little straw nests
Funny baskets we'd handmake.
Was the Easter Bunny watching?
How we hoped so, for our sake!

Bright and early Easter morning
In old slippers, flannel gown.
To our nests we'd run and gather
Lollipops of pink and brown.

Yellow chickens, chocolate bunnies
Colored eggs, marshmallow cremes.
All the goodies we had hoped for
Even in our wildest dreams.

One raw chilly Easter morning
As we hurried to our nests—
There was Lady, with five puppies!
Yes, we loved her present best.

Memories crowd: today I wander
Recall childhood days of mine.
To those special Easter mornings.
To that precious Easter time.

Esther E. Harris

THIS I REGRET

This I am sorry for—
    This I regret.
Having the kind of heart
    He could forget—
Having the sort of soul
    He could misplace—
It is no comfort
    His knowing my face.

Carol A. Price

ROSE HAVEN

The roses that you planted here,
    The Cecil Brunners by the door,
Have seemed more beautiful this year
    Than they have ever been before.
The mocking-bird has built her nest
    Within the rose bush, dear,
Well-guarded by the leaves that rest
    Upon the slender trellis tier.

The feathered friends you fed each day,
    The water left to quench their thirst,
Return to me in songs so gay
    As though their tiny throats would burst.
The mother feeds her baby birds
    And guards them here both day and night,
While singing precious, tender words,
    In lullabies so sweet and bright.

She seems to me to symbolize
    Your gentleness, your love and care,
A memory I dearly prize,
    And lift my voice in fervent prayer
To God who gave me, Mother Mine,
    A precious, priceless love like yours.
So sweet and true, so near divine,
    It still enfolds and still endures . . .
And will until God calls to me
    To share with you Eternity!

Cora May Preble

95

THINKING

I love to sit beside a fire,
And think of the by-gone days.
To sit and watch and never tire,
As the flames seem to sparkle and play.

And think of the past—those wonderful years,
When never a care had I.
Playing down by the boats and forbidden piers,
Loving the big blue sky.

Tasting grandma's homemade pies,
Devouring every bite,
Getting spanked by Dad whenever I'd lie.
Or being tucked in at night.

I can still see Mom—oh how she cried,
When I said Tom asked me to be his bride.
And the hours and hours it took of debate,
Just to settle my wedding date.

But now I'll stop for the flames grow low,
And soon they too will end.
But in my mind my thoughts are aglow,
Of people, places and my loving friends.

Deborah Osinski

TO BE NEEDED

To be needed is
One of life's goals.
To be wanted is
Another.
But what are you
To do when you
Have one, but not
The other?

Linda Prins

96

FOR AN OTHER

Life was a
different color
yesterday.

My thoughts and feelings
more intense
because they were shining
in that peculiar subtle light
of your being here.

We sat in a dusty garret,
illumed with musky vintage sunlight,
carelessly stacked on empty shelves
and tossed into private corners.
A pleasant room . . .

But you were sad.
When I reached out
to brush away the mist
on your face,
the drops fell into tears.

You smiled,
sighing,
to tell me.
And I quietly carved letters
on the teapot
in a different color.

Nora B.

REALITY

The world is full of hatred and of strife
And pessimistic attitudes abide,
Each a counter-ideology.
Yet even amid the hate and lust,
Amid that foul tongue and underhandedness,
A small flame burns incense to the gods—
A flame of sanity and good—
A flame of trite friendship.

David M. Kling

CHRISTIAN JOY

We cannot hope for sunshine every moment of our days,
Into each life some rain will surely fall.
We cannot have the knowledge of salvation full and free
Until we heed the Master's gentle call.

Our prayers cannot be answered till we have a trusting heart,
Each prayer must bear the words "*Thy* will be done."
For only as we ask of Him unselfishly in love
Can we expect to have His answers come.

We cannot see the glory of a perfect Easter dawn
Till Calvary's shadow makes our vision dim.
We cannot know the secret of a joyous Christian life
Till He abides in us, and we in Him.

The Calvary cross—a symbol of humility and love—
Becomes a glorious victory Easter morn.
It gives to us the purpose of a loving Father's plan
When in Bethlehem His only Son was born.

Charlotte Hagedorn

RABBIT IN THE GARDEN

There is a rabbit in my garden
Eating all my young and tender beans
All my cabbages and carrots he has eaten,
Now he's nibbling here and there and ruining my greens.
I catch the rascal at his villainy
And call him names galore,
But he just twitches his nose at me,
And returns again to nibble more.
I know that I should set a trap
Or get my gun and shoot—
I guess that I'm an awful sap,
That rabbit is too darned cute!
Say! How about *you*?
You like rabbit stew?

Dorothy C. Henderson

HOW CAN I TELL HIM

How can I tell my only child
his father was killed in the jungle wild?
He plays with his siren
and his little toy gun.
Just like a soldier
(he pretends he's one).
Look at him there, standing so tall,
just like his father when he was small.
Men are dying everyday,
why did mine have to go that way?
Should I tell him,
or should I wait?
Something inside me says tell him now,
but how can I tell him?
Please! Tell me how!
Soon he'll be drafted and killed in a war,
just like his father a few years before.
Oh how I wish this were but a dream,
but I know it's not, though it may seem.

I just told him his father is dead.
He looked straight at me and then said
with tears in his eyes, "My father is dead."
I grabbed him and squeezed him, oh so tight,
partly to ease my awe-stricken fright.
And partly to help him through his own little plight.
He was only nine,
and awfully small.
But by now my son was ten feet tall.
I hugged him close,
and I knew right then
my son was a MAN,
a man among men.

Glenn L. Simpson

THE BOOK OF LIFE

The book of life,
A never-ending book
Into the depths of which
None may take a glancing look.

Each life,
A chapter set apart.
This book contains
The great depth of a heart.

Each page,
A small event which once took place,
Whether great or small
Each has a space.

So we,
Must careful be,
For God looks in,
What *should* He see?

A life
That lives to gain,
Some worldly things and
Covers up a heart that's vain?

Or a life
That seeks to feed its soul,
This heart that reaches for
A heavenly goal?

So ever
May we better be,
A heart of gold,
For God to see.

Glennis Cleveland
Age 12

I'M THANKFUL

I'm thankful for the simple things—
A new-born calf, a bird that sings—
For air that's cool and clean and sweet,
Far from the city's noisy street;
For cattle bedded in the barn,
Content, well-fed and safe from harm;
For stars, away up in the sky,
Reminding me that God is nigh;
For neighbors who drop in to chat,
Of weather or of this and that;
For clean clothes drying in the breeze
And blue sky shining through the trees.
To plant a seed and see it grow,
And when the fruit is ripe, to know
You've had a partnership with God!
(Our greatest wealth are soil and sod.)
The well-earned joy of work that's done.
And rest that comes with setting sun;
To share life's joys and sorrows, too,
With one who loves and cares for you,
Not for the wealth and pomp of kings,
Would I exchange these simple things!

Esther C. Fethke

SUNSHINE REVOLUTION

i started in wholeheartedly
to write a little poetry
but i was thwarted thinking of
another word to rhyme with love;
and so i let the subject ride
and wrote a sonnet telling pride.
i wrote of sullen things and worlds
until the sun revealed a girl
and now i've made in meter worse
an ode of love in freer verse.

don julian

101

MY PLEA

Gentle Jesus, hear my plea;
A favor I would ask of Thee.

He and I are far apart.
Please grant these wishes from my heart.

Grant him peace that he may know
The meaning of happiness here below.

Grant him hope that he may see
The beauty of the world to be.

Grant him in Thy loving grace
Wisdom, so that he may see Thy face.

Grant that fame and fortune find him,
That the past he keeps behind him.

Grant that he may e'er speak true,
Be kind, and good, and strong, and pure.

But Heavenly Father up above,
Grant first that he be ruled by love.

Teresa Posey

BELOVED ABSENTEE

Where you are not—neither is the sun
Where you are not the day has not begun—
The hours portray a vacant scene
Where you and I have often been—
The mourning dove still calls his mate
Around our old and rustic gate,
No childish prattle neath the orchard trees,
The vacant cottage of the "keeper of the bees,"
The autumn maples, sumac too
All have on their gayest hue
A courtesy to winter's dawning
Bringing to flowers that gentle yawning
All these things come back to me
With hope they will come back to me.

Eva E. Favreaux

102

DUDE RANCH'S STAR BOARDER

He's old and bent,
His youth is spent;
To work hard, he's not able,
He wears a fancy vest;
And talks with zest
And lends color to the table.

His step is slowed,
His legs are bowed;
To dance he isn't able,
But he talks with zest;
Wears a fancy vest,
And lends color to the table.

He talks with a drawl,
And says "you all";
And has a girl friend named Mable,
He wears a fancy vest,
He's from way out west;
And lends color to the table.

Jennie J.

TIRED EVENING

In the tired evening
I rest with spiritless ruffles,
　　arm upon a sill.
Through bleary eyes I watch
　　black lace trees
　　almost blend into the dusk.
Hope, the illusion star hasn't risen
　　to stretch the drive from my soul.
Frustrations, breath quietly like sleepy dogs.
Fears, deep night, is a color yet unmixed.
Perhaps this is the final blessing
　　of the day.
And I should go to sleep
　　like all weary animals.

Jingle

THE OLD LEAF

It stood all alone
Like a speck in the sky
The others were gone
It was ready to die

And the lonely old leaf
Blew gently and calm
The tree had protected
The branch it was on

When all of the others
Had blown clean away
The one leaf was clinging
And there it would stay

Till finally at twilight
In the evening gloom
A slight breeze was blowing
Its death was due soon

When at last all was quiet
The tree gently sighed
And the leaf floated down
At last it had died

Kimberly Susan Allison
Age 14

THE HUMMINGBIRD

Wondrous whizzing bee-like bird
Be still so I can see—
Your softly feathered countenance,
Your lovely symphony.

As colored as a carnival
I need but only mention,
Your path disturbs a listless breeze
Too weak for intervention.

Margaret E. Anderson

AND THE FLOWERS WEPT

A piece of gray stone
rested heavily in the soiled snow.
A thickness with an etching
of someone's name and a few numbers
equalled the life of someone
dear to me.

And the wind blew
that saddened day,
forcing the flowers on the casket
to quiver and throb
like the bowed frame
of the widow who wept in quiet.

The hardened ground gaped
and welcomed the shining coffin
to then enshroud it quickly
and soon make anonymous
the face of the grave.
Unknown but for the heavy stone
struggling to be seen
above the deepening snow.

Margaret A. Waechter

MEDAL OF HONOR

Did it do any good
To take their lives?
Did folks rejoice,
And congratulate their wives?
Did their children at play
Learn the good news,
That their dads were killed
So our side won't lose?
Will a medal of honor
Ever replace
In a dead man's home,
His familiar face?

Marsha Rust Kirkwood

PILLARS

Tall columns,
Supporters of the
Past
And towers of the
Future,
Rise high o'er
The fallen
Marble of your
Sisters gone.
Tower above
Them proudly
But nobly.
Be ye not
Of conceit:
Ye are but
A little stronger
Than your
Sisters fallen.
Look up to the blue
Of the sky,
But forget not
The shadows
Of your base,
But for a
Stone's strength,
There lie ye.

McDonough Croom

BOTH

A man, he is a wondrous thing,
With eager zest for living;
A woman is a gentle thing,
With woman's gift for giving.

But both may climb a hill together
And never say a word,
And both may love the dark flight
Of a lone, winging bird.

Sara C. Stevens

106

THE OCEAN, THE SAND, AND THE SKY

Where the blue of the night, meets the gold of the day,
    and rainbows are chasing the dark clouds away;
Where songbirds are singing to the tune of the breeze,
    as it glides swiftly onward through spring-adorned trees.

Where the ocean waves meet with the sands of the shore,
    then roll back in fury before coming once more;
Where the rays of the sun turn dust into gold,
    and far away mountains look majestic and bold.

Oh! Let me stay here where freedom is found,
    where the soul is set free and the mind is not bound;
Just let me here linger while ages roll by,
    Just me and the ocean, the sand, and the sky.

Shirlee Sims

THE SEA OF LIFE

The wind tossed waves on the ocean,
The rise and fall of the tide;
That on a storm's provocation
A bilious surf seems to ride.

It bursts into floods of vengeance,
Its anger a white foamy heat
Then a calm like childhood's repentance;
A breeze rocks the surf waves to sleep.

Like the wind tossed waves on the ocean,
We are tossed on the maelstrom of life;
Blasted hopes and shattered ambition,
Must be built up again through the strife.

Kay Flemming

YOU, ATHEIST

Drive him out? You cannot, he has a way
Of nestling in some small corner of the
Mind and heart, of placing there the
Wonder seed—of at least, is he, or isn't he?
Berate him with hate, shellac him over
With the pride of the devil, but so help you,
You cannot, atheist, completely ignore him.
He's there because he loves. Each of every
Race and creed, among them you, atheist,
Have known his mercy. If he isn't why the fuss,
Why the driving-out, if he isn't?
He is, believe it, he's there because of love.
It's his world of want and suffering,
He was born to it, remember? It cannot be
Improved upon without him, its pulse is
His command, and its complete destruction
Will be at his holy will. Make no mistake
You, he *is*, he's the God for you, atheist.

Mary Agnes Johnson

FOR H—

All things I find gay or lovely
    Siamese cat or willow tree
Silver bowl or children's laughter
    All these things you are to me.

Lyric music, made for dancing
    Rainbow arch across the blue
Baby ducklings, golden downy
    Find their counterpart in you.

Dry martinis, crisply icy
    Old men drowsing in the park
You are all of joy or beauty
    Gold of sun, or velvet dark.

Ellyn Coley

ALONE

Speech is silver—
Silence pure gold—

What does one know
Of the gold of my days?

Synthetic—tarnished
With my aloneness.

Like a heavy iron hand
    On my heart,
Pressing, ever pressing.

Desperate to still the
Magnified sounds of an
    Empty house
            into
    Nothingness.

Our lovely home—
This familiar room—
Your easy chair—
A pipe you once smoked,
'Gainst glowing embers
    in the night.

Only a moment
The grey veil parted,
While time moved back.

Yet even now—

With music filling
Every corner of our room,
Encircling, and enfolding me
In blue waves of sound.

Once again—
    Only stillness—
        My tarnished gold.
            Nothing!

Earline Elsie

I AM THE FARMER'S SON

I can't explain the feeling
That I get each time I see,
A bed of red, red roses,
An enchanted bumble bee.

The whole world is my palace;
The sky it is my all;
The green, green grass my carpet;
The bugle is my call.

The setting sun's my glory.
The night it is my day.
The little stars are lanterns,
That help me light the way.

The dewdrops are my diamonds
That sparkle in the sun.
Mother Nature is my keeper;
I am the farmer's son.

Michelle MCmay

SMALL TALK

The little child comes in from play
And begins to talk, to sail away,
On his sea of adventure as he tells me
Of his rendezvous with the honey bee.
And of the flowers that tickled his nose
And of his battle with the garden hose.
He tells of the wind, how it whipped his clothes
And how the trees move when it blows.
He speaks of the birds: How do they fly?
Up and up to touch the sky.
Why is the grass always so green?
But then his eyes close, he begins to lean
More heavily upon me while he sleeps.
His small talk forgotten, now is for dreams.
There's time for tomorrow's small talk and all
Another day when small adventure will call.

Ruth Craig Leasure

110

THE KINGDOM

There is a land where demons dwell,
And iron chimes are known to knell
On blackened hills and falling trees,
And ogres ride the sullen leas.

And tombs are set upon a hill,
Where people, silently, there dwell,
And none dare move, and all are still,
And iron chimes are known to knell;
And dire notes of music rise
Among the darkened leaves of trees,
And all are seen in somber guise,
And ogres ride the sullen leas;
And all are chained and can't elude
This land, this cave of muted pleas,
This kingdom of dark solitude,
Where no light shines on fallen trees.

There is a land where demons dwell,
And iron chimes are known to knell
On blackened hills and falling trees,
Where iron chimes are know too well.

Art Steiger

THE MOCKINGBIRD

The mockingbird in the orange tree,
On yonder branch called out to me
A whit-ahoo, a whit-ahee
Sang the mockingbird in the orange tree.
A challenge, then, he offered me,
The mockingbird in the orange tree.
I'll whit-ahoo, you whit-ahee
Sang the mockingbird in the orange tree.
And though I listened carefully,
I simply could not whit-ahee
That's for the birds, said I, with glee,
To the mockingbird in the orange tree.

Maxeyn Swords Potter

111

AN AUGUST AFTERNOON

On a lazy, hazy, August afternoon
We hear the wheezy locust's tune;
And soon we'll hear the little katy's song
Which warns that frost will come 'ere long.

The robin sings his farewell song
He says "I'm leaving for the South, real soon
But I'll be back again next year
To charm you, in the month of June."

The squirrels are busy storing food
Which feeds them through the winter's cold;
As overhead, an airplane's drone
Is heard in dreamy monotone.

Nellie Goldy

WINTER COMES

See now virgin days of spring
When all about me there is born,
A promise of the days to come,
The pulsing life of summer morn.
And summer comes and all its days
Are filled with sweetness, too soon gone.

Then autumn comes, my heart despairs.
The fiery brilliance on display
Tells only of the sleep to come,
And points a finger to the day
When winter's quiet blanket falls,
And ends a tired way.

Keep the spring within my breast
And the joy of summer morn.
Stay autumn from my frightened heart
And tell me that I can be born
Each day, to feel my life anew,
Lest winter comes and I am gone.

Theresa Milton

LANTERN OF LOVE

The moon is a lantern of love, you know,
Sending its beams to earth below;
Beckoning to shadows with its glow;
The moon is a lantern of love.

The moon is a lantern of love, so fair,
With beams lightly dancing without a care;
They peek into a lion's lair;
The moon is a lantern of love.

The moon is a lantern of love, so grand,
Guiding two lovers holding hands,
And leading them into a magic land;
The moon is a lantern of love.

The moon is a lantern of love, so bright,
Lighting dark pathways in the night,
And hastening two hearts in love's delight;
The moon is a lantern of love.

The moon is a lantern of love, indeed,
And always has been so decreed;
Surely without it the night has a need;
It remains a lantern of love.

Bonnie M. Burt

THE NEW LITTLE FROG

There was a froggie in the bog,
Who perched himself upon a log;
With bulging eyes he viewed his world.
He croaked a timerous croak, and waited,
And was so relieved to hear it mated,
By another froggie.
A duet soon developed broadly,
The two did face the world so loudly;
And soon other froggies joined the singing;
Then the bog was really swinging!

H. Rala Scheel

113

CITY-BRED, IF YOU WOULD

City-bred, if you would work with him,
For just one day,
Then you would know how much
And why he loves the land,
And you would feel
His deep, unspoken gratitude,
For those who labor
In the mill,
Melting, forming
Bars of steel, that one day
Will be machines
And tools, that are his
Constant need.

A vital spark, in a demanding world,
His needs are great.
Buffeted by subsidies
And economic whim—
City-bred, he needs the best you have to give,
For no computer can assay—how much—
Your livelihood depends on him,
And how much, he in turn,
Depends on God.

Edith B. Fassler

TIME

Time goes by and we get old.
It is one thing we can't hold.
The bygone days we recall.
And many things when small.
Horse and buggy days are passed.
Now things are going fast.
Time brings night and day.
Brings and takes things away.
Here we are to journey on,
Just for a time and gone.
Many changes from time we see,
And many more there will be.
The time comes and goes.
What to bring, God only knows.

Poem Time

CONTENTED SQUIRREL

As I sat watching a squirrel in a tree,
I suddenly thought how happy he must be.

Did he ever want more than what he had?
Did he ever know sorrow or was he ever sad?

Was he always so contented with the life that he led?
Or did he want to start over or wish to be dead?

If humans could be as contented as that squirrel in the tree,
I couldn't imagine what a wonderful world this would be.

William E. Williams

A tiny wren
Perched on my plum tree
And sipped sweet raindrops
With its beak.

A gentle breeze
Swept through the sunbeams
And taught the grasses
How to speak.

A little girl
Plucked daisy petals
And blew their softness
To the wind.

A quiet word
Brought fragile teardrops
For joy is best a
Silent thing.

Dagmar Lagnado

GOODNIGHT, LITTLE COWBOY

Well, my little cowboy, guess
It's time you were hitting the hay.
You must be doggone weary,
You've been riding the range all day.
I've watched you when you weren't looking
And smiled for a while at your schemes,
For the big corral has a picket fence,
And the cattle go by in your dreams.
How you love to follow the lowing herds
Beneath the wide western sky.
Content to live for the moment yet,
Never noticing days drifting by.

May God bless my cowboy's childhood,
May the days all be cloudless and fair,
While your prairie is only a backyard lawn,
And your horse is a wooden chair.
For someday the wide world will call you,
And slowly our trails will divide.
You'll leave us behind at the homestead,
Down roads of your own you will ride.
Yes, you'll bid us goodnight, little cowboy,
And the long, happy hours of today
Will pass into memory's keeping
As a young man goes out on his way.

Julia Ransom

MOTHERS LULLABY

If I could take the sunshine
    From out the sky of blue,
And the fragrance of a lovely rose
    Kissed by the morning dew,
If I could take the bluebird's song
    And a fleecy cloud on high
I would put them all together
    For a mothers lullaby.

Lena McMinn

116

CHINESE GARDEN

The lanterns hang
In the cherry trees
And swing
And sway
In the soft, cool breeze.

The air is filled
With the magic sound
Of Chinese
Chimes
Hanging far from the ground.

The cherry bough and
The lotus bloom
Grow soft
And light
Giving sweet perfume.

The high arched bridge
O'er the silver stream
Lovely
Maidens
Cross as they dream

Midst the beauties of the
Chinese garden.

Christine Pasanen

THOUGHTS AND STARS

Seemingly silhouetted against black velvet,
Stars share a silence unknown to the world.

A quiet peacefulness pervades the still night air,
And myriads of wee lanterns twinkle,
Lighting the vast expanse of heavens.

And here am I,
An insignificant being among many,
Like one star in a galaxy.

Diane L. Klimt

STRANGER PASSING BY

As I was walking,
  Along the side of the road;
An old man came stumbling,
  With a very heavy load.
His burden was heavy,
  And unable to see;
In his great darkness,
  He confided in me.

"Please mister don't tell,
  Anyone of my fears;
Of how I'll get by,
  Through the forthcoming years.
My family's all gone now,
  I'm left all alone;
I've nothing to do now,
  But to wander and roam.
I've traveled so far,
  But nowhere can I find;
The hardest of all things,
  That's peace of my mind.
Mister please help me,
  Tell me what can I do;
Until I'm with my family,
  In a life that's all new?"

I forced back my own tears,
  To help him feel strong;
Not knowing his journey,
  Would not be too long.
Then he said "Thank you mister,
  For listening to me;
I'll remember you in heaven,
  Where I'm going to be."
As he bowed down his head,
  As if in a prayer;
I knew that the Lord,
  Had taken him there.

Glen Virgil Steller

I MEANT NO HARM

"I meant no harm" she cried
  No, you meant no harm
But it hurt just the same
  You meant no harm
Yet the tears did fall
  Doubts were born
But you meant no harm

No words can erase
  The hurt you caused
Yet you can only say
  You meant no harm!
Because of you and what you said
  Someone has been hurt
Someone's faith in you has died
  You meant no harm!
And yet it's done—if you could have been
  A little more careful
Perhaps you might not need to say
  "I meant no harm!"

Gloria Fish

WHY RUSH?

Rush! Rush! Rush!
What's all the fuss?
You'll catch the train. You'll catch the bus.
You needn't rush to get a seat.
Why do you think you have two feet?

Slow down! Slow down!
Don't hurry so!
Oops!
Pardon me, I've got to go.
I've got to run and catch the bus.
That's all it is, is rush, rush, rush!

Rosalia Barbera

119

A VALENTINE FOR MY HUSBAND

You're more than just my Valentine,
    You're everything to me.
To be your wife and love you
    Is all I want to be.

The years have passed so quickly,
    And yet I love you more
Each day that passes by, my love,
    Than I did the day before.

Mere words can never tell you
    How much you mean to me,
Nor can a lifetime spent with you
    Be quite enough for me.

Whate'er may come from this day on,
    I hope we'll never part.
My love for you will never end.
    Remember this, sweetheart!

                    Lorraine Claybaugh

LOVE'S TICKET

Come love, with me
And exchange dreams
Pawn a hope of tomorrow
Later to be redeemed
When time is up
And feelings down
You will leave the pawnbroker's
With the sun shining warmly on your back
And a good feeling in your heart
That you once more have
What you had given up

                    Brian Kelley

THE DREAM

As a child, I opened dream-filled eyes in the
    early morning hours
    and greeted each new day as though it were the
    moonflower,
        tumbling forth its blossoms of delight.
Night, as the closing of the blooms,
    brought the promise of rebirth . . . .
And then one day—so suddenly—I entered the
    rainbow-world of love, where soft-spoken words,
    a gift from my beloved, wrapped round me
        like pale velvets.
Here, in my isolated, much-populated, world, I
    sang away the days of autumn and laughed
    through the warm hours of winter.
But in spring my love was gone and with him went
    the season's beauty
        and I could find no reason to
        justify my existence.
So, until my moonflower days return, as eventually
    they must, I will drift slowly into the
        shallow days of summer . . .

Anne Johnson

ANOTHER DAY

Another day,
Turning the pages,
I came upon a clipping.
And it was an announcement.
The cutline read,
"Today Mr. and Mrs. announced
    the engagement of their daughter
    Miss, to Mr."
And I picked it up,
And it crumbled—like everything else.
Another day,
Turning the pages . . . . . .

Michael DeArmond

121

MY GEM

This so-called thing is a gem to me
For it is my very first car you see,
A big front end and painted black
A mile and a half from front to back,
The radio works and the heater is good
It has a smooth motor under the hood,
There's one experience I shall never forget
That's when my car and fence first met.
It started back at the old fairgrounds
Where I drove my gem around and around,
I followed a car through this gate you see
And onto the highway went my gem and me,
Then around this corner my house I see
I couldn't believe it was happening to me,
Well, into the alley I turned so-o slow
Crash, bang, boom, the fence did go.
Oh yes, that's one spot I'll never forget
Cause that's where my car and fence first met.

Esther (Collins) Washburn

TO YOU

Little boy
Making palaces by the sea;
The child at whom I smiled
But was far too busy to notice me
As you pat, pat, patted
The grains of sand
With the chubby, stubby fingers
Of your nimble, dimpled hand.
Oh build your castles high
As high as they will stand.
Toy with them
Enjoy them.
They will not be protected
Nor so easily erected
When you become a man.

Karen Springer

122

CAN THIS BE MINE?

Dear Creator,
      I know the world is mine . . . . yet . .
I cannot touch my heaven of clear blue, nor hold in
my hands, the purity . . . . and . . . white softness of
              one cloud; . . nor can I
catch the clean wildness of the wind, tho it touches
me . . . . as the lacey laps of ebb tide tease my feet. I
cannot fill a cup with the startling lure of the sea,
              but . . . .
Thank you, Lord,
          . . . for the pearly-pink shell that laid
              on its bed of sand.
Sea-sculptured, its translucent beauty touched lightly
by Time, it was teased . . .
                  and rejected,
by the ruffled coverlets of gentle shore waters.
It lay . . . . ignobly cast aside . . . by some slimy
denizen, an empty house from the sea . . . .
                 to be filled
with sirens' songs . . . . and . . . . thunderous roars
           of
Neptune's waves echoing thru its pink fluted lips.
Now . . . . I can touch and hold this symbol of
eternity . . . . and in wonderment, and in
               new awareness I
can listen to its endless symphony of the deep . . .
and forever, keep its beauty . . . . . . for my own.
Can this be mine?

Nelle Riggs

FISH

The green fish leaps high;
Then returns to the cool depths
Of his damp castle.

Samia Martz

123

SCHEDULES

"Rise and Shine," means on your feet,
To the bathroom, brush your teeth,
Gulp a cup of coffee down,
Grab the paper, get to town.

Work till five, catch the train,
Sometimes even catch a plane,
Destination, still watch clock,
Time will never, ever stop.

What if it did, you'd stop too,
Stop doing all the things you do,
Nothingness, dullness, vegetables all,
But you think you would have a ball.

Try it sometime, wait and see,
All of you will agree with me,
Schedules, bless them, knock them not,
Without them, we would all be rot.

Joyce Medow

AN AMERICAN'S DREAM

I'm going to be strong if it kills me
I'm going to be stout and brave,
I crave to be independent
I can be no one's slave.

I'll travel and search the world over
I want to learn much but fast,
For when I lay cold and silent
My soul will remember the past.

I want to love and live freely
No sorrows or regrets I keep,
For life is so brief and so short
And reasons for living so deep.

Sharon Dearing

124

REFLECTIONS FROM THE MIRROR
AT FORTY-FIVE

Mirror, mirror,
All florescence—
Reflecting
All my addled
Essence.

Little leaf, little leaf
Hold on tight—
Did you feel the wind last night?
Urgently it whispered "go"
Did you answer "no wind, no"?

Clutch the bough of frosted white
Hold time back with all your
Might
Gusty winds, swirling round
Little leaf, little leaf . . . down.

Jet mixed with snow—
Tiny furrows that go
Uninvited in a row

Summer is gone, it's November
Fires flame, now ember
Mirror, mirror, do you remember?

Chris Ford Lyons

Yesterday
was a restless pacification but
Today
was a painful realization and
Tomorrow
will be all too true.
Yesterday
I feared the things I had felt and
Today
I saw in your eyes that
Tomorrow
I would be dead.

Jean Fowler

125

MY MOTHER

Though my Mother's hands are getting wrinkled
Through the years with care and toil
Her hands still bring comfort
To those entrusted to her care.

My Mother's love is like a well—deep
Where waters flow
For her strength and her love never waver
As she works for those she loves.

Though my Mother's heart may break and tears
May fill her eyes
My Mother's love shines brightly
Like the thousands of stars at night.

God placed my Mother here to care
For those He loves
He gave her strength and patience
And an understanding love.

There is no end to her labors
For as she goes about her tasks
He gives the strength, the love, the hope,
The extra touch of His hand.

Robert James Gard

MICHELE

Who greets us with a heavenly smile,
Who makes life so well worth while.
Whose little arms reach out to us
      for comfort and a kiss,
Who fills mummy's busy day with
      perfect bliss,
Who, like the flowers in early spring,
      becomes more exciting day by day,
Who has that certain something
      to steal one's heart away.
Whom do the angels know and love
      so well, God's precious gift—
Our jewel—Michele.

M. J. Donly

A LOVE NOT YET FORGOTTEN

Far away on the distant horizon
I caught a glimpse of the last
Fading rays of the golden sun,
A touch of richness,
The gold in a day of dust.
Like love in a life of waste,
It's the rose that lends her beauty
To the chimney now standing in ruin.
It's the torch of memory
That lights the dark paths of the mind.
Two eyes so often remembered
Give faith to the fainting heart,
A caress not yet forgotten
Gives strength to a dying soul.
A smile shadowed by tears
Challenges hope for a brighter tomorrow.

Joyce Dean Stokes

AN APRIL SNOW

It came suddenly on a drab, windy,
    April evening . . .
From the pregnant clouds . . . falling
    ever so softly on the bright green
    world . . . coating each new bud
    and blade—even daffodils.

The next morning . . . it glittered
    when the sun's light shattered
    each crystal . . . then quickly
    disappeared . . . as a new warmth
    permeated the earth.

Diane Land

A TRUE FRIEND

To you a goodby.
To the one whose friendship and
    nearness I cherish with
    all my heart.
To you whose warmth and compassion
    give to life its true meaning
I give the love, that beautiful
    but limited love born the
    day we met.
And this love, which will never
    be given the chance to mature
    and grace you as I dream
Will forever be reason for you
    to call, write, and remember
    me when you desire;
And for me to hold till eternity
    and ever, your memory deep
    within my soul, so I may not
    feel so sharply the bitter
    cold of loneliness.

Karl R. Bosselmann

SOMEWHERE, A YEAR

We slipped through a breach,
Where future and present meet,
Gathered shining moments
Sprinkled at our feet.

Relentless thread of time
Called us back to a clime,
Where life is uncertain,
And events are out of rhyme.

Somewhere beyond space,
A year is sealed in grace,
Locked in silent reverie,
Only the heart can trace.

Audrey McKay

128

CINQUAINS FOR SPRINGTIME RAINS

The earth
is all aglow
with cherry blossoms and
pussy willows, babbling brooks and
new love.

The rain
tinkling on my
windowpane works magic
as a sweet symphony delights
my heart.

Springtime—
a mountain stream
leaving its frosty bed
trickles its way over death to
warm earth.

A dog-
wood tree standing
in the midst of the for-
est erases the cold bleakness of
winter.

Inhaled
are the perfumes
of freshly turned soil and
newly sprouted greenery; sweet
fragrance.
                    Helene Dunne

THE ELEMENTS

Where the sky meets the land,
And the land meets the sea,
Where fishing boats flock,
And sea gulls fly free,
The angry waves with dashing zest,
Rise up to a foamy crest,
Then they crash on rocks below,
Unfurling fury as they go.

Janet Jones
Age 14

The end has surely come
To an era of love
Time can never erase the splendor
Of a love that was so tender!

Steaming silence tries hard to melt
A heart of diamond strength
A mind fights hard to wrench memories away
And time the total healer by day;
Takes its toll in the darkness of the night.

Oh! God please give me the strength to bare
The loss, when his love
I no longer share.
Please, Dear God, help me sleep
When my life no longer has love to reap
Make me stronger.

Louise Martin

Life
Is brief,
Its stay short,
Withering into . . . .

Death,
Is darkness,
Overshadowing all life,
But blooming into . . . .

Eternity,
Is luminescence,
Shining forth in darkness.
Changing, unchanging into . . . .

The beginning,
In the end,
As the light producing life
And making it . . . .

Forever.

Tonda Fran Rush

130

FOOTPRINTS

You've come today; I know you have,
For you have made your mark
And left behind the sunshine
Where once the world was dark.

Though no one can explain to me
The magic of your feat,
There's gloom when you begin it
And joy when it's complete.

Though often you're unnoticed as
Your magic greets the ear,
There's no mistaking where you've
    been;
Your footprints are too clear.

You spread such happiness about
Before you go your way,
For you're a word of kindness
On a busy, hurried day.

Susan Frances Baker

WORDS

Why should a poet seek acclaim
For penning little words that prod
Unbidden at a tranquil mind—
Like small messages from God?

While he hopes to tap the wellspring
Of the happy and the good
He captures—more to understand
    himself
Than to be understood.

Having reached out, as it were, to
Grasp them, he sets them down in
    rhyme
Grateful when they guide the
Tracing of life's intricate design.

Doris Garvey Simo

131

TIME

Cruel time! Inexorable as fate!
There's none may stay its passing,
The humble or the great.

How often we would hasten
Through some trial of grief or pain!
But time cannot be hurried
To relieve our stress and strain.

How oft we'd hold the beauty
Of a moment that's sublime!
But none may stay the passing
Of the awful "march of time."

So, whether joy or sorrow
Is the order of our day,
Time, like a mighty river,
Will bear it all away.

Dorothy E. Whitney

I HAVE LIVED

I have lived to see the sun come out
    to make a sunny day
I have lived to see the moon at night
    and the milky way
I have felt the breeze upon my face
    and walked in ice and snow
I have seen the beauty of each spring—
And heard a robin sing—
I have climbed the highest mountain—
And built an open fire—
I have watched the restless ocean—
And tasted apple pie—
I have had true friendships
And a love to call my own
I have held a baby in my arms
And prayed my thanks to God—

Claire Anderson

EVERY TOWN

Each house, a treasured book
    With cover thick and strong,
Love fills up the pages
    There, the home is found.

Each fence, a colored jacket
    Rambling roses winding thru,
Each title's on the mailbox
    Each doormat welcomes you.

Open door the introduction
    To love's content, inside
Each room an illustration
    Of loving care and pride.

Each family has its chapters
    A book unto itself,
Every town's a bookcase
    Every street a shelf.

Isabelle M. Wall

WHEN AUTUMN WINDS BEGIN TO PLAY

Our golden dreams will soon appear
In radiant sapphire atmosphere,
To drive the darksome clouds away
When autumn winds begin to play.

The heart is filled from summer's yield
Of ladened tree or fertile field,
While maples dance in bright ballet,
When autumn winds begin to play.

The soul gives thanks on bended knee
In reverential liturgy.
Then voice is raised in roundelay,
When autumn winds begin to play.

Gertrude Whitehouse

HOME

The house a man lives in is his castle they say,
A joy to come home to after each weary day,
Whether a home is elaborate or a more modest style,
That it's lived in and loved in, that makes it worthwhile.
A home is as happy as folks dwelling therein,
It cheerfully reflects laughter from deep within,
How nice it would be if we all would decide,
To make *our* house gleam with a warmth from inside.
Home's where the heart is, our loved ones are there,
A place we are comfortable and a place where we share,
It makes my heart glad, this "castle," our own,
For loving, to dwell in, a place to call home.

Nora LaBryer

TRANSFORMATION

In solemn silence,
Nude trees stood
Shivering in the
Lonely wood.

Then mysterious changes
Overnight,
Adorned them all in
Crystal bright.

From top to bottom
They were decked
With frozen dew drops,
Rainbow flecked.

Intoxicated by beauty,
I stood to admire
The dazzling brilliance
Of icy fire.

Irene Wilson

I AM LIKE ADAM WONDER-FILLED

I am like Adam wonder-filled
On his first seeing an egret in flight
Muted and tremulous at glimpsing
A plane's silvery-ghost belly
And shadowy wing tips that taper
And diffuse into blue-gray mists
Making the configuration disputable
As though this particular flying machine
Will never land on any field
And I, chained by my Reality
Can not reach skyward and grasp
This missile of the intellect
But only watch its transcendental flight
Neither can I join in its merge with Space
For the price of a ticket to Somewhere
I remain earth-bound
Wonder-filled
And
Double-ironed
To the ground
Until my line of continuality
Is refracted across starry time.

Michael J. Skidmore

TRUTH

Deceive me not for moment splendor
   Nor cast me away while in a mood
Protect me with what you most treasure
   For I am the truth and I am good

Do not bend me to cause you shelter
   And do not use me only half way
For I, the power, will not suffer
   But you, the foolish, will have to pay

Do not let me drift from your meaning
   Place me in front of the wind and sea
Breath me in like it's life you're breathing
   And the breath of life, that shall I be

Don Wright

SO LITTLE TIME

Cease your haste, children of mine
For I would speak with you.
Cease your merriment, your drinking of wine
Behold! Chaos is coming in view.

I've given you minds to know right from wrong
Immortality dwells within your souls.

I'm weary, my children, my patience grows cold
These wars between brothers saddens my heart
You kill the young and even the old
My children, my children, we're drifting apart.

Soon the birds shall cease their song
There shall be no bread to fill your bowls.

So heed my words, children of mine
This is the last you shall hear from me
Heed my words, as best you can
For if I'm angered, you cease to be.

Jim Rabner

THE YEAR OF LOVE

It was a year of tears,
 A year of jeers.
A year of sureness,
 A time of insecureness.
A time of bashfulness,
 A year of rashness.
A time of sudden matureness,
 And surprising demureness.
It was a time of pure ecstasy,
 A time of bitter jealousy—
It was the year I first
 Fell in love.

Angel

136

WALKING WITH A GRANDCHILD

Grandma, why is the sky so blue?
Where do the turtles go?
What do the baby birds do?
Why do we walk so slow?

Where is the calfy's mama?
Why do horses snore?
Where are the fish now, Grandma?
What shall we get at the store?

Can chickens swim?
And why do birds eat worms?
Why are the leaves so red?
And why do pigs eat corn?

My legs are tired, Grandma,
But let's go see that cow.
Is it time to go home, Grandma?
Will you please carry me, now?

M. Elizabeth Radke

MY GRANDMOTHER

My grandmother is so sweet and dear,
She's got a hearing aid in one ear.

My grandmother loves us all,
And when we go there, we have a ball.

She thinks of us all day,
And we think of her in a special way.

She raised my mother and my aunt,
And she is very good, even at that.

My grandmother is so nice and kind,
That I hope she'll appreciate this
    poem of mine.

Nancy Ellen Brewer
Age 10

THE SPUTNIK

Not so long ago
In the year fifty-seven,
The Sputnik was launched
In a flight toward heaven.

A million miles high
Into outer space,
That little old Sputnik
Showed its face.

The flying saucers
Forgot to fly,
The day that Sputnik
Took to the sky.

A shiver was felt,
The stars gave a wail,
That Sputnik had cut
Through a comet's tail.

In the outer space world
A new era was begun,
The day that Sputnik
Moved around the Sun.

Mary Doran Schwinn

TRANSPORT

Night sounds
a creeping
sleepy train.
Snoring in the darkness
purring rhythm on aimless tracks.
Carrying
dreams of
half sleep
to a distant morning.

Blythe Ann Tilman

138

THE STEP

Three little boys, salty brown
    with summer,
Setting out upon a lovely mystery
As small boys will.

Waving good-bye as they turn
    the corner,
My mother-heart stopping with
    unhappened grief.
Will they return?
Will they be safe?

As hours pass, my heart grows
    pale.
Three little boys . . . . . where
    are they now? The adventure
    met and conquered?

A rush of voices at the open
    door, small ones returning.
They are safe home, a step
    completed into the world.

Thank you, God.

Saralee Lawson

SPRING WALK

Sun rays penetrate softly
    through delicate maple leaves.
Many have fallen, they rustle
    as you walk upon them.
A crystal glass rainbow, with
    softly shadowed colors, touches
    the earth.
The late droplets of rain fall
    gently off the leaves as if
    they were crying for some
    lost friend.
Spring sheds off its cocoon
    and butterflies into summer.

Deborah Plunk

THE BIG YELLOW CAT

You can see the swaying
  Of the large trees;
As they are blown,
  In the cold-stiff breeze.

That way and this,
  This way and that,
From across the road,
  Comes a big yellow cat.

Shaking and shivering,
  In the cold wind,
Where will he go
  At the cold day's end?

He'll probably crawl
  Down under the floor,
Until someone opens
  The big wooden door.

Then he'll walk in
  With an enlarged grin,
And be cuddled under
  A tiny girl's chin.

That's the way it is,
  With a big yellow cat,
And the trees are still swaying
  This way and that.

Acena A. Dyer

SALES RESISTANCE

I'd buy everything in the catalogue—
The sales "pitch" really gets me—
"Enclose check or money order"
Is the phrase that never lets me.

Evelyn Leeds

140

TO A SIX YEAR OLD GRANDSON IN A TOY STORE

"No, dear, I won't buy you a gun!
There are other ways to have fun.
Let's buy something to create skill,
Like a dish to tile, for a thrill."

"Let's buy some checkers, for a change,
Or a puzzle you can rearrange;
Look, here are flash-cards, please tell me,
The colors and the words you see."

"I know your dad is a marine,
Come, look at this gay tambourine!
Yes, I do want you to have fun . . . . .
Alright, come on, I'll buy a gun!"

Anne Esch

my butterfly,
fleeting
in its
beauty,
wistful in
its
primal form.
castled in
elysian fields,
pursuing the
path of
evanescence.

i long to
follow.

b. shields

141

THE HILLS OF HOME

I miss the hills in springtime, when dogwood
    blossoms glow
Amongst the forest's haze of green, that
    once were graced with snow
I miss the hills in summer, when garbed in
    robes of green
They add, with stately grandeur, their
    magic to the scene.

I miss the hills in autumn, when colors
    "stage" the "show"
The "back-drop" is a mixture from
    rainbow's lavish flow
I miss the hills in winter, when clothed in
    ice and snow,
Memories of their beauty still keep my heart
    aglow.

I wandered away from that land, seeking to
    find new thrills
But my thoughts always return to the
    beauty of the hills
For no matter where I go, nor how my
    feet may roam,
I'll always miss the splendor, found in
    the hills of home.

Evelyn Garton O'Brien

OF SUMMER NIGHTS

Heat, discomfort, humidity.
Sticky clothing, sweaty bodies, sleepless nights.
A flash of lightning—
A roar of thunder—
The steady pitter-patter of falling rain.
Coolness—comfort—sleep.

Victoria E. Laskowski

STEPPING STONES

While walking down the road of life
    A rocky path I see;
Are these just stumbling blocks of strife,
    Or stepping stones to Thee?

The way looks narrow and forlorn
    But, yet, it has an end;
Perhaps before we are reborn,
    We must stumble, fall and bend.

A little trouble on the way
    Seems but a minor thing,
When at the end of life's highway
    We hear the angels sing.

So walk the rough and narrow road
    For at your journey's end,
You'll feel your perils all unload,
    And there you'll be with Him.

J. L. Barber

THE LAKE

I sit in the tall grass
On the steep shore
And dangle my toes
Just an inch or more
Above the small ripples,
Out of reach of the waves;
Oh, this is the feeling
My hungry mind craves!

The sun drops her diamonds
On the water's bright crest;
The lake hold them gently
And close to her breast.
Along her steep banks
The calmness I find
Is good for the body
And good for the mind!

Christine Pasanen

TO YOU

Remember the first day we met?
Your smile and friendly ways
Made me want to know you better.

The days and weeks went by,
But not without a great accomplishment
For we soon became good friends.

We shared secrets and jokes.
We teased each other, and
Many hours were spent in laughter.

You became ill one night,
And I sat beside you
Trying to instill some sort of comfort.

My only hope is that I succeeded
For it is my way of saying,
I treasure our friendship.

Donna C. Spranger

SHIFTING SAND

Your love is like the sea
Calm, then exciting it can be.
It is silent—
Then it roars.
All at once a love soars.
My love is like the shore
Without sea, it is no more.
I await the returning tide
Once again to be by your side.
I would be as shifting sand
If the sea took away her hand.
Let me know the thrill once more
When the sea touches the shore.

Joanne G. Looper

DEDICATED

My heart is filled
With a joy that echoes
Throughout my whole body
In a way
Which is not too outstanding,
But worthwhile
In making a difference
Between the ordinary
And the extraordinary.

My face reflects
The inner happiness
Concerning satisfaction
Of things accomplished
Or not important at all,
For after all is gone
My mind remains
In a state
Of love.

Rene Mathieu

MOUNTAIN BROOKLET

Happy little brooklet
Rippling in the sun,
Dancing, dashing,
Sparkling, splashing—
Ever on the run.

Merry little brooklet
From the mountain side,
Tumbling, hurrying,
Frisking, scurrying—
To meet the river wide.

Jolly little brooklet
Springing to and fro,
Slipping, sliding,
Tripping, gliding—
Everywhere you go.

Olin C. Bissell

MY LITTLE LEAF

My little leaf of autumn gold,
I heard the story that you told,
While lying there so all alone,
No other leaf to call your own.

You wished to dance the autumn song,
While winds were singing loud and strong,
The other leaves all danced in pairs,
Shedding their colors and their cares.

But there you lie, my little leaf,
As I ponder my disbelief,
Why, a wind so strong, so bold,
Cannot grasp you in its fold.

Then I knew why you were alone,
With fragile beauty all your own,
There was none other to compare,
You were special, you were rare.

You were not meant to join in song,
This interval of music is not long,
The winter ermine soon will press,
All autumn music and its dress.

But you, my little leaf of gold,
Shall have a home when you grow old,
I'll keep you in a special book,
Your page is where I'll always look.

So, I'll pick you up, we'll both go home,
And you will never be alone,
For to my eyes you will always be,
The dearest leaf I'll ever see.

Anne Freeze

GRASS IN FALL

A golden blanket over green
Captured dewdrops in between.

Peggy Dehn

TWINHOOD

I speak to you on being a twin.
One is always going to win.
I was slow; she was fast.
I was usually coming in last.
I did not want to dress alike.
Neither did I want to share the one
    bike.
For awhile, when she did as I did not like,
    I would pinch.
And somehow, we both knew she would
    give in the inch.
For mistakes, she was given the blame.
For me, things were still the same.
Authority she always gave.
Decisions she surely made.
Being a twin is not all fun.
People see the two as one.
Each is her very own.
As so, she should be known.

Sally Kirkland Shirley

THE BEGINNING OF SCHOOL

Children gather by the door
Vacation time is no more.

Excited voices, laughter and tears
The beginning of the school year is here.

Pretty dresses, nice new shirts,
Deep pressed trousers, pleated skirts.

Bright new blouses, shining shoes,
Gather in groups for summer news.

The doors fling open, the teachers appear
Study begins for another new year.

Leona S. Rossi

A FRIENDLY HAND

When you haven't got a dime,
And you're feeling mighty blue,
You just can't see the sunshine
And you don't know what to do.

Then a fellow comes along
And takes you by the hand;
You straighten up your shoulders,
And all the world seems grand.

You almost thought there wasn't one,
That you could call a friend.
Just because you had no job,
No money you could spend.

There are two kinds of people
In this old world today;
The ones who pass you on the street
And look the other way.

Then there are the others,
They take you by the hand,
You can feel their interest in you
And know they understand.

They realize you're not to blame,
Misfortune came your way.
Somehow the load is lifted,
And the sun breaks through today.

Your heart begins to flutter,
You hold back the gathering tears;
With real friends, when you're in trouble,
There's no worry, no more fears.

Lotta R. Drake

RAINDROPS

I love to watch the raindrops
Slide down my windowpane,
I catch them with my finger
And push them up again.

Lillian V. Piner

THE BLOOM OF DAWN

In yawning reddness, infant morn
Half lifts its head as night is worn,
And tiny fingers stretching out,
Unveils a blurry world of doubt,
Like small retrievers, golden beams
Have filtered away a world of dreams,
For dawn no more content to lie,
Now creeps and crawls across the sky,
The shaded figures—ghosts of past—
Are now a more familiar cast,
Like giant brushes sweeping hues,
Subduing sketchy night previews,
The master's handiwork is shown,
The bud of dawn is now full-blown.

Bethel Arthur Angus

CHICAGO: A MOSAIC

Chicago:
A mosaic of peoples;
Where lie the hopes of the future;
Where thousands upon thousands
Seek for contentment and advancement;
Where thousands more lie in fallow waste,
Unwilling to seek, therefore
Cannot find.

Chicago:
A city with many faces—
The new and the old
All intermingled with the masses
Who labor together, knowing and unknown,
To build a city of dreams—

Chicago.

Eloise Dunn Bryant

APRIL

Waiting on the threshold
   We saw her yet afar—
And opened wide the welcome-gate
   That so long stood ajar.

Her arms were filled with flowers,
   There were joy-tears in her eyes—
There was sunshine in her laughter
   And she bore a glad surprise—

For a mighty bird-song chorus
   Echoed through the distant hills
To the joyous melody and splash
   Of a thousand rippling rills—

While the western breezes whispered
   Of nature's glad rebirth,
And the scent of Easter lilies
   Enshrouded all the earth.

Stella B. Arancibia

FLOWERS

I sit beside the daisy fair
And stroke its softly yellowed hair.

Its round green body
And oval arms—
Its pretty face—
The charm of charms!

The tulip with her upturned nose
A crisp spring breeze: She strikes a pose.

And there upon the meadow hill
Are many buttercups to spill.
Upon the unset table green
The buttercup shall reign as queen.

Donna Conroy
Age 11

INSOMNIA BOUND

There are so many little things,
  That I find really boring;
But the one that bothers me the most,
  Is to hear my husband snoring!
I roll and toss and turn at night,
  And count so many sheep;
Then finally I do relax,
  And try to go to sleep.
The noise starts, I'm wide awake,
  Oh my! Why must he snore?
I punch and pinch and kick at him,
  And push him on the floor!
Now he's awake and angry,
  And as grumpy as can be.
Just why he would get mad at me,
  I really can not see.
So by the time he crawls back in,
And starts again to snore,
It's nearly dawn and I'm so tired—
  The noise, I ignore!

Ann Bear

CONTENTMENT

I walk among the flowers,
  And feel that God is near,
And He, who marks the sparrow's fall,
  Has bid me have no fear.

And as the days go swiftly by,
  I know His constant care,
I need not seek in a far off place,
  My God is everywhere.

So, I'll be content in my little sphere,
  Doing my daily tasks;
Worshiping, serving, praising Him,
  For this is all He asks.

Esta A. Hart

151

THERE HAVE BEEN . . .

There have been times when I have looked at life
From out of the eyes of sorrow.
There have been times when I have wept warm tears
And tasted of their salt.
There have been times of deep heartaches
Which have cut my vision.
There have been times of utter loneliness
Found in the emptiness of nights so dark.
There have been times I've wanted to cry.

There have been times when I have loved
Only to remain unloved.
There have been times of frantic despair
When I've felt like ending everything.
There have been times of terror
When I've known not what to do.
Yes, there have been bad times.
They have been many—but fear not, for
There have been good times, as well.
They have not been so few.

There have been times of happiness
When I have bubbled, like a child with joy.
There have been times of complete gladness
For life has been wonderful to me.
There have been times of laughter
Thanks to happy thoughts and cheerful looks.
There have been times of sunshine
When my heart has been empty of its rain.
There have been times of contentment
And of well earned rest.

Cheryl Paulsen

LOST

A dried blade of grass drifted by
On the graveled roof outside my
Dirty window.

It tumbled about, very tired and
Lonely, wondering what it had done
To deserve eternal exile from roots.

Gayle A. Hansley

152

A SCREEN PLAY

Deep, dark depression
   shadowly shows
itself
   upon the narrow
transient screen of life.

Tragic, troubling trials
   myriadly mirage
themselves
   across the stage
in panoramic view.

Slyly, slowly, softly,
   death dances
inevitably
   out and up
freely forming fast finales.

Daniel R. Lakeman

HEART'S SEASONS

The dogwood in spring lifts yearning branches bare;
Deep in her heart the buried dream begins to waken.
Petals white appear . . . promise of a love most rare;
Clothing her in modest organdy—as befits a maiden.

Leaves now—where once blossoms white have been.
For in the fruitful summer—occupied with living—
She wears her soft, full gown of homespun green;
Growing, loving . . . she fulfills herself in giving.

In the fall she proudly dons her richest garment;
Fashioned of shimmering tafetta—deep, heart-red,
With an underglow of gold. For this brief moment,
Glorious . . . by the promised love fulfilled.

Frost now, revealing in her heart a silent grief.
Must proud glory go ever so . . . . . .
Slowly falling, leaf—after stricken leaf;
Bare branches mutely praying for the quiet snow?

Jane Ridenour

MY FRIEND THE CAT

Old ladies and cats, like old men and dogs,
Just naturally go together—
An easy chair, and crackling logs;
Who cares about the weather.

Something dependent to wait upon,
To cheer the lonely hours,
To fill the void of a family gone,
You turn to cats, and flowers.

When you miss the ones who have left the fold,
And the hours seem empty and long;
A cat is warm, and soothing to hold,
And its purring is like a song.

Its head is lifted to listen,
Its tail waves to and fro;
Its eyes are bright and they glisten,
Watching your will to know.

You speak, and it strains to hear;
You move, and it's by your side;
Oh a cat will bring you cheer,
And still stay dignified.

Their love and trust, they bestow;
It can't be begged or bought;
Yet once it is given, you'll know
A true companion you've got.

Anna V. Shive

GOOD MORNING

Good morning and a good today!
May all things happy come your way.
And may the light of the new dawn,
Find all your cares and worries gone.
So much the simple words convey—
"Good morning—it's a lovely day!"

Muriel Baker

154

DEATH OF A SPIKE BUCK

As steaming mists of morning rose
And hounds were loosed at break of day,
A tiny buck did run, then froze.
Too late! So still in death he lay.

Oh, God, what a tragic deed is done!
To fell a kingly, valiant beast
With triple blast of hunter's gun,
And watch its noble life surcease.

No longer will he rub or flail
His crown upon a tree or stake,
And leaping, bound away, and sail
Into a cane or cypress break.

His snowy, gallant flag will fly no more
In teasing classic flight,
Nor will he hide and quietly lie
'Til dreaded danger moves from sight.

As sunset falls upon the lake
And creatures of the wood do drink,
This tiny buck can never take
A cooling sip from off its brink.

Frederick T. Shepherd

WAVES

Silver folds of cloth stretched across the
    wide, wide land,
Rising high and falling, as if water all there be,
Thus gently, softly, slapping the sparkling
    golden sand,
Then, drawing back slowly and blending with the sea.

Waves that splash our sandy beach and beaches
    far away.
Clear, blue waves, like sapphires in the sun—
Rolling, roaring, rocking across the land each day,
Night comes, the sunlight fades, and another day is done.

Patricia Schuler

155

OUR PASTOR

When a baby is born,
    Pastor is there.
When a man dies,
    Pastor is there.
When a man and woman want to
    Live the rest of their lives
      Together,
    They come to him.
When they are fed up,
    They come back to him.

Our pastor, must be able to go from
    Death to birth in a matter of hours,
And from a marriage to a divorce in
    The swing of his office door.
Our pastor, thinks of the young woman
    With laughter tumulting from her lips,
    As she talks with her husband to be.
He thinks of the little boy in an oxygen tent,
    With his teddy bear near.
He thinks of the mother smiling,
    The smile of first mothers,
    As she tells of the birth of her child.

And then, he thinks of himself and his
    Being there, and of God's coming
    Somewhere, out of the nowhere
    Into the now, here, and being there,
    Too . . . .
        Our pastor.
            Diane Schutt

Because God made us builders all,
Unbounded is our worth;
In answer to each worthy call,
Lord guide our talents forth.
Deliver us from selfish gain,
Enrich our hearts to build;
Resplendent may our works remain,
Sublime, each task fulfilled.

        Ervin H. Strub

COME HOME, COME HOME, COME HOME TO THE SEA

Sand churns beneath my feet,
As the soft light of evening is covered
By the dark inrush of cold cold sea.

In the dwindling light I stand,
Silently on the shore;
My heart flys out to briny depths,
Neptune touches my hand
And golden throated sirens call longingly.

I am alone with the sea
With each roaring pitching wave
Calling out to me:
Come home, come home, come home to the sea.

Heaven has hidden her jewels,
No flickering guiding lights,
Only blackness overhead and below
Nothing but sea, oh endless endless sea.

Orion and the North Star,
Guides of ancient mariner,
Have vanished from the sky above.
The horizon has melted into the sea.
The sea: a cold blanket that longs to cover me.
The sea: a kingdom rivaled only by heaven's majesty.

Vastness of ocean, you will not cover me.
I am trembling on your threshold,
But magnetized by your call,
Come home, come home, come home to the sea.

William Elton Houck

The whistling wind
Howls through tall, barren trees,
Then weaves through the grass.

Carol Brodaczynski

THE REGAL BEAGLE

There's a regal beagle that lives on our street,
   he walks erect on dainty feet.
With a neat little sweater to keep him cozy,
   at times he's inclined to be a little nosy.

When passing by the butcher shop,
   he always comes to a sudden stop.
And looking up expectingly,
   hoping for a wiener, or two or three.
But if by butch he is ignored,
   by passers-by he is adored.

"Isn't he sweet, a doll, I'll bet,
   I know he's just the perfect pet."
He looks as if he understands,
   and prances forward like the leader of a band.
He's quite a sight this little fellow,
   his leash bedecked with stones of yellow.

His mistress looks at him with pride,
   as he walks devotedly at her side.
You can see his elegance from his head to his toes,
   and by the toss in the air of his little nose.
There are pets of all kind;
   from chimpanzees to the bald eagle,
but none can match the regal beagle.

Chris Nelson

NOW

Yesterday's laughter is comfort,
tomorrow's laughter is fear
Best of laughter is what we share,
laughter now and here
Yesterday's love is sadness,
tomorrow's love is death
Best of love is what we share,
breath to passing breath

Katherine Kastler Young

158

THE CHINESE ELM

Beneath its shade I used to play
All the long, unhurried day
Crowded years away.

My world, not yet begun
Was that place of light and sun
By childhood won.

Its green and gold of chequered light
Its temple song of bells in flight
Made pure delight.

I pledged returns with happy sigh.
Countless days have since gone by:
Now, traitor, I

Turn aside and revoke
All that might now evoke
Nostalgia's cloak.

Zenobia Stockton

A SHINING STAR

Long ago in days of old
There shone a star as bright as gold
Brighter than any other star.
Three shepherds saw it from afar
They traveled here, they traveled there
Till they came upon a stable bare.
Inside the stable were oxen and sheep
A mother and father, and child fast
    asleep.
Then from the heavens an angel came
Saying this was the Christ child born
    to fame.

Rowena Middleton
Age 14

159

TEARS AND SHADOWS

I walked out in the moonlight
To watch the stars above,
But little did I know then
They did not shine of love.

For only tears and shadows
Shown bright up in the skies
Only to match the sorrow
That shows up in my eyes.

Why did you ever leave me
To go with someone new
When *all* I did was tell you
That my love was always true.

Now I walk out in that moonlight
To face those stars alone
That only match the hurt and pain
That's deep within me sown.

Linda A. Hollingshead

I leave to my son
   the weeping willows,
The birds who in heaven fly.
The clouds drifting above
   giant trees,
The sun up in the sky.
The clover fields, the
   daffodils,
The silent babbling brook.
And all the good things
   he shall learn,
From God and His great Book.

Melva Blakley

I WONDER

As I burst forth year after year,
I think of brave men lying here
Who gave their all that men be free,
And then I wonder, could it be
That wars are fought time after time,
Without a single reason or rhyme,
Because the world is full of greed,
And hate of color, race and creed?

I am the Flander's Poppy.
I represent them all,
The black, the white, the short,
The tall, who died for right
And now I pause to wonder why,
Men still must fight.

Will I be worn in memory
Of those who did their best,
And who now rest in Flanders
Field?

Or will they be forgot
Amid the present strife for
Others to be free,
And prove that neither war
Was fought for liberty.

I wonder.

G. B. Evans

THERE MUST BE A SPARK

There must be a spark
To be kindled by a dream;
To burn in the realm of genius
And glow in the borders of creativity;
To smolder in the thoughts of others,
To grow cold in the waves of time
And turn into ashes of the obscure.

Kenneth Record

A GRANDDAD'S SOLILOQUY
Dedicated to Bonnie Anne Logan

How in the world did we get along
Before you came to town?
We had forgotten that jet black hair
Could be as soft as down.
We had forgotten a lot of things:
A baby's cry and coo,
The dance and sparkle of bright blue eyes,
The cute things babies do;
The cuddling love as they nestle close,
Early attempts to smile,
The thrill of watching them fast asleep;
These make life so worthwhile.

How in the world can you be so good?
Seldom you fuss or fret,
Requiring little to be content;
Small wonder you're our pet.
Each passing day as we see you change
Brings happiness anew.
You're a heaven-sent bundle of joy;
A bonnie lass, are you.
The happy hours which we spend with you
Are worth far more than gold.
The pleasures you bring us every day
Are myriad tales untold.

How in the world could so small a tot
Instantly steal one's heart?
Almost, it seems, you planned it that way;
We loved you from the start.
Looking ahead to when you sit up,
Or your first baby tooth,
Or your first steps—what thrills are these,
But Bonnie Dear in truth
Perhaps the greatest thrill of them all
Will be the day you speak.
We wonder what your first word will be:
"Ma Ma," "Da Da" or "Peek"?

How in the world can such boundless joy
Be wrapped in one so young?
As you go up the ladder of years
We'll glory in each rung.
The brightness of stars, seen in your eyes,
Foretell, to us, it seems,
Life will bless you with sunny bright rays,
The sparkle of moonbeams.
And as the years go rolling along
A richer life we'll know.
Ahead of us lies a whole new world—
Watching our Bonnie grow.

Tom Logan

A CHILD'S WORLD

A child's world is in color:
    Pink clouds that hold dreams,
    Blue waters that hold adventure,
    Red fire that holds schemes,
    Yellow flowers that hold wonder.
    Green grass that holds life,
    Purple doors that hold mystery,
    Orange anger that holds strife,
    Golden pictures that hold the future.

Why is my world in black-and-white?

Joan Damoth

THE UNKNOWN

I haven't the right to question
or the knowledge to answer but I
do have the curiosity to wonder.

Joyce E. Flowers

ADOLESCENCE

Why do I forget myself so often?
Why is she considered sensible
    and me giddy?
Why do people respect her
    and look down at me?
What is my purpose?
What is my talent?
What is me?

She sings, the other dances
She draws, the other thinks,
But I exist.
I dwell, I do nothing
I do everything and yet nothing
What is me?
What do I mean?

Why does she know what to say
    always at the right time?
Why are my comments tossed aside?
Why do people hold her up as beauty,
    as grace, as goodness?
Why am I a child?
When do I mature?
When do I know what is right?
When do I gain wisdom?
When do people stop making comparison?
When will I be me?
When?

Alice Greenwald

CONTEMPLATION

Let us not fail to glean every vestige of
    joy from our todays—
For these todays become tomorrow's
    memories.
How tragic to rob ourselves of
    rejoicing in remembering.

Wanda G. Orr

A TIME FOR PLANTING

How quickly pass the seasons
that form the years called YOUTH,
those precious years of sowing
the seeds of Right and Truth.

The first shoots spring up slowly
from under fertile grounds;
the strangeness of their growing
is done with wind-swept sounds.

The green leaves spread and blossom,
the slender stalks fill out,
and as they stretch up higher,
the fruits begin to sprout.

The beauty of their growing
is often never seen,
but truly there is beauty
as leaves turn darker green.

The fruits begin to mellow,
the branches bow and bend,
and as they quickly ripen,
the harvesters descend.

The orchards then are empty,
the cycle is complete—
the fresh-picked crop is scattered,
to go forth to compete.

But in some distant orchard,
among the new-plowed rows,
the process is repeated,—
another seedling grows.

Raymond J. Harms

Seven swallows sang
Soft, solemn lullabys and
Sipped honeysuckle.

Brenda Crawford

In the autumn's middle days
People sit under twilight trees
  Some sketch fallen branches
  Some contemplate life's wounds
  Others tantalize sweet conversations
But many just sit, knowing how to

Carol Phillips Rosenberg

A STAR FOR HOPE

I am a stranger on this lonely hill.
My thoughts, bat-like, dart noiselessly too near.
Mouse fears creep close and nibble at my heart;
And doubts, like owls, hoot eerily about.

The small cicadas beat their serenade
Incessantly upon the midnight air.
And from the ebon that encircles me,
I lift my eyes to heaven; there a star,
A little star shines brightly from the heights
Communicating kinship with my soul.

K. Stevenson Shaffer

DAWN

Gathering softly, the world of darkness waits,
  and holds its breath
til gray and silent, the dawn comes
  and they blend together,
fighting silently, the battle of
  dark and light
until at last the victor emerges,
  bringing the day.

Kathryn C. Walton

COSMIC IMPETUS

Outside; black shrouds of night
   have fallen . . .
Above; the naked moon
   gleams thru!
Inside; I feel
   the universe calling,
"Come, burst these bonds
   binding you!
Come, soar through celestial
   heights!
Come, scan each blue
   nodding star!
Come, alight and rest on the cool
   waning moon . . .
Be the free spirit
   that you know you are!"

Russ Michael

THE COMING OF NIGHT

Velvety tenor of fading light—
Splashes of sunshine 'midst shadows a-tremble.
—the coming of night—

Frantic, the elfins, of a sun-rayed day,
Are flooding the exits:
They must away!
Stained by shadows; athirst to be
Free from this light-born
Mystery—

Phantoms careen o'er the dark'ning sky—
Shrilly defying a petrel's cry—
Then silence, musing—ineffable delight—
Such is the coming of night.

Tilly Stratton

OH HANDS, MY HANDS

Oh hands, my hands, how you have
    changed since our journey first began.
From small un-co-ordinated objects,
    to steady tools of my life's labor.
You have seen the passing of time,
    the memories of first learning, and
    the caressing of loved ones.
And now, old friends, as I look down
    the veins are large, the calluses hard,
    the knuckles red, the fingers swollen.
But, even tho you are unsteady now,
    never fear, for you have been faithful,
    and fulfilling,
And all the time I have been watching
    you—my hands!

Virginia M. Cutshaw

TO GOD

I love your beautiful earth with its beautiful trees,
Its hot summer days and its evening breeze;
Its fields of flawless, waving grain,
Molten gold along the lane;
Its songbirds singing, sweet and shy,
Brilliant specks against the sky;
Its flowers beside the garden wall
Perfuming the world you made for us all;
Everywhere gifts no money can buy,
Free to enjoy—and they reach to the sky—
So I thank you, dear God, in my own small way,
For the blessings I've shared on your earth today.

Peggy Ann Lawson

DEATH

They say I'll never regain my health
But I'm grateful for having lived.
I've known sorrow but also good cheer
So I'll not complain as I lie here
I'm just grateful for having lived.

They say that before long I will die
But I'm grateful for having lived.
I've never achieved a great ambition
Nor completed a daring heroic mission
But I'm grateful for having lived.

I've known hate but I've also known love
So I'm grateful for having lived.
Since death is an inseparable part of living
I'll accept it, also, in thanksgiving
Because I'm grateful for having lived.

Jim Brophy

THE DAYS OF TIME

The beautiful days of summer
Days filled with singing and humming.
Childhood bright and gay
No cares to dismay
These are the days of summer.
Now autumn has begun,
With her darker hues
Of gold, bronze, and orange.
Days go by too swiftly
When autumn has come.
How will winter be spent?
Will it be cold and dismal?
Time will tell what the days have meant
Oh Lord, you will be my strength,
In you these days will be complete.

Rita Evans

HIS LAST LETTER

Mother, I received your letter,
It just came to me today,
And I know your heart is aching
Ever since I've been away.

How I long to see you Mother,
And to know that all is well,
Oh, the heartache every moment,
No one else can ever tell.

As I write the shells are falling
And our tanks are rolling through,
While your love to me is calling
Now my heart will answer you.

Please tell Daddy that I miss him,
And I know he'll understand,
Though you never hear him say it,
Just because he is a man.

Tell him that his son's a soldier,
And will ever do his part,
Though my Dad will never know it,
He's the hero of my heart.

If I could but see you Mother,
And that little rose-trimmed shack,
When my work out here is finished
Mother, I'll be coming back.

Keep on praying darling Mother
That these days will soon be through,
But if I do not see you Mother
Then we'll meet beyond the blue.

I can hear the bugles calling
Deepening shadows falls the night,
Now may God protect us Mother,
And be with us in the fight.

Good night Mother, heaven bless you,
You are all this world to me,
Only God can bring the answer,
He can bring the vic-to-ry.

Soon to her there came a message,
We are very grieved to say.
Please accept our deepest sympathy,
For your son was killed today.

James E. Curtis

170

NIMBUS CUMULUS

Towering omniscience in the sky,
   Mutely searching the earth.
Slowly moving, deliberate scorn,
   A nimbus cloud is born.

A small scud cloud flees in fear,
   As if to lead the way.
Swirling west wind gathers dust
   And scatters it away.

Moving grandeur, right and left,
   Cloaked in silver and grey,
Muttering oft in the distance
   As it mantles the summer day.

Growling and muttering angrily,
   Impatiently racked and torn,
Spewing forth its vengeance,
   Heralds another storm.

Bellowing angry malice,
   Re-echoing down the valley,
Bending trees before its wrath,
   Over the earth it sallies.

Darkened earth, hushed in fear,
   Quaking before the storm,
Eerie shadows dance in glee,
   The sky above is torn.

Then the rumbling grows weaker,
   The sword's lost its flash
The towering lashing nimbus,
   Is dying, dying, fast.

Now the earth all aglisten,
   Warm beneath the sun.
All is fragrantly silent,
   The towering nimbus gone.

George S. Hurst

NAILED TO A CROSSROADS

My mind awakens from its restless sleep
White dawn drenches my soul in darkness
Words on walls wither before my questing hand
Ivory towers beckon believers
The neon touch of silence entangles me
Ripples of sound reach distant children
Wasted old men hasten to heed their master
Crumbling parchment walls fade in my mind
I cannot live today for a vague tomorrow
I stand alone reflecting my yesterdays

Sandra Harpster

GIVING

Oh! Why in our search for happiness
Do we look over yonder hill?
When all the time it is here close at hand
Just waiting on our window sill.

For giving is joy: You get while you give
A hand to the man with a load
A word to the lonely, a smile for the sad
Or a kiss on the brow of the old.

But that is the way with us all you see
'Till we learn to take His hand
And not go wandering over the hill
After something that's close at hand.

Yes giving is joy: You get while you give
The lift of a word of praise
And life will flow on like the words of a song
To brighten your own cloudy days.

Ida Combs Donnelly

172

WONDERING

The rain began gently
   Falling softly to the earth.
Now it is beating the ground in a torrent
   Rivulets flow here and there.
Now it is gentle again
   Falling in a sweet repose.

My life began gently,
   My fears softly allay'd by my mother's hands.
Now it is beating the world in a torrent
   Rivulets flow here and there.
When I am old, will it be gentle again,
   Falling in a sweet repose?

Amy Guess

LOVE

The soft warm sun
Shining on you and me as
We walk along the cool,
Wet sand, so near the
Water.

The birds fly overhead
Singing soft warm songs
Of love and contentment.

The wind, mussing my hair as I turn
And smile at you, says to me, "Love
Him always as you do now."

And the water rushing
Up to lay the cool splendor
Of gold at our feet as we
Walk together.

Linda L. Wilcoxson

FRIENDSHIP'S DOOR

The paths that lead to friendship's door
Are paths where kindness trod before;
Little lanes where memories tell
Of pleasures shared and sorrow as well—

Of a kindly smile along the way
When someone needs a brighter day;
All goodness found at friendship's door
Comes from the heart where love is stored.

Marion Amedick

OLD MAN

Schoolbells
Ring out sharply.
Without hesitation
He reaches for his slate, but finds
A cane.
Dorothy Maxwell

WHY

And you brought warmth into my life.
A hand to touch, a heart to share . . .
When I cried, yes, you were there,
And told me just how much you cared . . .
But there was something missing.

For all the times I needed you,
I had but to call and so you came,
To hold me close and still the pain.
So much like love, yet not the same.
Why couldn't you have loved me?

Pat Mitchell

SONG FOR LOW VOICE

Relinquish now your hold upon the bough.
No fruit is there; you must prepare
For hunger and thirst to come—this is the first
Of the harsh replies. Here are dark skies
With a promise of rain and hail to beat on the frail
Leaves clinging to boughs. Go back to your house,
The familiar place, wearing a kind face.
Leave this unfriendly grove, that denies love.

Loretta Roche

The politician,
And the chameleon,
Are very close akin;
Each can change their color,
To match the *fix* they're in.

Marie Scola

THE WALK

And we shall walk in the dark moonlight.
I hear your breathy footsteps,
You feel my full heartbeats without touching me.
For you cannot touch me and grasp my soul,
As I lose you in holding your hand.
Our souls can be one, apart,
More than together.
And we must walk in the dark moonlight,
Apart,
Until souls are one, together.

Andrea G. Nelson

175

THE LIGHTHOUSE

When mighty storm-gods ride the skies
In battleground array
And flash the order "mobilize"
Alert storm troops obey;
Staccato sounds like hand grenades
Echo o'er land and sea
Followed by rumbling cannonade
Of massed artillery,
Sharp flashes like a surgeon's knife
Cut patterns in the sky
And waters deep, with billows rife
The rugged shores defy;
Yet through it all your beacon warm
Sends dawn of hope to man
Assures that calm has followed storm
Since first this world began.

Clifford Carle

SPRING COMES ONCE MORE

A snow-clad morning
With sparkling diamond glow,
Wind-swept trees, silver tasselled;
Flowers under white coverlet
Waking now from dreamless sleep,
Lift adoring eyes
And smile at an unveiled sun;
Winter gustily withdraws,
And, clothed in leafy garlands,
Majestically, spring appears.

Beth Briggs

ODE ON A HOT TAMALE

The food of Mexico is hot.
It peels the paint right off the pot.
And though it's chili,
Cold it's not.
I like it!

Yes,
I confess,
"Me gusto" plenty
Latin dishes "caliente."

So fire up! There's no fiasco
When I tackle the tabasco!
And though from hell's own cauldron sprung,
With sauces sure to scorch my tongue,
I still cannot admit to folly,
Because I love a hot tamale,
     by golly!

James F. Blewer

ARKANSAS

Arkansas's the Wonder State.
She really is the most.
I say this 'cause she's wonderful.
And makes a pretty host.

She is just a little state.
But full of pride and hope.
She loves the country atmosphere,
Every tree and slope.

Angela Lunday
Age 11

IN TUNE WITH NATURE

I love the water, sand and air,
A gentle breeze to toss my hair,
The fragrant flowers, shady trees,
The cheery birds and humming bees,
For I am in tune with Nature!

I love the sky, the stars, the moon,
Twilight, midnight, sunshine of noon,
A snowy cloud, a gay rainbow,
The feel of rain, icicles, snow,
For I am in tune with Nature!

I love the spray of a waterfall,
A valley green or a mountain tall,
A mossy rock, plateau or plain,
And pebbles on a winding lane,
For I am in tune with Nature!

Hulda LaZerte

AUTUMN RAIN

Autumn rain, autumn rain,
  Nature's tears, shed in vain.
Summer's gone, so are dreams.
  Fate and nature, unforseen.
I too cry, for you and I,
  And a love that used to be.
Once we loved, as love should be,
  A tender, haunting rhapsody.
And tho I lost, like winter's frost,
  Your memory clings to me.
Autumn rain, autumn rain,
  In my heart still burns the flame.
And I live, tho you have gone,
  Like a muted bird, without its song.
And the raindrops, that you see,
  Are the teardrops shed by me,
That fall as the autumn rain.

Ray Rockwell

WHEN YOU CRITICIZE A NEIGHBOR

When you criticize a neighbor
Or some kind and loving friend,
Why not ask yourself the question,
"Was it not I that did offend?"
When you find a fault in others
And you're inclined to pass it on,
Stop and think a minute, brother,
The fault may be your own.
When you criticize a stranger,
For some act or unkind deed,
Why not ask yourself the question,
"Is that the way the Lord sees me?"
Come, my friend, and let's be honest;
Just the two of us reflect
All the things in this mirror
That both of us respect.
Let's admit no one is perfect,
Your neighbor, you, or I.
This world is full of all our errors
No matter how hard we try.

Elsie Hatter Bales

FRIEND

Come to me when you feel pain
And I will empty out my crucible of love upon you.
We will talk of many things, and laugh, and cry,
And share some dreams.
Then when I see you smile and know the hurt is
    gone,
Go on your way—free, restored, and full of life.
But return if need be.
What joy you bring me in your coming!

Mary Lou Hewitt

A MORALOEM

Let's look for an abandoned Hut
In a very secluded place.
Then lock up forever the word But,
And even its memory erase.

This word was never bonafide,
It doesn't team up with ability.
A little nook in which to hide
And evade some responsibility.

If you have talent for doing good,
That's a trust, considered divine.
Don't ever say, "I would if I could"
But—You know the rest of the line.

So if this little rhyme rings true,
Or possibly touches your heart.
Remember, talent was given you
Not to hoard, just to impart.

Deane Hickman

IF

If I could put time back within its darkened place
And send the rushing rivers up their beds
If I could make the present just a memory
And pick up every footstep I have tred
If I could make each man to be a child
And every mighty oak, an acorn be
If I might make all creatures to be wild
And drive the angry waves back out to sea
If I could put once more into the earth
What man has taken from it in his stride
And give him back the innocence he knew
Along with every long forgotten pride:

I'd make the world a better place to live in
Just as the Great Creator meant t'would be
But this is idle fancy, merely dreaming
And I must now awake and let it be.

Catherine S. Engstrom

180

DESTINY

A beautiful but overpowering swell of water
Arises unexpectedly
And disturbs the quiet solitude
Of each pebble and grain of sand
On life's eternal shore.
Great masses of tiny particles
Seemingly attached before the attack
Can be seen in their true isolation
As each is carried individually
By the roaring advance
Of an overwhelming force
To an unknown destiny.
Each grain, separate and somehow unique,
Is tossed to a new location
And becomes part of a new world
That it helps to create
And to which it may contribute to the whole
In ways of which it has no awareness.

Esther Kevelson

ON THE DEATH OF A LOVED ONE

Alone, afraid, lost without your love.
And yet I remain whole, when once
I thought I would be amputated without you.
And yet my heart still beats with life
And my soul still flows with love.
For there is the ocean, and the roses,
There is a sunrise and a sunset.
And the rooster still crows at five,
And the evening breeze still blows,
The flowers bud, and the grasses rise,
The tides come in, the tides go out.
And God remains within, and man remains a friend,
And Existence continues to flower into Being.
And there is the miracle of time
And a sureness of tomorrow.

Leah Hass

181

THE FLAG OF GLORY

This is the story
Of war and glory.
Of how men fight
And die for the right,
While under the cover of night
The enemy attacked.

One by one they took aim—
Their job was to maim.
Day broke through
And the terror came to view,
Beneath a yellow hue
Lay the ruins of man.

The battle was won,
The job was done.
Men cheered for the victory
That made their place in history.
Up rose the flag of glory
Over a battleground of blood.

Nellie Ann Buck

WHAT LIFE IS TO TEENAGERS

Life to teenagers is just a game
In their life there is no aim,
They just want to play life for kicks
Pulling a bunch of immature tricks.

They don't realize what fun really is
They try to act like adults but they're
   just little kids,
Someday they'll face up to the fact
How old you really are is how old you act.

Cheryl Griffith

A DREAM'S WORTH

Terri with the brown eyes
limpid, and lanquid lips
parted softly in a sigh.

I saw her on the beach
behind her the mirrored sea
created by the sun . . .

Her silhouette swaying peacefully
danced across the water
innocently, though she knows,
one can tell.

She came once to me
through a cavern by a mountain
to blow a gentle whisper
into my empty ear.

Caressed my longing desires
longingly, to recreate a
something which was not there.

Now she stays
and I . . .

Clay Garner

TO THE DAY STAR

You, golden love, my summer sun,
Shine down on me
Standing, bright and cool as May.
My quiet stream a chattering brook becomes
Before you, and then
As my pent-up winter passions pass
Silent I fall into the bed
In which I flow and lie
Beneath your burning golden kiss.

June McDonald

183

SPRING REVERIES

Tho winter's chill is still in the air,
You can feel it's spring just everywhere.
Friendly pussy willows swaying in the breeze
Trying to waken the rest of the trees.
Maple buds showing their tints of red,
While crocus and daffodils peep thru their bed,
Even showing and glowing thru drifts of snow,
We can feel that old winter is just about to go.
Grass slowly turning to shades of green,
With pines and the firs, and the birches between.
As the birds start their mating and singing sweet songs
We should rejoice and thank our Maker, to Whom all
    praise belongs.

Elsie B. Willenberg

CINQUAINS

Interwoven, colorful,
    textures of feeling—
hot red and warm pink
    pulsing together
encased in misty cinnamon as one—
    these be our hearts.

Neither the silent, silky snow,
    nor the gentle, caressing rain
can compare
    to the dove's touch
of my beloved's hand
    upon my face.

The essence of silence is found
    in the twilight
of your eyes;
    the lapping of a love wave
against my heart's shore.

Susan Petrosky

REFLECTION

A silver moon sailing thru the
    black waters of night
Leaving a wake of clouds
    billowy white -
An artist's portrait of night.

A crimson sun setting,
    extinguished by the sea,
Like an orange poppy out
    on the lea -
A poet's poem of sunset at sea.

A golden flute tripping out gay
    notes on the air
Trimming sound with a colorful
    ruffle-like flair -
A musician's song of little care.

A brook babbling over rocks
    of green jade
Flowing through a garden
    of flowery shade -
A dreamer's dream that fades.

A world shining bright in
    the heavens above
Sparkling in serenity with
    the calm of a dove -
An American's world of peace and love.

June H. Garrity

ETERNAL LOVE

As the silver moon is
To the rushing tide,
The friendless person is
With a friend by his side.
As the almighty God is
To the heavens above,
Is as you and I are
To eternal love.

Debbie Coslop

AUTUMN'S GOODNESS

So dearly dressed are you this year,
So sweetly scented and charming.
So all out to capture the hearts of all who
    see you, and feel your soft gentle air.

So reposed, and designed just perfect for
    your time.

So right for the after summer break,
So needed for contentment, and rebuilding
    of dreams and new projects to attain with
    "your presence."

So all inviting and unselfish are you
So willing to share with everyone
    just for the taking the sweetness and
    joy of your company.

So lovely fall, oh lovely days
    that I might stay outside this way
    and keep the winter far away
    this time, this year.
"I love you truly fall."

Elizabeth Warner

SPRING

Spring reminds me of beauty
In many different ways
It reminds me of the blooming of flowers
And of the sun's golden rays
Of the annual April showers
And beautiful warm days
Of nice fresh air
That always stays
As long as spring is around.

Rolf Freter
Age 10

186

SUNSET

The sun sinks silently into the western sky
And casts its golden rays upon the waters blue.
A gull flies by; gently, so gently waving his wings,
Gliding, landing upon the receding sea.

The sail is being drawn—
The wind has gone to another land
Until the rising of the sun on the morrow.
Silence prevails.

Two lovers walk hand in hand down the sandy shore.
Two birds fly to their nest.
The golden sky is giving way to the darkening night;
A lone star appears.

And there are some who claim no God to rule the
     universe,
But there must be a Hand that
Closes the eye of the sun unto rest,
And guides the lovers, and birds to nest.

I leave my place of sweet repose
And turn my homeward way.
The moon will soon light my path—
The night is come.

Emalea Faunce Jamieson

LIFE

Life is not a box, from which you can withdraw
     your daily wont,
Without a care or thought,
Of ever having drought.

Instead it requires a certain amount of daily
     reimburse;
And constant care,
Is ever there.

Unless—you carry an empty purse.

Thaddeus W. Stevens

SEA GULLS

I found a haven by the shore
Where sea gulls come and go,
A place to think and dream my dreams
And watch the white waves flow.

There is peace and joy in simple things,
In a sea gull on the beach,
And in the breeze that blows so free,
Many lessons these things teach.

As the sea gulls take to quiet flight
And they higher and higher soar,
My cares and worries fly away too,
And life's serene once more.

Gertrude Gehl Shook

OCEAN SYMPHONY

This morning, on a quiet, windswept knoll
Beneath a tree
Where gulls stood by in watchful, stately line,
I watched the sea.

Its music reached beyond the distant waves,
Serene and clear,
As though to rest all tired and troubled souls
And banish fear.

A million white caps bobbed and danced in glee
Far out of reach,
While breakers swelled the chorus in great cheer
All down the beach.

My dull heart joined the mighty symphony
And found new peace
Just knowing that the ocean's constant song
Shall never cease.

Alice E. DuBois

TWILIGHT LONELY

Sitting on a log
on the beach
while the twilight sun
filtered the grey of dusk
and washed the sky
and ocean pink
writing your name
with such love
so beautifully etched
in the sand
but it was sad
I was alone
and the tide
    would be
        coming in soon

Patricia Lawry Humme

RETREAT

Let me retreat into my shell of silence
Filled only with the faint echo of my own thoughts,
Where I can be alone with myself;
Where intruders are forbidden.

Don't speak to me, don't break the spell;
Don't destroy the solitude that envelopes me.
Don't trespass on the sacred grounds of my sanctuary;
Don't force me back into the noisy world of reality . . .
Not yet.

I crave loneliness, solitude, silence
I want to hear my real self speak.
Go away—give me time to interpret myself.
Give me time to listen to the silence.

Susan Ross

SORROW AD INFINITUM

These days of melancholy,
This abysmal loneliness,
Those anxious days, grandeur.
Terrible fear and loneliness!

Find a happy man and I will show you loneliness.
Find a happy man and I will show you a life not living.
Find a happy man and I will show you troubled dreams
Awake and asleep.

I am a happy man,
A cynic at love,
A cynic at religion,
A cynic, a happy man.

He searches for more.
He reaches for something,
He flings away truth.
He reaches,
He searches,
He finds!
He cannot have it.
Too bad, happy man.

He laughs at the world,
He laughs at her,
He laughs at it all.   Then
He cries deep but none sees,
He is laughing.
He hears laughter, his name,
Happiness of then is still around him.
He cannot see it, he is laughing.
Weeping and crying,
Terrible sorrow!

It is the time for love.
It is the weather for loving.
It is the time and the weather.
He loves and waits, loves and waits.
Loving and waiting.
Useless! She has gone, he has died,
Loving and waiting.

Drink deep, happy man,
Drink deep.
Drink and laugh, laugh and drink.
Drinking and laughing,
Then weeping, terrible sorrow!
Drink deep, happy man.
It was another day.

David Wiseman

MIND'S EYE AND ME

Prism of mind—refracting inner thoughts
Colors of pride and greed and joy
Spectral moving things of dreams to come
Shapes of places past and far away
Thoughts
Joyfully alone
Short as life itself
Preserved in amber glass of books
These colors of my spectrum

r. e. blume

QUIET HANDS

There are many hands that work
And two hands can clasp in joy
Gentle hands of a young girl
Strength seeking hands of a boy
Mending at evening's repose
Tired hands of a mother
Making lifelight spark anew
The hand's touch of a brother
Facing, fearing no future
Hands that I look for again
Loving, praying—quiet hands
Quiet, gentle—hands of man.

Vaughn Powell Cofer

ADOLESCENCE

Quickly come the startled tears
How silver is the rain
Halfway between the splash of years
A smiling face that disappears
Not far behind, the trusting child
How yellow was the sun
But now the thunder darkly wild
And first awareness has begun

Swiftly comes the passion now
The fever of a dream
The look of longing on your face
The fumbling fear of first embrace
But now too soon suspicions creep
How sweet is privacy
Softly doubtful comes the sleep
And with the dawn—maturity

Faelynne Clarke

A friend is someone who cares.
A friend is someone who takes with joy
all of you that you will share
and knows that some things are not to be shared.
A friend is someone who indulges your fussing
shares your laughter
cries with your tears.
A friend is someone who forgets her own problems
to help you worry about yours,
because half a problem
hurts less than a whole one.
A friend is someone you can depend on.
A friend isn't always helpful.
A friend doesn't always understand.
Even friends make mistakes.
A friend is someone who cares.

Margaret Andrews

DID YOU?

Did you ever press your nose against a thistle
And feel its fuzzy fur upon your face;
Did you ever watch a tiny-legged creature
That caught the sun upon its web-strung lace?
Did you waken to the cool, sweet gray of predawn
That chilled your ears, your nose and feet and toes;
Did you see bright flowers stretch their faces sunward
And envy garments painted such as those?
Have you ever lain upon your back in grasses
And heard the creakling crackling earth does make . . .
Have you sat on sandy shores bathed pure in moonlight
And watched the lamp of night dance on the lake . . .
Have you dared to let your feet hang in the waters
That bubbled merrily upon their way . . .
Beneath the swirling, dashing stream that wanders
Have your toes sought out and found the softest clay . . .
Does a meadow lark perchance entrance, intrigue you
As gently, sweetly clear his song is played . . .
Do the scarlet glowing hues of evening sunset
Still hold you as they dim and close and fade . . .
If of these things you love to drink most deeply
And verily upon them seem to thrive,
Then never fear my dear that life shall ever
Take from your heart the joy of being alive.

Linda Jean

ORCHARD IN EMBRYO

One russet apple clinging to the tree
Defying rain and hoar frost's piercing dart,
Joining the wind in wanton revelry
While guarding summer stored within its heart.

Out, out it swings upon its fibrous stem,
Undaunted, unperturbed by buffeting,
With autumn on its brow for diadem
And in its core the mystery of spring.

Margaret Furness MacLeod

ON THIS HOLY NIGHT

Oh downy flakes tumbling down to earth
You spread a white carpet of twinkling mirth.
In a little village, church bells ring,
On this Holy Night, the village children sing.
"Gracious," Santa whispered, "what a beautiful sight!"
Yes, peace rules one village, on this Holy Night.

Down a stone chimney to a moonlit hall
All were asleep, no one heard Santa at all.
He crossed the hall, opened a door,
A peaceful picture with a kitten and four
Little girls cuddled so tight,
The world is troubled, but one homes' alright.

Santa tip-toed to the parlor, trimmed the tree,
On opening his sack with the striking of three
The dolls came to life, then sat on the floor,
As Santa stepped quickly through a French door
His eyes came to rest where a star shone bright,
The symbol of Christmas, on this Holy Night.

Soon he was over the village church steeple
Santa's echoes returned, "God bless these people."
His spirits were warm, on this moonlit night,
As he rushed along by the moon cool and light.
He uttered a prayer, "God make it right,
Give all the world peace, on this Holy Night."

Elsie M. Westrick

SO LITTLE TIME

There's so little time
To get things done . . .
The clock ticks
The feet run
The clock chimes
And still, there's so little time.

Tarey McGuire

A COLLEGIAN'S NEED FOR EXPRESSION

Expression-filled etching en mass
   cover this desk.
They struggle for expression . . .
Prophets of doom, and lovers
   and people driven by depression
Voicing to all their apathy, their
   grief, their hilarity
   Whatever . . .
Some scribbled "John Hancocks"—
Some significant dates—
Some rhymes—familiar and original
"Go to hell" written-embedded in the
   wood.
Their pen scratches into the once
   satin-like smoothness
Tattooed memorabilia . . .
The blue ink—not to write—
It is the blood of the mind given
   as a transfusion
   to the anemia of the desk.

Linda D. Colello

CELESTIAL DIAMONDS

While standing on a lonely hill one night so long ago,
I spied a star, a huge white star, it held my attention so,
As I watched its yellow light
Penetrating through the night,
I asked aloud for some insight
As to a reason for its celestial flight.
When suddenly it came to me
There are ships upon the sea
And planes within a lonely flight,
Also girls who wish at night.
Now, with some thought, one can see,
That all throughout our history
Life has continued amid toil and war
And probably will forever more;
But remember, a dictator's loudest cry
Is infinitesimal to a starry sky.

"Skip" Moyer

FOG

Light, damp fingers of darkness,
   Silently slipping, silently creeping,
Caressing the midnight
   Under cloak of the darkness.
Soft, cool, encircling arms of night,
   Waving, luring, white and cold
Curling lips that come with the dusk
   Kissing the lar d with a dewy softness
Cold, foretelling prophet of death,
   Rising over the water.
And, finally, toward the morning, lies
   Like a quilt on the patchwork land
Enveloping all as a halo,
   With the red morning sun at its back,
And slowly dissolves at the sight of the dawn
   Leaving dampness as its signature.

Nancy Griffith

HAVE YOU EVER . . .

. . . been sprayed in the face
with a garden hose,
or held a fragrant flower
close to your nose?

. . . locked yourself up
in your room to brood,
or ever tasted
Chinese food?

. . . stepped down
upon a tack?
Had an itch you couldn't scratch
in the middle of your back?

. . . cut your finger
on a knife?
If you haven't
you can't really enjoy life.

F. Allen Kelliebrew

CAPTAINS OF MY MIND

Ah! Who are these fiends
Closing in on me—
And tearing me apart?
I try to fight them
But their constant gnawing
At my heart—
Poisons all my dreams
Of what is right and
Takes command of me.
As the captains of my mind
They lead the way,
So all I find
Are cold hello's—
And groups that shun;
Painted smiles—
And love from none.
The more I hate—
The more I'm hated.
The more I'm hated—
The more I hate.
This vicious cycle's in my soul;
I've known not love—
Nor reached a goal.
Who are these fiends
Who did this deed?
Damn them!
Jealousy—and greed.

Vicki David

LIFE, WHERE IS DEATH?

Oh! Life, where is death?
How far is he? How near
Can he be? Someone is
Always asking. But I only ask
How close am I to he?

Lee V. Smith

CHRISTMAS IN VIETNAM

The wonders of winter are not seen here,
And deep in my heart I know how I care,
For snow-covered pine branches bowed
    in prayer,
And icicles melting as if shedding a tear.

No white covered fields or roofs
    blanketed with snow,
Or brightly decorated houses with
    happiness glow.
No trees bare of leaves lashed by a
    windy foe,
Nor a gentle kiss stolen 'neath
    mistletoe.
No frozen lakes filled with skater's glee,
No little children from snowballs to flee,
Or a child asking Santa to answer his plea—
No my angel there's no Christmas this
    year for me.

Ron Stinson

LOCK AND KEY

When 'ere the sun forgets to shine,
When 'ere the lovers hate;
I shall then, my love,
Flee beyond the gate.

The gate that holds me true to thee,
With lock and key unknown;
You'll find then and only then,
My love for thee has grown.

But if I flee beyond the gate,
Think not unkind of me;
For I turned not my love to hate,
But found the lock and key.

Cheryl Dawn Sullenger

198

come with me to
eternity—
the infinite destiny
that graciously
suckles
mankind
and nurses him
into a
fearless being

walk with me
around the
edge of death,
and lean against
the cardboard wall
called faith

run with me
in fields of
spiders
and broken dreams
and peel the
thick layer of the
human race from your bones
and walk hand in hand—
like lovers—with death.

Connie Collins

Search not for a brighter tomorrow,
Strive not for wealth untold.
Success isn't measured in dollars,
It lies in the depth of your soul.
Fill not your cup with envy,
Be not consumed with greed.
Those who lack peace and contentment,
Theirs is the greater need.

Rachel F. Bryant

WINTER'S SNOW

As the day creeps into twilight
And the wind begins to blow,
The clouds appear to blossom
With small miracles of snow.

While our horses trot with vigor,
They blemish up the snow
That was lying soft and silent,
Just a mile or two ago.

The trees that once stood barren,
Have now the purest coat,
Which builds and builds in richness
As the tiny snowflakes float.

And as the night approaches
Its black against the white
Leaves everything so tranquil,
God must have sent the sight.

Deborah Sorrentino

A MOMENT I LOVE

Black clouds hovering
In a greying sky.
Wind bending trees
And whipping my hair.
A cool moistness
Caressing my cheeks.
And a smell, oh a smell
Of coming rain,
Newly turned earth,
And dewy grass.
I stand
Suspended in time.
And then,
A spatter on my brow,
And I go in.

Judy Tillery

TO A BEAUTIFUL ROBBER

Without your presence—you have robbed me.
I am robbed of my peace,
For only with you, have I known true quiet
    in my heart.
When I stand before fine art,
I am robbed of total appreciation . . .
I wish only to retain the best of it so that
    later I may share it with you.
The sounds and rhythm of poetry have no
    meaning unless I read them to you.
    (Or you to me.)
I am robbed of the pleasure of my oldest
    friends—my books—when you are not
    also there.
The very beauty of a spring day is
    nothing compared to the joy of
    springtime with you.
Before God, my soul is robbed of its
    completeness without you.
But during those precious moments when we
    are together:
Our kisses—the kisses that only we know . . .
The almost painful tenderness of those
    kisses.
And the gentleness you evoke from me,
My hand on your soft cheek—
The quiet gentleness of that touch,
The angle of your neck,
The perfume of you,
The softness of your hair,
Your trust—our freedom—my joy!
Dear one, please rob from me.
Beautiful robber, take for a lifetime.
Beloved thief, lovely robber, loved one.

J. A. Jackels

THE CALLER

How could he know instinctively
it was warm inside: the gray kitten
who failed to yield submissively
to the fields which housed him since his birth?

Personally, I've never cared
for cats. But *personality*
in a cat is different somehow. He dared
to yammer softly at my door

and lift a sanguine paw to vent
his cause. The charm was overwhelming;
now he lies in sleek content
upon my hearth. (I swear he's grinning.)

Evelyn J. Boettcher

COMPATIBILITY

If I'm lacking in courage, I pay it no mind.
You're brave, and you're strong, and
    courageous.
Little by little, I'll try, 'till I find that
    strength, that is so advantageous.

If you're lacking in laughter; the capacity
    to soar;
The feeling of life surging through you.
I'm well versed on these, and you will learn
    more than you ever dreamed you
    possibly could do.

Don't figure it out—please pay it no heed
    as to why we are thus mental-blocking.
We've discovered a gift, very rare;
Realize;
That our psyches are just inter-locking.

Harriet Namm

THE STORM

The weather at sea is strange.
There rarely is forewarning.
So if you are not careful,
You may get caught one morning.

You'll awake to find it clear and calm,
With a gentle wind a-blowing.
You'll go below for breakfast,
But take notice, the seas are growing.

Then all at once, it strikes.
The fury of the ocean,
Is tossing your craft about,
In a horrible rocking motion.

You look skyward at your sails,
And see they're torn to threads.
Above the wind you hear a crack,
And you'd better duck your head.

The mast comes tumbling down,
And hits the deck with force.
Because you're unable to steer,
You're blown many miles off course.

And when it finally ends,
Your ship is all but wrecked
And you realize your plight,
A drifting derelict!

But this is if you're lucky,
And your craft withstood the gale,
For many never return,
With life to tell the tale.

Robert Gloss

DAWN

The dawn doth break the morning mist,
The birds their songs do sing.
A happy song, this song of theirs
Across the meadows ring.

To gladden each and every heart,
And grant our souls delight.
So happily we greet the day,
And bid good-bye the night.

Lawrence E. Thomas

AFTER READING PICASSO'S
DEFINITION OF AN ARTIST

I am an artist . . . and a man.
What other men do not see or hear, I can.
The music and the motion that life gives
I soak in the spongy substance of my brain.
And when it's saturated to a suitable capacity
I wring it on my canvases like rain.
My ears and mind and heart and eyes
Work separately, yet in accord.
Sometimes my deepest thoughts I never know
Until at last my hand begins the cultivation
Of all the separate factors—and they grow.
Strange things, and real appear before me.
Odd symbols of a world inside the mind.
They are the flowerings from my experience
I can't erase the things I find.
They grow here on the canvas
The ground is fertile, the air is free.
Look life, here is your substance—
At least the way it seems to me.

Linda Millen

FAR WINDS

The winds, high-crying in urgency
Draw shuddering breath after breath
Outside the door, latched fearfully.

The firm-clasped roof, the sturdy beam
Deny them any passage through.
I light the fire, reprieved, and dream.

Those winds, far-journeying today
Saw so much sorrow that my soul,
Ungirded, dare not hear them say.

Louise Ingram

SOUTH CAROLINA SWAMP

Black-lace trees reach up to sun-filled skies,
Moss-hung fingers brush twigs of long-leaved pines
While small birds twitter in the great swamp beneath;
Waxen-berried mistletoe bushes adorn high branch
And graceful bamboo-vine entwines all within its
    reach.
Below, gleaming black water reflecting smoky
    purple of cyprus knees,
And muted autumn colors of lingering foliage
    portray splendid tableau against azure sky.
Wild pampas grass waves ethereally—glowing with
    rosy radiance atop isolated hammock,
And a white crane flies across in majestic splendor—
In deceptive serenity the swamp reposes,
Silent in this mid-winter hush—seemingly dormant
    with all life in abeyance—waiting—
Waiting for the magic hand of time to bedeck
    sweet bay and magnolia tree in profusion of
    perfumed beauty,
Festoon all trees in golden jessamine vines and
    carpet dark water with iris, lily and
    hyacinth's blue;
Waiting for shafting sunlight to flash on
    cardinal's brilliant wing,
For the swamp to awaken.
And sing again the eternal song of spring.

Virginia du Pont Davidson

RESPONSIBILITY

I once tried to plant a garden
And make it grow pretty and tall
But being a silly child
I watered it not at all

Now the ground is bare
And has no foliage left
It now lies as a reminder
Of the responsibility of which
    I was bereft

Carolyn Brown

NOW IT'S I WHO MUST GO

Hold my hand.
It's dry and cold.
The veins stand out
For I am old.

I held your hand
As you learned to walk;
Answered your chatt'rings
As you learned to talk.

Then we were striding,
Hand in hand,
Marching in rhythm
To your unseen band.

And for a time,
Side by side,
We marched shoulder to shoulder,
Matching stride.

Then your call came!

I couldn't go,
And you couldn't stay,
I lifted my hand
And turned away—

As eager for life
You had never known,
You waved farewell and
I was alone.

Now my life is ending.

When that door opens
Only I pass through.
But it's lonely waiting
Even with you
Near me, to give of your strength
As my strength ebbs away.
Now it's I who must go
And you who must stay.

Mabel B. Shaffer

ENCHANTMENT

I was enchanted not by his thoughts,
    but by his smile.
I was not interested in his bravery,
    but in his height.
I did not care about strength in his heart,
    but that of his body.
I did not listen to what he said,
    but concentrated on the voice that
    was saying it.
I did not search the depths of his eyes
    for emotion, but for their color.
No, I did not care until I watched him
    smile, as his tall, strong figure walked
    away and his deep clear voice spoke
    her name and his bright blue eyes
    looked into hers as he took her hand.

Susan Grabowsky

This spot I love, has drawn me back
    With precious memory
It tugs so gently all year long
    This place beside the sea

So I return, year after year
    To sit in reverie
Of happy times, when we were young
    The children, you and me

Now, children laughing in the surf
    Or playing in the sand
No longer bring me shells to keep
    Or take me by the hand

Tho time has changed our family
    It has not changed the sea
The shells, the birds, the sand and tide
    Is as it used to be

Marie Yandle Guinn

A PAPER PAD AND A DOT OF INK

With a paper pad and a dot of ink
I can sketch a picture to make you think.

With a splash of ink and a paper pad
I can draw the good or paint the bad.

On a crinkled scroll with a feather pen
I'll etch the future or the might have been.

I can stroke the dreams of a yesterday
Those shadows and hopes that have gone away.

The triumph and tears of your very soul
I'll put in colors to show your goal.

The hopes of man and his godlike link
I can place on a pad with a dot of ink.

Lee Gorman

WHAT MIGHT HAVE BEEN

There's one secret we can never win,
The secret of what might have been.
No turning back—to what's past and gone,
No way to know—were we right or wrong;
No chance to change the course we took
Nor to retrace one step with a backward look;
But life has a way to save only the best;
They shine like jewels in our memory chests;
Each a symbol of treasured gold,
But the secret of what might have been
Has never been told.

Ethel Todd Marshall

WILD DEER

Resting in a quiet glade
    Beneath gay autumn's dappled shade,
I see the last leaves drift and laze
    Through October's golden haze.
Content, as I often am, to dream
    In drowsy languor by a stream.

I lift my eyes and there I see
    A great pronged deer across from me.
He stares at me in mild surprise
    A baffled question in his eyes.
Then, moving on his wingéd heels
    He, in that very instant, wheels,
And on the spot where he just stood
    Are only shadows in the wood.

I blink my eyes and wonder if
    I really saw him, mute and stiff,
Then flashing into liquid grace
    Go bounding off in limpid space.
"Did I see him?" I think fretfully,
    I'm sure he wonders, did he see me?

Bee Noble Vickrey

SNOW

After it snows and it is night
The snow sparkles in the soft moonlight

All is so quiet and peaceful and still
Way up there on the snow-covered hill

Such beauty makes me think of my love
While the moon and stars shine down from above

Judith McCullough

GOD'S TEARDROPS WE CALL RAIN

As I stood to admire the massive trees,
That framed my windowpane,
They appeared so aloft and blessed
When touched by the gentle rain.

While the raindrops sprinkled every leaf,
Even those that seemed to hide,
Somehow it made me feel real blue,
As if the heavens dropped and cried.

I wonder if the Heavenly Father
Weeps as He looks down.
I wonder if He's sorry
For those who wear a crown.

Are these raindrops, "tears," God has shed?
As He watches from above;
Is He sad for those who went astray
And ignored His teachings and His love?

In the early fall, the leaves
Turn from green to gold.
They make me think of me, myself
And others who will grow old.

Thru fall, then into winter,
Then back to spring once again;
These trees with all their beauty,
And God's teardrops we call rain.

Catherine Ryan

Exact
To be precise
To know all that is true
To bring forth evidence, and yet
Be wrong.

Diane Carillo

THE FENCE POST

The fence post is all battered and worn—and
The wind blows around him as if in scorn.
Cracks and crevices are embarked in his wood.
We just don't treat him the way we should.

He stands like a sentry—bold and true;
And his tiresome job is never through.
He holds up the fences and guards the gate
To save the animals from some terrible fate.

Then, in some savage storm and wind
The fence post may fall and God will send
His guardian angel to bring him to guard
The little critters in heaven's yard.

Shawn Lee Holve

REFLECTION

Birds sing gayly in the apple trees
Butterflies flit in the summer breeze
Flowers sway to the honeybee's hum
Here I sit and there are chores to be done.

The woodbox is empty, the waterpail dry.
The cows need milking and I need to mow rye.
But summer joys as a boy I did know
Are before my eyes in the sunshine's glow.

So I sit and rock in my cane-bottom chair
And the chores need doin', but I don't care
'Cause it's seldom seen through an old man's eyes
The beauties around him, and summer surprises.

So the chores will go untouched for a day
As the honeybee's hum to the flower's sway
And the butterflies flit in the summer breeze
And the birds sing gayly in the apple trees.

B. Daphne Johnson

211

WE LIVE AGAIN

As we pick the roses fair,
From their sturdy stem;
Never once do we think,
We must perish too, like them.

We feel a sadness for the faded buds,
That in our garden lie;
And seldom think they'll bloom again,
Beneath a summer sky.

So like the roses, fair and frail,
Are we upon this earth;
Some live their seasons out,
Others wither at their birth.

But as life, again to them
By summer skies is given,
So shall we arise above death's door,
And live again in heaven.

Fredrica Williamson

CHRISTUS '68

Happy is the man
Who's heart is consumed
In flames of love.

In the crucible of life
He finds the essence of existance.

Tempered by life
He becomes
The Christus of our day.

Kenneth Kulinski

TODAY

Today can be so many things:
The first . . .
The last . . .
The inbetween.

Today could be:
So special,
So joyous,
So sad.
Today could be anything.

But
It's what I do with
Today
With its sorrow, pain, joy, love:
That makes today
Something
And tomorrow
Something even more.

Clarice Fehskens

QUESTION TO A HYACINTH BULB

Alone, forgotten
In twilight,
Unloved, unwatered.
What happened in your inner core?
What silent change took place
On that cold cellar floor
That pushed the sprout
Which sought the sun
And turned to blue these milliard
Curls of fragrance,
Announcing spring
When winter's done?

Lois Drew

MY PRIVATE WORLD

To wish for riches is not for me
I'd like to wish for a roaring sea
I'd ride upon the crest of a wave
And go down deep where the mermaids
    bathe
I'd dry myself with the golden sand
And think of myself as alone in my
    land

The waves would be loud like a clap of
    thunder
The wind would blow my hair asunder
Then dusk would drop like a curious
    cat
Upon the waves now quiet and flat
How quiet would be my private world
No one else's eyes could see
My kingdom there
Just God and me

Betty Cocherl

SOFT THE WIND

I have been told that love can be
A silent, subtle thing
With ne'er sign
Nor thought expressed;
A kind of gentle, tender thing
Like a soft, caressing wind,
Wafting your hair or
Brushing your lips.
Did you ever feel the caress
Of a soft wind,
Wafting your hair or
Brushing your lips?
You know . . . it just might not be
The wind at all!

B. Morceau

214

COULD I?

I could reach as high as heaven's door,
Draw hearts on the ocean's blue
And never find a thought so sweet
As the love I hold for you.

I could beat a path through gardens sweet,
And still not be as wise
As the hope that shines eternal
From the deepness of thine eyes.

I could raise my head in humble prayer
To my Lord Devine above
And still not find the mortal peace
I find within Thy love.

I could build a mansion filled with gold
On Canaan's happy shore,
And sitting in its marbled halls
I could not love thee more.

L. James Coe

DEATH COMES SOFTLY

The raindrops run down
    the window, leaving trails of
glistening silver.

The spider spins his
    web, only to catch raindrops,
dew, and bright moonbeams.

Death comes softly, sometimes
    violent, never cares who is
left behind.

Katherine D. Marshall

DEEP IN THE WOODS IN MARCH

I hold the silence in my hands
   my heart
   my soul.
The air is sharp with frozen strands
   of wind, warmed by a winter sun.
Bare branches form a radar screen
   to catch the sound
   of crocus breaking ground.
March and I are one.
The cold green creek goes burbling by
   the north bank's icy shelf
   while I
   upon the thinking stone
Cry silently for you
   for spring
   and for myself.

Lois Drew

The cat sitting before the fire licked its
   paws and washed its face
Then curled up in a snug little ball and
   sang a song of delight before drifting
   off to sleep.
Is this security?
The mother ran from her paper over
   to where her son sat crying.
She gently picked him up from the
   sidewalk brushed off his knees and
   kissed his cheek.
Is this love?
Folding their hands and bowing their
   heads the couple pray in silence.
They thank the Lord for their daily
   bread and singing birds.
Is this faith?
Is the cat secure? Is the child loved?
Does the couple have faith?
Or is this all just habit?

sara thompson

216

SOLSTICE

Summer is
A song of bird
That speaks your name
At daybreak; lilting, gay.

It is the mist
Soft-circled
Round your head
At morning
That urges me
To let your hair
Run through my hand.

It is the clearing
In the wood at mid-day
Where sunlit eyes
Are smiling up at me.

It is the shadow of
An elm in afternoon,
Protective shade
Caressing gently
As your arms.

It is the moon
That touces on
My cheek at night-time,
Lightly, with the
Memory of your kiss.

Helen Roche

LUCK

Ain't got no talent, no education
Guess I'll never know fame
Ain't got no Cadillac, but I guess I'm lucky
'Cause I gets there jus' the same.

Florence E. Allen

SLUMBER JOURNEY

Out of my lowly bed at night,
I look up into the sky so bright—
Up into "God's window of heaven" I peep,
Then fall into a wonderous sleep.

I dream that angels high above
Are guarding me with tender love,
Guarding me each night and day,
At my work and at my play.

I'm riding on a star so bright;
What a wonderful, glorious night,
Riding high into "God's heaven of blue,"
What a wonderful, marvelous view!

Slowly I descend again into my bed
And lay me down my sleepy head—
Ready for slumber, now am I,
After a make-believe journey in the sky.

Gloria Winifred Squires

RED, WHITE & BLUE, APPLE PIE, MOTHERHOOD, DRIVE-IN PACKAGE STORE, AMERICAN WAY, T.V. DINNERS & GREAT SOCIETY SONNET

Falls of morning sunshine
warming melting light
parading unsoiled flowers
joyful to the sight
missionary songbirds
sing arias of light
to yellow children's laughter
undaunted by their plight
then sharp explosions join them
and orange jelly sprites
engulf the scene i write of
and attack the coming night
the napalm sperm of freedom
has made that bad scene right

Denny Wells

FLEETING

Close not your eyes against the glorious light
Which brightens Earth today. It may not
Linger or it may; but we know our rapture
Lessons not the glow of its bright light.

Close not your hands against an innocent
Joy that thrusts itself within your reach.
It may not linger or it may; but grasp it
Ere 'tis past and on you a sad reflection
Cast for future day.

Close not your heart against God's child
Who needs your love today. Time may not
Linger or it may; another day, if you should
Wait, may be, for life on Earth, too late for
Love's great joy.

Daniel W. Horner

MY SECRET SPOT

I know a little spot
Where only I can go,
Near a little wooded place
By which a blue stream flows.

Nature's beauty is all around,
Her mountain peaks reach high;
Her fluffy clouds form animals,
Which seem to pass me by.

To me, there is no lovelier spot,
To come to just be free;
No better place to think aloud,
Or to be alone with "THEE."

Kathy M. Irwin

MEMORIES AT SEA

How lonely the day ends, seeing its golden
crimson death, leaving a sense of melancholy
when summer is passing and fall is creeping in.

Standing alone, watching, listening, smelling
the bitter sweetness of the air, like a veil of
serenity floating around me, the coolness of
the air. It takes me back to the memories of
a place I knew as a child; the green hills, a
forest, and the many scattered ponds,
glimmering like diamonds; the old road
twisting and turning where the moon is
right, looks like the river rushing on its own
way.

Standing alone, seeing you with the gentle
wind blowing through your hair, memories
of when we were one, seeing, exploring the
beauties and mysteries of life—the one painful memory of the last time I looked upon
your face seeing the tears like the dew on a
rose.

Standing alone, watching, waiting, looking
at the sea, thinking how peaceful it must be
to dwell in your world, a world of blue
sleep; waiting for the day when you and I
are together, together for an eternity.

Arthur L. Webber

NEVER JUDGE

Never judge a man by his past,
What matters most is his life today.
Everyone can change in contrast,
To the things they used to do and say.

Evelyn L. Fleck

UPON BEING IMMORTALIZED IN BRONZE ON THE WALL OF A COLLEGE LIBRARY

Didn't feel a thing—
At first.

But now
I feel a wizened Puritan,
Staring down on flocks of errant freshmen—
Kids in church.

No wiser than they are,
No more religious—
Only older,
And bronze.

James E. Fletcher

HAIL TO SIR WALTER!

Sir Walter Raleigh did one
Day
Spread his coat o'er a
Puddle of clay.

The queen stepped on it,
With dainty toes,
And charmingly threw
Sir Walter a rose.

Oh, those days when
Knighthood was in flower
When men were gentle
But men had power.
When ladies were feminine,
Soft and weak;
When the art of gallantry
Was at its peak.

Lisa Ann Walker
Age 14

THE SHELL

There beneath our blinded projector
Lay a porcelain edifice surrounded
By what seemed to be the impossible.
The sea rolled over on its side
And called for us to adopt our vision,
And snatch our desire and hold steadfast.
Nothing now could extinguish our attempt.
The sunburnt sand whispered endlessly
For relief and emancipation from its
Subservient role to the tiny treasure.
The grains soon parted East and West
And left the poor sea corpse unprotected.
Our chance came in an instant,
And slowly the afterdeath spiraled
To the surface and lay restlessly in my palm.
A duet of sun and sea sang out:
"The shell, the shell is yours!"
I looked at my love, and we smiled.

Philip Raymond Smith

TWILIGHT

I sat in the cool of the shade
And watched the bright day fade
Into twilight.

The busy rush of bees was gone.
Lights of many fireflies came on
In the twilight.

The roses, now no longer wilting,
Listened to thrush calls, light and lilting
In the twilight.

Donna M. Biggs

222

I CANNOT . . .

I look, but I cannot see
The world which seems to be
Shadowed by this strange person.

I listen, but I cannot hear
The mysterious way he plans to
Enter my heart and linger there forever.

I touch, but I cannot feel
The warmth of his hand as he
Leads me toward a new understanding.

I eat, but I cannot taste
As a remembered kiss awakens
Me into another world.

I sniff, but I cannot smell
The scent of his body as he
Approaches closer and closer
To capture my heart.

I cannot see,
I cannot hear,
I cannot feel,
I cannot taste, nor
Can I smell;
For love has weakened all of my senses
Into a world of enchanted bewilderment.

Marcia Va. Bradley

WITHOUT YOU

I think about you every day
And count the hours that you're away.
And I pray to the Lord, up above
That He'll protect you, the one I love.
For if you should ever be taken away,
Upon the earth I could no longer stay.
For it is with you, I want to be
Until the end of eternity!

Linda S. Stephens

THE RICH MAN'S GAME

The pawns are growing tired of the moves
    by royalty,
They find themselves in danger and some-
    thing must be lost;
A sacrifice, we know, there has to be
And the pawn is the cheapest cost.
The bishop preached his sermon for
    everyone to hear,
But the pawn is first in battle when
    the enemies appear.
The knights are out for glory and a good
    word from the king;
As the battle continues to grow longer,
    someone has to fight.
At home, there's immorality and peace is
    what they sing,
While the pawn is on the battlefield
    doing what is right.
The pawn is losing numbers, morale is in
    a wreck,
The king—although he's safe at home, the
    foe, still mumbles "CHECK."

D. R. Memmott

LOOKING BACK ON US

And this,
This must be a toy
From some previous
Generation
And war,
War was the game
They used it in
And death,
Death was when the game
Was done
And everyone went home.

G. C. Ahrberg

KEEPSAKES

Far beyond the haunts of man,
Where no human foot has trod,
There he stands amid the splendour,
Gazing o'er the woodland sod.

There among the hills and vales,
In another world he dwells,
Sure that in the morning glory,
Nature—all her wealth foretells.

With his hawk-like eyes he watches,
Hearing every slightest sound,
Waiting for his chance to capture,
Unsuspecting life around.

Not for him the rod and gun!
Not for him the knives and bows!
Shooting memories forever,
With a lens is best—he knows.

Winifred Brown

WHEN I DIE

When I die—
Fuse my body with the fire,
Mix my ashes with the black earth,
And salute the sun.

When I die—
Say only that I loved
And felt at home here,
And knew kinship with the universe.

When I die—
Let those who loved me, not weep—
But continue to love, even more,
Not me, but each and all—

Till they themselves die.

Dotte Turner

WINDOW PICTURES

When I look out of my window
Sometimes I see a haze,
Or the world in vivid colors
Seems to be ablaze.

Sometimes the snow is falling
Silently—never a sound
As it piles snowdrifts here and there
Upon the frozen ground.

Or maybe the rain comes
   tumbling down
From high up in the skies
Making beneath my window
A tray of small mud pies.

So I look out of my window
Always eager to see
Today's beautiful picture
Painted there for me.

Lucy B. Saunders

THE WAITER ON THE EXPRESSWAY

Expressway choked with traffic, weaves and curves,
It satisfies the artist's view from tower tops;
Bold postcards show lights' lines in whites and mauves,
Reds and blues from beams on streets, in shops.
The motorist is tolled and taxed for this
New maze of wide, expensive miles of road.
He seethes and swears as each new day, he'll miss
Green lights and catch the reds; then he'll explode!
His temper flares from crawls to stops. He lights
A cigarette and thinks of how he should
Be planning roads, not serving tasty bites
In Toby's Tavern where the food is good.
He parks his car beside the restaurant sign
And leaves the stress of life to serve fine wine.

Patricia Campbell-Hardwick

226

IDENTITY

Who am I? A voice within me loudly cries.
Who am I, most Gracious God?
A tooth? A bone? A hank of hair?
Who am I? I long to know!
Am I but a footprint on the Sands of Time?
A footprint to be washed away
By the eventide? A footprint
To be seen no more, but mingled
Anonymously with the Sands of Eternity?

Am I but a speck—a mote—
In the Eye of Life?
A mote to be cursed and cast
Away into Meaninglessness?
Am I but a Word in the
Journals of Time! A Word
To be scribbled, read fleetingly, and
Forgotten in the fleeting lifetime?
Or am I, oh God, a Seed of Life?
Tucked into a small corner of Your Heart?
A seed which will take root,
Blossom forth into a beautiful fragrant flower
Whose fragrance will forever entice the Nostrils
Of Forgetfullness?
A seed to be nurtured, and loved
And fed, and guided, and blessed?
    OH GOD!!!
    Only to say
I AM!!!!

Judith Grisham Clabes

DOUBT

I think if you should leave me dear,
my life would cease to be.
    I gave my heart and soul to you,
as your's you gave to me.
    I'll love you dear when I'm turned to dust,
and in the grave, so deep.
    For love like mine will never die,
but gently fall asleep.

Kay Van Arsdale

It's cold; and that chills and huddles
The wind is slapping and slashing
Not so brisk as to freeze,
But once in a while a warm puff comes
And that softens and mellows somewhat.
The trees bend without argument
Shrubbery bustles about
The water caps and laps
And asks not to be so disturbed.
The people are stiff and rigid
And travel their way well-bundled.
Not so cold that they can't enjoy
Ole Sol and his games today.
The chill of the air blows memories back
And one remembers other such winds.
For instance, atop that naked mountain
Or even in the midst of dunes and sands.
After the winds have blown themselves out
The calm will again settle down
The trees will relax and reach upward
The shrubs will rearrange their positions
The water will sleep and be still
And the people will carry on again
Better for having played the game with ole Sol.

Marlys L. Cutler

It is inevitable
I must be your love.
Through the light
And the darkness of life,
As the seasons
Bless the world.
I may never learn
To share the joy
Of your laughter,
Too deeply—
For I will ask
A greater gift
Bring me
Your tears.

Roberta Whitten

TO BE TWENTY-ONE

I have to laugh when I am told,
By some young miss they're getting old.
Yes the years gone by is quite a sum,
They're every bit of twenty-one.

How I chuckle as I ascend from bed,
Twenty-one? I just shake my head.
I try to spring on to the floor,
My poor old legs won't go no more.

They check their tresses so very bold,
And find one grey hair amid the gold.
I pause before the mirror there,
To see a lady with snow-white hair.

I get so "tired," they do reply,
Cannot do nearly as much as I.
I just smile as I take my cane,
Oh to be twenty-one again.

I'll not reveal what's in store,
Growing pains, that's what they're for.
Twenty-one? And so carefree,
That's the age I'd like to be.

Margaret Smith-Snyder

LAMENT

I heard a step behind
And turned to see

Death in pursuit of me.

I turned with arms open wide,
And he seeing who it was

Stopped and turned aside.

Virginia Anderson

LOVE

The rose and weed grew side by side
Along the garden wall.
They grew and grew till their leaves combined,
And their roots beneath it all.

The gardner saw them and he said,
"Is this really what I see?"
This gorgeous rose and ragged weed
Are one or seem to be.

The gardner took and with a hoe,
The weed's life gave an end.
The rose she wept some bitter tears
For loss of such a friend.

And as the years flew by on wing,
The rosebush took her fall;
And the rose and weed once more combined,
And their roots beneath it all.

Shirley Jean Pitney

The wind before a storm is not quite wild,
Not quite demanding, like love.
It tears through tall grass and falls
Face down on the earth, making love
To Nature.

Trees stand firm—unmoving—unbending—
Hiding the act.
The sky remains untouched, but pales
On seeing what the trees attempt to shield.

The torrent of air consumes the earth,
Leaving it trembling, shivering,
Worn from the effort.

Trees sway, the wind moves on.
The earth appears untouched.
But the clouds that were witness
Begin to cry.

Jan Crawford

MORE WONDERINGS

The mother sees
Only the best
In, for and about
Her dearly beloved
Offspring . . .
Will they succeed
In life ahead;
Be compatibly
Espoused, beloved
And true
To old, as well
As the new
Family ties?
Only the best
    . . . best
      . . . best!

C. Fielding Pearce

REFLECTIONS NUMBER 35

when i look into her eyes
i think of the good things we've known
    when we were young
      and the world our own
when her breast heaved against mine
i thought of wealth untold
    a heart of pure gold—
      gems of priceless worth
        patience
        understanding
        sympathy
        and mirth
in her person i found all that is good
    but she is now contained in a box of wood
yet she is living
    and as near me as is this picture
      for the love she instilled into my heart
      is as vibrant and full
        as life itself

Rick Kellas

231

KITTENS FOR SALE

Kittens for sale! Any one want to buy?
You've the pick of the litter and that
    is no lie.
There's black ones and gray ones and yellow
    ones too,
They're a source of amusement and pleasure
    to you.
Just watch them at play they are hard to
    resist.
Take two, not just one, I really insist!

They're old enough now, they're almost
    eight weeks,
Their tiny "meows" really sound more like
    squeaks.
Just look at that gray one rolled up in
    my rug,
And there goes a cute one, chasing a bug.
There's one on his back with his feet in
    the air,
Now see that one peeking from under the
    chair?
Oh look! There's a fight, one's ears are
    back flat,
And the other one's standing there, paw
    poised to spat.
The black one is kicking his little toy
    mouse,
And getting the catnip all over the
    house.

Oh you will take the one with the longest
    white fur?
Oh dear, can't tell if it's a "Him" or a
    "Her!"
Please Miss, have a heart, if you don't
    want to pay,
I know what I'll do, I'll just give them
    away.

Marilyn Mead

MOORLAND MEDITATION

I climbed up the meadow trail
To the rocky, windy moor;
To the earth where it melts in heaven,
On the ledge where the cold winds roar.

I heard the moan of the sea
As it crashed against the cliff,
Where slime and foam and rivulets run,
And moss and seaweed drift.

I saw the last warm glow
Of twilight softly fade,
And night as it settled over
The silent forest-glade.

I watched the world around me
As it silently grew cold,
And the stars fly all around,
And fall to the ocean's fold.

I felt the chill of the winds
In their sweep across the sky,
To gain the angry heather
And the sullen clouds near by.

There's a sadness and a loneliness
That smothers all your soul
As you stand atop the moorland
When the wind is running cold.

So I turned from the ocean's world;
From the moaning, seething sea
To a path on lonesome moor,
And a trail on the far-off lea.

Frances W. Tribble

WHEN A HOUSE IS A HOME

A house is a home where neighbors call,
Where children romp and run and fall.
It may be painted white or green,
Back in the trees it may be seen.
Curtains at windows trimmed in pink,
Dishes piled in the kitchen sink.
Doors are opened to let in the breeze—
A house is a home if it has these.
A hinge is broken here and there
And by a window a worn-out chair.
The carpets are worn to almost bare
Showing signs of living there.
Out in the back where grass is green
Borders of flowers may be seen.
Coffee perking on the stove,
Homemade cake that looks like gold.
Rows of cups are standing there
Some show cracks and handles gone.
By the sink a dog's nice bone—
If a house had these, it's called a home.

Azalia Blanche Gaiser

HOME

The stars no longer glisten
The sun is breaking through
The flowers are looking upward
Their faces wet with dew

The night was so refreshing
The sky so cloudy blue
The quiet night so restful
Dreaming of friends so true

The alarm broke the silence
Smell of bacon in the air
Happy for home and loved ones
I breathed a thankful prayer

Myrta B. Brollier

A MOTHER'S SONG

Eyes so bright they seem to shine,
Hair that's never in place.
A little hand clasped tight in mine,
That always dirt-smeared face.

The banging door that never stops,
The cuts, and bumps, and tears.
The wondrous dreams that turn out flops,
Dirty footprints and hand smears.

The terror of those tiny fears,
A smile that shames the sun.
His laughter ringing in my ears,
A miracle, called my son.

And even when he's left the nest
His own family, for to raise,
I'll thank Our Lord, for I've been blest
In oh, so many ways.

Kathleen Laugherty Harbarger

PACKS OF UNIFORMITY

Man is the Master of creation,
The paradox of virtue,
The epitome of intelligence,
The ruler of his own destiny,
Each individual a different
    God-like being.
Why, then, does he choose
    to live in packs of
    uniformity—
To disguise his uniqueness in
    masks of drab sameness?
Because for all the splendid
    things men have and men are,
They lack the one most important
    thing.
And, that is the courage to be
    what they are.

Sibby Savaro

235

MAN?

They say man has become civilized,
And more peaceful, too.
But I sometimes sit and wonder,
Is any of it true?

Is man really civilized?
I truly doubt it for
Men seem to want to fight and kill.
They're always craving war.

And man dares to claim himself peaceful?
Always longing to draw blood.
Yet, throughout the human race,
There is a small, tiny bud.

A bud of hope for man to exist,
And prosper as he should.
For if that bud should bloom and grow,
Prosper? Surely he would.

Never has there been such racism,
Trouble between Black and White.
And apparently there will never be an answer,
As to who is wrong, and who is right.

And riots! Those terrible riots!
People revolting for no reason at all.
Destruction is plentiful along the way.
Mobs bring down many a wall.

And yet, there is an Imperial Being,
Who watches over us every day.
Only He knows the Ultimate Answer.
For man can go either way.

Yet, man's actions will affect the outcome,
As only He supposedly can.
But only His decision will decide,
If we are worthy of the title MAN.

Mendy Lyle Pozin
Age 12

How green is my valley!
How aching my back!
My checkbook is empty
From sack after sack
Of gypsum, and lime, fertilizer,
    and peat,
Seeds sown, watered, mowed—
Ah! My joy is complete!
Now, I'll rest—look upon it,
    contented, and smile
But the thought comes to
    mind that in just a while—
There'll be a white flurry
    and then many more
To cover the ground and
    add a new chore
And so—down to Sears
    to buy me a shovel
To dig me a path
    from the road to my hovel
And then spring at last
    finds its way through the mud
And the trees burst their limbs
    with the new leaf in bud

But!—the joy of next summer
    when friends have to sod
I'll rest in my hammock
    and leave it to God!

Mary C. Haubrich

Crawling along the twig
The caterpillar passed
People,
People who spoke
But knew little,
Spoke of ugliness—
Spoke, but knew not
Of the beauty
Of the ugly creature.

Jenny Harrison
Age 15

NECESSITY

A flower needs water to make it grow.
A scholar needs books to make him know.
A fish needs the river to help him spawn,
And I need you to carry on.

A bird needs wings to take him there.
A child needs a mother to make him care.
Man needs hope to live through strife,
And I need you to go through life

Trees need sun to stand so tall,
Tender words are needed to ease one's fall.
Laws are needed to guard one's land,
And I need you to hold my hand.

I need your smile so warm and bright.
I need your touch so soft and light.
I need your kiss to reassure;
I need your love forevermore.

Only you can ease my sorrow.
Only you can fill my tomorrow.
Only you can happiness bring;
Only you can wear my ring.

Elliott H. Davis

INCOMMUNICADO

Isolated
With a shield around me
With a wall between us
You speak but your words seem distant
They cannot touch me
I need to feel that we are
In the same world—
That I am here too
But no one will touch me—
The one who is here—but is not here.

Ramona Teresa Kanellis

MAN'S SIMPLE GLORY

The glittering lake, alight with a spectrum of
    dancing fragments—
The quiet, moist stillness of the fragile forest haven—
The whispered majesty of the wild doe as she nurtures
    her soft-skinned young—
The soft, violet, shimmering, dew-drenched face of
    the woodland flower—
The serene magnitude reflected in the aqua, mountain
    sky—
Out of all these, man's simple glory: his oneness
    with God.

Barbara Sherman

A TIME FOR EVERYTHING

There's a time to be born, and a time to die,
A time to laugh and a time to cry
A time to learn and a time to teach
A time for contentment, and a time to reach.
A time for youth and a time to mature
A time to aggress, and a time to endure.
There's a time to love and a time to hate
A time to give and a time to take.
A time to work and a time to play
A time to rest and a time to pray.
There's a time to be silent and a time to speak.
A time to advise, and a time to seek.
A time to win and a time to lose
A time to be free and a time to choose.
A time to be serious and a time to be gay.
A time to leave, and a time to stay.
There's a time for great joy, and a time for sorrow
Use this time wisely, for there may be no tomorrow.

M. Therese Roling

MY SPONSOR IS DEATH

I sit, unseen, at each motorist's side,
And tempt him to use more speed.
Where signs read cross roads or dangerous curves,
I urge him to pay no heed.
I delight in maimed bodies and property loss.
I promote reckless driving, it pleases my boss.

I love thick fog or a slippery hill,
Their coming I hail with glee.
I smile with joy when the traffic grows thick
Each crash means success for me.
My assistants are striving with diligence rare.
They are known as Impatience and Devil May Care.

I enjoy the shrieks and the children's moans,
I gloat o'er the victim's gore.
I convince the drunks they, alone, must drive,
Their misery I adore.
I rejoice in their groans, in their last gasping breath.
This is Accident speaking, my sponsor is Death.

Verne J. Weber

NO VACATION

If God took a vacation
What would we do
There would be no schedule
Of day and night—darkness or light

What kind of air would we breathe
What would time be like
Would it be all days with light
Would it be all black night

How thankful we should be
God takes no vacation
For it is He
Who supplies our every need.

Mabel B. Stevenson

240

THE BULLFIGHT

As the great matador steps into the ring.
The crowd gives their cheers, to their feet they all
    spring.
"Ole" they all cry to the idol below.
Taking his bow and his clothes all aglow.
His red cape in hand for that bull that he seeks.
Looks at the crowds—but no word does he speak.
The gates open wide as the black bull appears.
He thinks to himself, I shall have his tail and
    his ears.
The cape opens wide as the bull makes his run,
A slight turn of his arm the bullfight's begun.
"El toro, El toro," the matador cries.
As he looks deep within the bull's angry eyes.
He charges again in the cape that he waves,
His back to the bull this matador brave.
His posture so tall as the bull starts to seize,
The bull all in rage puts his head down to his
    knees,
Rubs his hoofs in the dirt, to lunge at the red,
    that he sees
The crowd is all silent as the sword comes in
    sight.
The glare of its power blinds in the light.
The matador is ready as the bull charges ahead.
One stab of his sword and the bull falls down
    dead.
Hats are all flying, as he holds up the ears.
"Bravo, bravo," from the crowds comes the
    cheers.

Dottie Palmieri

HAUNTED NIGHT

Haunted night;
    leaves are writhing in the mist
    hissing as they rear and twist
    within the forest citadel.
Animals have fled and crept
To hidden burrows, scenting death.
Wet, clinging mist
Invades the fur upon the predator's
    domed-skulking head.
He senses his own dread;
    moves through the haunted
    night.
Whole forest now is trembling.

Marjorie Ann Johnson

A WOMAN'S PRAYER FOR PEACE

Lord grant that great men of all nations
   Strive to form a peaceful plan,
Forever outlaw mass destruction,
   And proclaim a nuclear ban.

The world has seen too much of battle
   When battlefields were bathed in gore,
The soldiers wounded, maimed, or dying,
   Attest to the aftermath of war.

The wars have left a grieving mother,
   Or widow waiting at her door,
The crosses in a far off country
   Mark the hero—who lives no more.

We pray that we may live as brothers,
   And extend a helping hand,
Not only to our friends and neighbors,
   But to all across the land.

Extending hands across the ocean,
   And reaching all the way around,
Let's make this world a land of beauty,
   Where love, and joy, and peace abound.

Mrs. John Novak, Sr.

God keep you, husband dear, I pray;
Though steep and rugged be your way;
And grant that all your journey through;
My love and prayers will go with you.

God grant faith, steadfast and high;
And hope, a star to light your sky;
And love, to warm your heart with cheer;
I love you so, God keep you, dear.

Della Myers

WILD WINDS IN THE NIGHT

What are the wild winds saying,
As they whistle and rant and roar?
It's bound to be pretty important,
When they shake and rattle my door.
They cause the whole house to tremble,
As they shriek and bellow and hiss.
I turn and toss, and cannot sleep,
No ghoulish nightmare, this.
They hammer my windows with gusto,
While I'm lying here in my bed.
Their fingers tear at my roof top,
As if by strange forces they're led.
They call to me down through the chimney,
Every cranny and crack, they spy.
Reaching down, I pull up my blanket,
Trying hard to shut out their cry.
No use, for I can still hear them,
And they whistle and shout with glee,
To know that their storming and raving,
Has such an effect upon me.
The night is so long and so weary,
And I've even tried counting sheep,
While these nasty old winds get some pleasure,
Out of robbing me of my sleep.
Next morning, and they are still at it,
Sleepless night, and the sky is so gray.
But to me, 'twill remain a great mystery,
What the wild winds were trying to say.

Alma N. Bromley

ADDING UP A STORM

Cold feet? The chilling facts
Prompt me to wonder
If monthly blizzard of bills
Will snow me under.

Eleanor Willis

LOVE

Love is a friendship,
   Cherished and enduring.
Love is a shadow,
   Dark and fleeting.
Love is a smile,
   Bright and cheerful.
Love is a tear,
   Sad and lonely.
Love is a child,
   Teasing and gay.
Love is an enemy,
   Hateful and destructive.
Love comes,
   Warm and shining.
Love goes,
   Cold and dull.
Love rules all,
   Heart and soul.
What is love?
   The reason we live!

Cheryl L. Meurer

Send me no roses, for roses are gentle,
And I am not worthy of this.
Speak me no praises, for praises are falsehoods,
And bless not my lips with your kiss.
Make me no promise, for promise is sacred,
And I am a breaker of rules —
Love her forever, but keep me for pleasure,
For I am but one of your fools.

Linda Cayton

Yesterday I loved a man, and he loved me

Yesterday I held a man close to my heart
And breathed the warmth of my soul upon him

Yesterday I released the things within me
That had been stored for a lifetime

Yesterday a man held me in his arms
And spoke of the stirring passion within him

Yesterday I was touched by the words
Of a beautiful human being

Yesterday I felt a swelling of my heart
That I had never known before

Yesterday I absorbed the delight
Of being needed and wanted

Yesterday I knew the true measure
Of being loved unselfishly

Yesterday I was able to share a love
That was reflected back to me

Yesterday the happiness within me
Knew no boundaries

Yesterday I had great pity
For those who have never known love

Yesterday I loved a man, and he loved me
And today I love him more . . . .

Beverly Kramer Goldberg

PURSUIT OF HAPPINESS

We struggle for contentment
Each hour plan and plot it,
But sometimes our biggest mistake
Is not knowing when we've got it.

Kathryn McGaughey

LOVE

Lovers give it, scientists sieve it.
Oldsters recall it, lewdsters maul it.
Sheiks collect it, medicines affect it.
Drunks pursue it, derelicts rue it.
Athletes perform it, Eskimos warm it.
Moroccans cool it, actors drool it.
Rabbits adore it, turtles store it.
Braggarts tell it, madams sell it.
Angles 4-letter it, puritans fetter it.
Cynics deny it, tycoons buy it.
Youngsters test it, tramps molest it.
Bachelors rent it, old maids resent it.
Sailors vary it, anchorites parry it.
Poets dream it, infidels blaspheme it.
The lonely extol it, policemen patrol it.
Ministers preach it, Sunday schools teach it.
Musicians lyre it, the handsome fire it.
The lucky find it, the tolerant don't mind it.
In tennis they lose with it, the jealous get
    the blues with it.
The moon makes a mist of it, the wild get
    the gist of it.
Collectors marry it, morticians bury it.
Ghosts haunt it, I want it.

Lakenan Barnes

Cause and effect is
An affected cause
And a caused effect.

The dichotomy is a fiction
Claiming power of prediction.
The delusions of a past event
Are scattered by the baffling timeless
Prism of the present.

Peter C. Davis

THE INHERITANCE

At the time of the funeral
   they came from afar.
Bob took the quilts
   and a Dresden rose jar.
The twins chose the pieces
   they always loved best:
The rope-bottom bed
   and the sea captain's chest.
Beth has her pearls
   and a rare cameo;
The pewter and sterling
   were labeled for Joe.

We have the shell
   she found at the shore,
A bone crochet hook
   and the thimble she wore.
For long years ago
   we made the best choice
Those months of her smile
   the sound of her voice.
We had all the treasures
   that heart understands
The wealth of her stories
   the warmth of her hands.

Celia G. Stahl

SHARED BEAUTY

I planned and dug and planted with care
A few flowers here, a few flowers there.
These flowers will bloom next year again—
It may be I'll not be here then.
But it doesn't matter, for others may
Enjoy the beauty I've planted today.

Dorothy Fay Cooper

LOST NEIGHBOR

Throughout the years she lived there
We built this friendly sign
A slender curving pathway
From her back door to mine.

Sometimes she'd leave her sewing
To come and knit with me
And once I went to borrow
Her pickle recipe

She brought me bulbs, one autumn
To start a tulip bed
And after baking, often
I'd take her gingerbread

I miss her lively footsteps
And wonder since she's gone
If my new next door neighbor
Will want a pathless lawn.

Estella Walsh

Bright yellow
Green grows the stem
Turn into the ghost-like image
Carried on the wind's Smile
Breaks up into segments of a
New unborn dandelion
On the side of the hill
With all the clan
of Bodies and Souls.
They grow wild
And are wonderfully wild
And free.
And get along very well
Without thinking.

Rapt Reynolds

A CUP OF COFFEE

What does she think as she sits there
With pallid face and shrunken cheek?
She sips the coffee from her cup
And moves her lips, but does not speak.

The shadow there that crossed her brow
Bespeaks the painful startled moment,
When first she knew without a doubt
All lives contain both joy and torment.

The stare that's fixed above the cup
Held motionless before her lips
Holds me spellbound and as I watch,
She shrugs and smiles and slowly sips.

Then I relax because I know
The memory so painful then
Has been inspected and rewrapped
And placed back in the past again.

When her eyes grow soft and dark
And light the face we all adore
I know that all is right again
Her gentle heart has won once more.

She sips—I watch her past unfold.
I sit so still and make no sound,
But now she's relived all her life
And rising puts her blue cup down.

Cloie Carson

THE AMERICAN FLAG

The American Flag makes me proud
And makes me want to shout out loud
For every stripe and every star
Our country is known both near and far.

Billy Crawford

THE CHRISTMAS MIRACLE

This is the Christmas miracle
God sent His Son this day.
To be our Saviour, Guide, and Ligh
Our Comfort, and our stay.

So let us all look past the lights
The tinsel and the floss.
And see not a small helpless babe
But the Man upon the Cross.

Then let us at this Christmas time
Resolve to do our best.
To pay the debt we owe our Lord
And let us work with zest.

To carry out the tasks He left
For each of us to do.
Knowing you cannot do my work
Nor I your work for you.

And as we pray for strength let's ask
In Christian humbleness.
The good Lord to accept our thanks
And may He ever bless.

And keep us ever faithful as
We travel down life's road.
Loving our neighbors always and
Helping to share his load.

May we find the kindness and the
Compassion in our soul.
To all be friends as together
We strive toward the goal.

Remembering the Saviour said
I come to bring thee light.
I will walk along beside thee
Be it by day or night.

No matter what the future holds
Or how hard the task
Fear not for I am there to help
You, you have but to ask.

Thomas W. Yoke

QUEST VIA KIPLING

If I could lay
All worldly treasures
   at your feet
or press your lips to mine
   on your command.
Hold still each moment
   of all Time
and keep forever
   the Happiness
within your heart
   for mine,
I would make myself
   a pauper
to see you Queen
of every treasured good
and know your smile
   was wished on me
   with
   Love.

lief greneforst

EQUINOX + 2

A thousand minds lay shattered
   in the scarlet mist of forever

Searching
   for a withered yesterday's return

Waiting
   for tomorrow's unhurried promise.

R. Steven Graves

PRAIRIE-SCULPTURED

My soul has felt the Prairie Sculptor's hand.
The harsh unsoftened blows that lash the land

Have smoothed its roughness, chisled beauty there,
And left a sense of calmness everywhere.

The prairie knows the peace of gentle rain.
My courage soars with each bird's glad refrain;

The dragon breath of heat has sealed my heart
With fearlessness against each fiery dart.

That strives to tear this moulding from my life.
The vastness of these rolling plains is rife

With strength and hope and joy I understand,
My soul has felt the Prairie Sculptor's hand.

Ethel Ballard Terry

FOR WALTER K.

On your 80th birthday Walter
Do not let your footsteps falter
In 20 years you will be
Starting on your Century!

We wish you happiness and health
And if it's possible, some wealth
To keep your travels worry free
Is the wish of all—including me!

Lyn

WHEN THE GEESE HAVE
FLOWN OVER AND GONE

The sounds of the far-off geese, silver in the night,
   Beating their way overhead across the moon;
Their far-carrying calls
   that one hears before he can see, in flight
To spend one season South;
The melancholy of the failing autumn dusk
The clear blueness—the ache—
Venus—
The scarlet West
   and woodsmoke from nameless fires
Curling around the heart;
And again are felt the old wounds.
Staring into a landscape—a distance—
   I have never known,
Into a fire—the calling stars—
   I have never seen
At the drifts and drifts of snow
   and the ledges where the wind has swept it clean,
Is remembered—
   and reawakens—
The old ache in the old sores.

What more can this new year bring
   Except
A desolation at heart
   and a gnawing disquiet
      at the life inadequate, unfulfilled
An interminable search and search
   for
(—Can you tell me? Do you know yourself?)
Something forever drawn beyond reach,
A gradual and separate spring
   With the walnut trees
Remaining bare
   till all the iceskates
Have been packed away
   for another year,
And nothing but this emptiness—
   and the dirty, dirty snow.

Nannette Czernega

JUST LIKE DONNIE DID!

I hope some day I'll have a boy,
Who'll fill my heart with so much joy,
And have great love for each small toy;
Just like Donnie did!

He'll win my heart with baby powers,
And play alone for many hours,
And love the smell of all the flowers;
Just like Donnie did!

When he is tired, he'll rest his head
On his little pillow-bed,
With his knees drawn up 'til they both turn red;
Just like Donnie did!

He'll love his pets, and treat them well;
And he wouldn't cry even though he fell.
He'll cause my heart with love to swell;
Just like Donnie did!

When he is nine, he'll be a scout,
A cub at first, without a doubt;
He'll join their yells and really shout;
Just like Donnie did!

He'll have many friends and lots of fun;
And keep the little girls on the run;
And fight going to bed when the day is done;
Just like Donnie did!

I wouldn't want a naughty child,
Whose manner would be rough and wild;
I want mine styled like Donnie's styled;
Cause, gosh, I love that kid!

Marjorie R. Morrow

PERHAPS TODAY

Life's guarded secrets are revealed,
In most surprising ways,
Destinies are made and sealed,
On ordinary days.

Alice Robertson Pratt

CHILD'S SLUMBER

There's nothing so sweet as a
child in slumber,
A child who kicks off the
covers he's under.
A child who tosses around
in his crib.
Who quests for the toy his
mother has hid.
And finally after he has fallen
asleep,
He smiles a smile that goes
cheek to cheek.
And when Mommy recovers
him with his blanket again,
She sees little white sheep
jumping over his glen.

Linda Piper Jewell

FOR GUITAR

He heard a ballad and felt moved
    To write some of his own;
A ballad has an episode
    That's personal in tone.

He'd sing about romantic love
    And simply tell a host
Of tales the minstrels told who sang
    Of war and sad-eyed ghost.

Or balladeer who left his love,
    His songs to celebrate,
Bewailing loss of fickle lass
    And of man's tragic fate.

But gleeman, harpist, troubadour,
    The story must depend
On life and death, the brief refrain,
    A false or faithful friend.

Liboria Romano

NOT TWICE INTO THE SAME DAWN

Only by pain may Beauty claim the right
To be admired for Truth's and Virtue's sake.
It is the wound that makes the pearl grow white—
The field to bloom must know the rip of rake.
The cup of clay endures the oven's fire
In order to contain the cooling spring,
And strings are tortured to the curving lyre,
Yet at the touch they joyously will sing.
At jungle's edge the tiger takes the goat
And makes him into orange barred with black,
More beautifully bright than his old coat
Was worn. I wonder, would he ever want it back?
    Man cannot come but once to each dawn's light
    Without he first walks through another night.

Ralph W. Seager

IF I HAD NO ONE

If I had no one to hold me,
To kiss away each tear,
If I had no one to love me,
To smile at me, my dear,

If I had no one to care for,
To cherish and obey,
If I had no one to live for,
To share each precious day,

If I had no one to miss me,
To hurry home each night,
If I had no one to kiss good-bye,
When dawned the morning light,

Then life would have no meaning,
And I don't know what I'd do,
So I thank my lucky stars,
My darling, I have you.

Joyce Totten

NIGHT THOUGHTS

Although the sea divides us
Through the day . . .
When darkness comes,
I feel you near.
I hear
In low-breathed tones
Your promises
Of love forevermore . . .
And know
Who says the sea divides us
Tells a lie.

Clara H. Wenger

"Just look!" says Day,
"My sun is bright!"
"Ah, yes—but I possess
The moon," says Night.

"My strength excells!"
Boasts proud strong Wind,
But Calm remarks,
"I am peace within."

The Mountains claim
Peaks, high and keen . . .
While Valleys low
Are clothed in green.

The Sands—dry warmth,
The Seas—their tides;
You see, Life's Coins
ALL have two sides!

Mary LuAnne Campbell

BACKTRACKING

You could've found me
Had you turned around
And waited for the dust to clear.

You could've seen me
Had you
       looked
           down
Away from stars, this side of heaven.

You might not have lost me
Had it not started to rain
Back where I was.

Now you come back down my road.
Wondering when . . .
Pondering why.

But I've long since been gone.
I came across another straggler
Withering as I was.

Together we backtracked,
And found each other.

Andrew Jackson Borders, III

EVENING ON THE PRAIRIE

The prairie at even is wondrous fair,
The scent of silver willows fills the air,
The meadow lark is singing his lay
At the close of a long hot day.
The sun to the west is swinging
Crows and blackbirds are homeward winging.
Cowbells coming up the lane
Tell us it's milking time again,
All these things to feel and see
Mean a prairie evening to me.

Marjorie Stewart

THERE . . .

There . . .
Beneath the soothing tall timbers,
Which, in turn, look upward to the stars—
Unbelievable billions—
I and the cool night
Are content with being still.
Darkness is a must for my pleasure,
Or the stars would not be as they are.
I can see a face;
A vision seen as well,
If not better,
Than at day.
This relaxing, reverent eve
Unclouds my mind—
As was the twilight—
Making it possible
To brand one beautiful fleeting moment
Upon my heart;
Forever . . . . Unforgettable.

Thomas Jay Tozer

THE DEER

How quickly he goes through the brush,
How noiselessly and yet he is so very careful.
His young are put to sleep by the lull
Of the night owl.

His colors blend with the grass,
And yet he is so beautiful,
Every year he is slaughtered
Without mercy.

How is it that we do such things.
Artists paint him
And then they shoot him;
I do not understand.

Louise Thompson

WINTER SYMPHONY

The silvered sun,
slipping through
the drowsy duskiness,
sifts o'er slumb'ring clouds
its prismed hues,
to cloak the fleeced world
with an elfin veil
of rainbow loveliness.

Dirty icicles
dolefully drip,
sullen silhouettes
against the icy pallor
of steel blue slate,
as the leaden silence is pierced
by a tram's noisy jangle
and the shrill whistle shrieks
noon.

A velvet tent of darkness
enfolds in its mantle
of star-studded night
the dreaming drifts,
whilst, hov'ring o'er
the sleeping silence,
the pale moon peers,
a frosted face
behind the sombre lacework,
of a midnight pine.

Rosalind McKague

CLOUDS

A white mist of beauty,
A handful of loveliness,
Stretching far across the sky,
Like palaces of kings they stand
In everlasting beauty.

Patricia Howes

IMAGINARY TREKS

Let's take a stroll, or a moonlight cruise
   Or a walk down lovers' lane
Or let's take a bicycle built for two
   On a picnic down in the glen
Or, if you prefer—a bowling spree
   Or a movie, light and gay
But for me, I'd rather the moonlight cruise
   Along some scenic bay.

Let's go in a car 'long the skyline drive
   Down old Virginia way
Then head into old Nashville
   To hear country music, what say?
Or, if you prefer the mountains
   With trails and lovely streams
Then let's go there, or anywhere
   In our imaginary dreams.

Oh, this land of ours is beautiful
   In the sun of day, or night
With nature all around us
   Why would we e'er take flight?
And go back to the cities
   With all the city smell
But thru all, just to be near you
   Is more wonderful than tongue can tell!

Peggy Standeford

FUTILITY

When I die, don't cry for me,
Don't weep, don't rant, don't rave.
No matter how you feel my dear,
I'll never leave my grave.

Janeen Allen

261

RAINBOW AND RAIN

How is one to see a rainbow unless
　　he's seen rain?
How is one to know health unless
　　he's felt pain?
How is one to know peace unless
　　he's known war's toll?
How is one to know a friend unless
　　he's known a foe?

How is one to know youth unless
　　he's known age?
How is one to know freedom unless
　　he's known the cage?
How is one to know happiness unless
　　he's been sad?
How is one to know the good unless
　　he's known the bad?

How is one to know hope unless
　　of despair he's reaped?
How is one to know success unless
　　he's experienced defeat?

Rosalie Figge

THE GIFT

To think, to reflect, to feel—that is life.
Although sometimes slow—sometimes painful—
It keeps the soul awake.
How easy it would be—how painless—
To let moments like these slip by without
　　notice—
And how wrong.
What greater sin than to empty the mind—
Even in the darkest of night—I know not.
The greatest value lies not in the consolation
　　of forgetting,
But in the gift of remembrance.

Joel Simmer

FLORIDA

No island in the sun have we
 Yet nature gave us blue-green sea
Kissed by miles of sunlit sand
 This is Florida our land.

From ocean bed upon the shore
 Lie many shells which years before
Were treasures of the briny deep
 Where sunken ships their watch
  still keep.

Palm trees sway and birds still sing
 Near Ponce De Leon's magic spring
By drinking of its waters clear
 One ne'er grows old for many a year.

Old Tami Trail runs by our door
 Where Seminoles in days of yore
Hid in saw grass wild and high
 To watch the white man's boats sail
  by.

This land of beauty, sun and flowers
 Is yours and mine—forever ours
So why not come and work or play
 It's such a lovely place to stay.

     Elizabeth Sharp Brown

SEPTEMBER

There's something in the air tonight,
Branches whispering, birds in flight.
Chirping crickets cease their trill.
Shadows lengthen upon the hill,
While mellow scent of ripened grain,
Betokens summer's on the wane.
The moon shrouded with silver haze,
Heralds the coming autumn days.
Soon frost will paint with magic brush,
Dull landscapes bright, ere winter's hush.

     Patience Ann Bell

263

MY PLACE

With empty hands I came to you—
    my heart was empty, too.
My years were spent in seeking—
    roaming the whole land through
Looking forever for a love to whom
    I could be true.
So my hands and heart were empty
    when, at last, I came to you.

At first, I could not believe the
    things you said to me,
The love that you held out to me
    was too beautiful to be.
But as I gazed in wonder at your
    gentle, lovely face,
I knew that I had found, at last,
    my own loved, lovely place.

Lance Du Vall

ON THE PASSING OF A FRIEND

The seasons pass over them.
No longer do they feel the
Cold of winter nor the
Warmth of summer.
And oft times I think of
Them and ask "why?"
Often I say "Had it
Only been me, that
My friend might have lived."
But now I think of it
This way on the passing
Of a friend. She died so
That I might live and
Through my memories I
Will continue to live
For her.

Susan Joy Perry

TALK

We talked.
Such pleasant conversation
Without reservation,
   I thought.

You said
What you thought you meant
At least during the time we spent
   together.

I listened—
But I didn't hear.
Your words I fear
   got in my way.

We understood
What we wanted to understand
As if some giant hand
   covered our ears
      to the rest.

Though conversation's real
Thoughts conveyed are not.
What's said is not a lot.
   Damn Webster anyway!

            Gayle L. Evans

IVY

Crawling up the trellis white,
Is the ivy, shining bright.
It aimlessly grows on every day,
Without an eye to show the way.

Most men think it best to die,
Then live without a seeing eye.
But not the ivy! It has an aim:
To keep the earth from being plain.

          Peter Hollenbeck
             Age 13

MAIN THEME I

For Debbie

Driving around this evening
I so wanted to have you with me.
Such a beautiful night—
Not the kind to be wasted with trivia.

I would have called you—
But it was too late; you might have been asleep.
And not wanting to disturb your dreams
I went home with only your smell.

Perhaps tomorrow I'll tell you of these things.

Although I'd rather you'd know:
I never walk past the window of a hospital nursery—
    but what I look for my daughter.
Or—
If you'll stick around—hold my hand in the dark,
Touch my face—we'll discover each other.
But most of all—
You're a woman.
Have good dreams tonight—
Tomorrow I will tell you these things.

Larry Cosand

MY WISHES FOR YOU

A wish to make your prayers come true
The sun to make your skies all blue
A song to make your days all bright
A love to guide you through the night
These are the things I wish for you

A bird to sing your blues away
Someone to help you through the day
The wind to make your troubles fly
And nought but cheer to greet your eye
These are the things I wish for you

Kathryn Diehl

266

FOOTPRINTS

Together
        we walked to the sea.
And tired with the want of human understanding
    went to rest in a boundless room
        of azure ceiling.

A few lonely gulls protested our intrusion,
    but if we did notice,
Paid no heed.

How soothing the sound of the crashing waves
    and the echo of distant bells!

The wind blew my hair.
And I buried myself deeper into your arms—
Oblivious of all but your pounding heart
    and steady breath.

We spoke not a word.
But have two people ever said so much?

Dusk drew near.
And we rose
To walk hand-in-hand to the emptiness
    of civilization.

Two
        sets of footprints.
But the wind blew them into one.

Arlene Wydronek

THE QUIET VOICE

The wind blowing softly through the trees,
Seem whispering thoughts with every breeze,
As if God speaks to us that way,
Giving us comfort day by day.

Fay C. Moys

THINGS

The older I grow, the more
    "things" matter.
A Dresden cup, my Wedgwood
    platter,
My lovely China vase—by Ming,
A silver bell with its tinkling
    ring.
My Boston rocker, a brown bean
    pot,
A book with a pressed forget-me-
    not.

These "things" matter, the older
    I grow.
A pink petunia, a garden hoe,
A pot of ivy, an old lace fan,
A dimpled grandson, my
    grey-haired man.
Sweet organ music, soft and
    low,
These "things" matter the older
    I grow.

Hortence Goodfellow

ANVIL

Stars disclose us with scattered dust of blue
as lovers mold soft lips of dew
to rise and fall fearlessly
molten molded you and me
passion moist in fullness flow
gently lulling to and fro
oh gentler lover cling on fast
this burning anvil scours my hidden mask

Patricia Looker

CEASED BY REASONING

War is there,
What is war?
Mrs. Jones sued Miss Smith
a war broke out,
no notice.
Johnny punches Bill
in the nose
a battle occurs,
no notice.
Two countries fight,
notice death,
useless death.
Death that can be
prevented by adult
   reasoning.
What is war is there!

Larry Artale

LIGHT

My light growing brighter
Coming closer, nearer to me—
My light became dimmer—
Soon it exploded with new hope for me . . .

My life, but a water trickle
Comes light, it started to pour—
My light so fair yet so fickle—
My light was bright, an open door . . .

Her light was solemn and grey
Her light would not reach, reach to me—
My light now dying, it too is grey—
I live now in seclusion, no light in me.

Ken Hotard

TRILOGY

Looking for something that doesn't exist
I know that's what I am doing indeed
But I cannot stop, my search must persist
In spite of the fact that I shall not succeed.

I am in love with a girl but I am confused
I have the strongest feeling of being used
But I may be wrong she may just be coy
Whatever it is, she is my greatest joy.

Obituaries

Here rests in eternal downright peace
A man who was mentally obese
He had nothing at all to give
So he just ceased to live

and

Here rests a man of considerable note
Whom the world will eagerly quote
He worked himself to the bone
And was rewarded with a stone.

Gunnar Kullerud

IRISH GOLD

One moonlit night when all was still
A leprechaun I spied
Tip-toeing through a shamrock patch
With bucket by his side

I saw him turn to look about
For fear he might be seen
Quite satisfied he was alone
He skipped across the green

He wore a tiny tasseled cap
Laced shoes upon his feet
His little coat of scarlet red
Was buckled very neat

He started mending elf-like shoes
Not very far from me
An Irish lull-a-bye he hummed
And sipped sweet shamrock tea

The bucket shone beneath the moon
The Irish I'd been told
Entrusted, once, a leprechaun
To guard their precious gold

The Irish say this leprechaun
Is clever as can be
When spied upon he vanishes
Into the Irish Sea

With quiet step and thumping heart
I slyly stole his way
With Irish luck I'd have the gold
So close to me it lay!

Then quick as scat! I grabbed the elf
"Your gold!" "Your gold!" I cried
"My gold?" laughed he "look to the sky
'Tis moonbeams that I hide!"

I raised my eyes—the elf was gone!
His clever trick of old
He left me in the shamrock patch
With moonbeams for my gold!

Zelda M. Masten

271

THE PROMISE

Behold effervescent sunshine!
My soul's time-sores are healed
As I waken from my hibernation from Life.

Never dreaming in my hours of unsought sleep
That the deepening chambers could be filled
By your ecstasy once remote, now
Nakedly, honestly exposed.

Groping my way among dawn's first rays
I slowly dare to sip of your wine
Lest I become drunken with your splendor.
But I cannot restrain all my impatient hopes
So I drink deeply, and I am whole.

Do not mock me in my renaissance.
Be not a sorcerer—hypnotize not
My void feeling into dependency, submission
Only to cast me off with a shrug,
Worse—a laugh of conquest.
And repent not afterward with Freudian tears
To make yourself believe
You indeed exist in Purity.

For I will surely re-vanish into an abyss
With others who believed that
Crystal tears could be shed
By a parasite cloaked in love.

You are my final reincarnation
There is no other—

As you rise to the height of noon,
Your warmth is felt in the
   depths of vague twilight.

Once limp, lethargic arms,
Now beating sun-streaked wings.
I fly alone to the highest branch
   of the Olive.
Where, slowly, I begin to integrate
My shattered feathers. And in the quietude
Of your promise, I dare to open my eyes.

Diana Georgantas

THE END AND THE BEGINNING

The sky grows dark. The cold wind howls, forcing
leaves to follow it.
The rain slashes down beating a cruel tattoo upon
lighthouse roofs.
Waves crash upon the rocks, threatening to devour
them.
A thundering climax is contrasted by a dim ray of
sunshine
Trying to escape from the gray clouds' ugly head.
The clouds move slowly apart. The dim ray becomes
a momentarily blinding flash
Then transforms into a soft billowing pool of
brilliancy.

A soft breeze blows playfully at multicolored flowers
Carrying their sweet fragrance over fields of flowing
grass for all eternity.

William M. Turner

SHE

She went walking down the road
That led to hell.
She walked faster.
Then she ran.
Faster . . . faster!

And she found herself there and . . .

She liked it.

Her mind absorbed the ecstacy
Of hell,
As she slowly melted into the haze
Like a pat of butter over a freshly
Baked potato.

And she loved it.
Carol V. Von Ruden

HEART'S PATH

I walked the path you set for me, and left my
    footprints there . . . .
On the sands of good behavior, along the shores
    of care . . . .
Faithful in each step I took, my love for you
    my guide, ...
I walked alone, hoping someday . . . You'd
    walk by my side . . . .

But you went down another path, where love
    is stepped upon, ...
And trust is smothered by the weeds, until its
    bloom is gone . . . .
Your stride was long, Dear, and it carried you
    with speed . . . .
Into a forest of broken vows, where love is
    paid no heed . . . .

I have clawed, 'til my hands are torn, at the
    growth that parts our ways . . . .
But you've nurtured it with your unconcern,
    and so it thrives and stays . . . .

Now I stumble down this rocky lane, no one
    to lean upon, ...
Not knowing how to leave it, when all heart,
    all hope, is gone . . . .

Patsy Williamson

TODAY'S CALL

Today this child needs me.
Not tomorrow,
When other voices press upon her
And mine is lost or dim.
But now she is the charge
God gave me.
To fail to be here
Is somehow to fail Him.

Arlet Osnes Vollers

274

THE FRIENDLY TREE

Once as a tiny seed, it hoped a friendly tree to be,
So stretching forth its many roots it grew in ecstasy.
A graceful, friendly tree, it stood to shelter from above
The little things that came to rest, with understanding
love.

The deer, yet with her spotted fawn lay there in
summer shade,
And bunnies came to take their naps from out the
woodland glade.
Some happy birds came there to nest and sing their
even' song
And knowing well the friendly tree brought other
birds along.

Then woodsmen came, with learned eyes its
usefulness they knew—
The tree was glad to be of use as they began to hew.
It swayed farewell to all its friends and traveled forth
to see
What wondrous things the other trees had gone away
to be.

The stump remained for many years, one day we
found it there.
The tree was gone, the roots were left with beauty
yet to share.
Some parts were scattered 'round about with twists
and curves and such
And knots and rotted parts, as though just waiting
for our touch.

Now, woodland friends in passing, pause—and say a
little prayer
That soon another friendly tree will grow and shelter
there.
And so 'twill be when we are gone, if deeds have been
well done,
A little part, a friendly thought will linger on and on.

Myrtle D. Hulse

275

LOOK UP AND TOUCH THE GROUND

Look up
And touch the ground.
Hold fast
To the ladder of uncertainty
Rocking slowly—
On the edge of life.

Like a bird,
Vainly attempting
To take flight
With a broken wing;
Courage is fruitless and
The vague shadow of hope,
Just a senseless dream.

Candles,
That once
Shed the world with light, are
Instantaneously snuffed out,
Unveiling jagged pieces of timber,
Signifying remnants of shelters that
Once were inhabited with life.
And a muted black sky, stripped of
Its former color, stares blankly at
The bleak surroundings.

The silence,
Blaring with unholy quiet,
Raises its bizarre voice in protest,
Unaware that it is falling on deaf ears,
While sparse drifts of sand wearily move
Their littered grains along the
Newly acquired emptiness.

Only the wind,
Bears the heavy burden
Of being the eternal sole mourner
For a silent, now desolate,
World that was . . . . .

Eileen S. Clark

MY BROTHER

when i saw you wading through the grass today
my feet longed to walk where your feet went,
    feeling the feeling that knows no sister or brother;

your fair head was bent against the sun,
    your body weak from trying to shrug heat's arm
        from your shoulder,

only your feet
      (and mine, wistfully watching)
   knew deliciousness
     and smiling
        then

when i saw you wading through the grass today

Judith Anderson

TO A VIOLET

Every flower in God's garden,
Has a beauty all its own,
But to me, the modest violet,
Wears the royal crown.

So tiny, yet so beautiful,
With its rich deep purple hue,
And fragrance so alluring,
It has a message for me and you.

It's not always the largest, brightest flowers,
That make the bouquet sweet,
It also needs the smaller ones,
To make it quite complete.

So if you feel left out of things,
Feel there's no place for you,
Just remember the tiny violet,
And you'll bloom in God's garden too.

Ellen Hornigold

WHERE REALITY?

Stilted wooings, stilted yearnings, stilted desires—
These I felt beneath my feet, my very haughty feet—
Till, adventuring down my chosen path to conspire
my fate, I penned with ink ethereally sweet.

I penned my chosen way through—
quicksand—and
I wrote about a world—
unknown.

I wrote about a world
for which I alone was looking—
Then, at last—aghast—
I found it delicious,
To settle my feet upon
the hearth-rug of Common-Place!

Rose Wiley Chandler

LIFE

The happenings of tomorrow are unknown.
They could be what you've been waiting for.
And again
They could be what you've been avoiding.
We know not.

Life is cruel.
Was it meant to be this way?
I can't understand . . .
We live
To die.

Why are we experiencing life?
For the enjoyment of fighting, rejecting,
And killing our own brothers?
No.
For the fulfillment and happiness,
Of love—the source of life.

Linda S. Swanson

278

AN OLD FEELING

Where are the dreams of
A summer day in happy youth?
When blood-blossomed cheeks
Cheered merrily their calls
And then went unwisely their way
On their way . . .
Perhaps to where the life spring lies,
To the fount of youth
That the aged can not find.
Or was it on a spring morning
That I thought I felt
Or dreamt I thought I felt
The old sensation pulsing new
To a forgotten rhythm
To a sprightly rhyme
To a time that I once knew.
Or so it seemed to me
I could recapture the old
Newness in thee.
Or was it mature reality
Confronting a romantic notion
That led me to believe a
Sensation 'tween waking and sleeping?

Arthur A. Molitierno

NO TIME

There really isn't enough time,
you see;
To do the things that are left
to me.
I clean, sweep, cook and shop,
my chores go on and never stop;
If there were some way to hold
the sun;
Maybe then I could get all of my
work done.

Linda Dianell Glanton

279

HOW MANY TIMES, MOTHER?

Today is your day, and a day for all mothers—
But, you know that to us, you're greater than others.
Tho' I was the first one to call to you "Mother"—
How many times came that call from the others?

How many times did we call out at night,
When we had a bad dream, or some little fright?
How many earaches and toothaches did you
Get up and kiss better in the morning at two?

How many times have we cried on your shoulder,
When we were little and as we grew older?
How many times did we forget to do
Some little thing you had asked us to?

How many times did we call on the phone
And asked you to hurry and come to our home?
How many times did you sit with our babies,
And never said "No"—or not even "Maybe"—?

How many times did we bring you our troubles
Rarely in singles, mostly in doubles?
How many days, in thirty-nine years,
How many smiles, how many tears?

How many times?—that many and more—
And try as we might, we can't even the score.
We just want to tell you, all eight and three plus—
That of all of the mothers, you're the greatest to us!

Evelyn Ide Saltz

RESTLESS WIND

The
void or
tempest is
reflection of
mood.
Alyce Ersland Anderson

POTS OF CYCLAMEN

I brought into my own small room
As subject for my pad and pen—
Right in the depth of winter's gloom—
Some planted pots of cyclamen.

Some were simple twists of pink
And some were ruffled prettily
Then easily I grew to think
Of every blossom lovingly.

To me a cyclamen suggests
A sort of saucy jaunty thing
Pleasing both a host and guests;
A worthy flower of which to sing.

And, in morn's dusk when I arise,
Or, in the day if I look in,
They wait to greet my hungry eyes
Those pretty pots of cyclamen.

Alan C. Reidpath

DAYDREAMS

Dreams are spun of fragile thread,
Albeit bright and shining.
Shattered by a thunderhead,
Which tears the silver lining.

Indifference, or a thoughtless word
May ruin someone's hopes.
Despair, then, like an evil bird
Upon their shoulder mopes.

And all at once the happy dreams
Dissolve as soapened bubbles.
Leaden, now, the weight it seems
Of all their daily troubles.

Mildred E. Wright

WHO WILL REMEMBER

The world around is moving fast
   Things change by night and day
Philosophies that can not last
   Come and go that way
Nothing is allowed to stand
   Iconoclasts decide
All that is old and still in use
   Just has to be denied
But I still cling to orthodox rule
   I guess I always will
For I believe no man a fool
   Who values these thoughts still

I will not live for self alone
   Or seek only for gain
I will extend an open hand
   To ease another's pain
Self pity will not be my song
   I will not whine or cry
I should do right in spite of wrong
   And keep my spirit high
I will not live with prejudice
   Nor will I biased be
May every creed and each man's race
   Mean brotherhood to me
I must never take for granted
   America Supreme
And with God's help—I will protect
   Our founding father's dream.

Marie Yandle Guinn

HUFF-PUFF

The Wind
Shook the house
About.

And made His presence
Known
To all within.

Dean Zewan

282

SEARCH

O search young man
For the self now lost;
For the answers of a soul once present
And a conscience since removed.

Quest the dreams interrupted
And the unexplored desires;
The once happy individual
And the memories past.

O search, young man
For the reasons departed;
In the days which seemingly die
Or the sleepless nocturnes preceeding.

Past is the mind of high ideas
And present the damnation of repeating sins;
Sinking into the abyss of conformity
And despair of a soul once alive.

O search of the why not
And not of the why;
For the why is in you,
And you in it, oh dying faith.

O search for the hope
Which is never lost;
Less the searching is ended
And the too late comes the light.

Dennis Mason Adams

ATTITUDE

Lord, here I am again, on my knees;
With my hands in the attitude of prayer.
It's not that you are any closer this way,
Nor that I am any more penitent.
I guess it's just to make it clear
That there's no doubt about what I'm doing—
Clear to everybody—especially to me—
For there's no one else around.

Ida Mae Whittaker

THE ROYAL BIRTH

The snow lay deep upon the ground,
and stars were shining all around.
The world was filled with peace and joy
because of the birth of a royal boy.

In a stable small and mean,
a miracle of God was seen.
Carol, oh bells, peal long! Ring wild
in tribute to the small Christ-child.

The shepherd boys lingered near
while angels carolled songs of cheer.
And humbly came the Wise Men old,
bringing gifts of myrrh and gold.

In a manger did He lie,
while far above Him in the sky
a jewelled star shone bright and clear
proclaiming the dawn of Our Lord's year.

And God looked down upon the earth
in pleasure at the Baby's birth.
Oh, that there could be again
such peace on earth, good will to men.

Beverly Hall

A MOTHER'S PRAYER

Dear Father, watch over my boy for me
Where he's fighting across the sea
Not only him, but the others too
That are fighting for the red, white, and blue
Give them strength for every day
For they're fighting for the "American" way
Of freedom of worship, press, and speech
The right to laugh and the right to preach
Keep them safe and may some day we see
Our boys coming home to the land of the free.

Hazel Louise Garber

284

A PERFECT ROSEBUD

God found a perfect rosebud
Blooming on a tree,
He plucked it Oh, so carefully
And sent it down to me.

He said that I could keep it
To cherish and to love,
And it would stay as beautiful
As when it bloomed above.

That rosebud grew and blossomed
And it's made me very glad,
For it grew into the sweetest daughter
A mother ever had.

She's filled my heart with happiness
And blessed my every day,
It's just as God predicted—
She's perfect in every way.

Frances Rader

ONE DAY

One day the exterminator
Came and got 'em
                    all.
Time was already
Here clearing the
                    memories
Of you
From my mind.
Time is doing the job;
It takes longer, that's
                    all
And so I lived to be
One-hundred and three.

Connie L. Preston

WONDERING MYSTERY

You are a
   mystery to me.
For you are
   like the wind.
The wind blows
   never settling
     in one place.
You roam
   the earth.
Traveling
   from place to place.
You are as
   free as the wind.
For nothing or no one,
   can hold you down
     for long.
You are as
   the unsniffed
     flower.
But,
   once love is felt,
     you will be
       a mystery no more.

L. Joyce Anderson

WATCHING HER COMPOSE

She is composing over there,
   Breaking down nature
And putting it the way it is,
   The way she sees it.
Peering through the window,
   Seeing the dusky dark day,
She puts her mind's thoughts
   Down on the pad before her.

Kenneth W. Titt

THE SEASONS

It began in the autumn of the year one day,
When you had to leave and go so far away.
Sadness filled my life completely,
But for the memories of you, so sweetly.
I lived on letters and tapes and dreams,
Nothing else mattered to me, it seems.

Winter came on and brought ice and snow.
No matter what the weather, the time still goes slow.
I lost a dear loved one this time of the year,
And wished so much that you could have been here.
But the weeks go on and time reveals,
A purpose in life, the wounds it heals.

With the coming of spring a baby is born,
New thoughts, new love, a smile is worn.
Then like a dream one day in May,
I met you on an island far away.
What a wonderful week I spent with you,
Even then I could not believe it was true.

Then back to earth and home again,
Only a few more months 'till then.
All summer long I've nothing to do,
I care about nothing—only you.
Day by day as time goes on,
My love grows sweeter for you alone.

I know the time has come when the leaves begin to fall,
I watch them through the window as I wait for you to call.
My heart beat wildly and I cried with delight,
When you rang my bell in the middle of the night.
Now that you're home darling—safe and sound,
Let me say that it's wonderful to have you around.

Joan Callegari

FOREVER MINE

It seems so long ago now
That I watched you turn and go
Out of my life forever,
And into a falling snow.
I listened as your footsteps
Slowly died away, and closed the
Door upon my heart
For fear of what it might say
I still hear your voice at evening
When the twilight fades to night
Then I see your eyes still sparkle
In the stars that shine so bright
My dreams still hold a vision
Of one I loved so dear
Each little memory still holds fast
And lingers through the years
Though you have long forgotten
Why must I still remember?
For the ashes are cold
From our love of old
That once was a burning ember.

Georgiebelle Lusher

LONELINESS

So many times I've been surrounded
by it—trapped
    I'd want to cry out,
        But there was no one to
        answer
    To run
        But no one to stop me
    To reach out
        But no one to take my hand
        and lead the way
So many times it's engulfed me–
        So many times . . .

Joanne Criscione

THE ROAD

You say 'twas ever thus?
The younger and the older look askance
At one another.
A different time,
A different tune
Directs them.
One looking back, the other fore,
A different view,
A different tempo
Stirs them.
The old ones say,
"Our deeds are done.
"We cleared the path
"That you may tread it free.
"Unhampered by the pitfalls
"That marked our way."
"Not so," the youth replies.
"Where once you thought the way was clear,
"Lo, many new obstructions now appear.
"And these require
"A new approach,
"A new resolve."
But when the task
Becomes too great,
The older ones stoop to
Share the load.
And help the struggling
Younger ones to clear the road.

Wilma Ramp

CAMOUFLAGE

Smile though the heart be a garret of gloom,
Be clever, when wit is approaching its doom,
Be strong, though you're apt to succumb to
    a nudge,
Be glib, when the tongue is reluctant to budge,
Soar into flight on weakened wings,
Life is forever demanding such things.

Louise-Gallo

289

EPITAPH

"Clarance Parakeet" is dead.
"Just another bird," they said,
Never having heard his cheery
Chirping, on a morning dreary;
And his comic antics could
Drive away a grouchy mood.
Picking bread-crumbs from the table
Just as fast as he was able,
Drinking from your water-glass;
Falling in, sometimes, alas!
Bathing, on the window-sill;
Climbing on the chain, until
You would wonder; as you sat,
Were he bird, or acrobat?
Flying to your shoulder when
You returned home once again.
Looking in his mirror, the
Epitome of Vanity.
And I often wonder why
Things, so beautiful, must die;
Did God need another sweet
Blue and yellow parakeet?

George J. Peace
(ASCAP)

LAYETTE FOR LINDA

I spun a shirt of downy cloud,
Moon-pillows for your head.
Braceletted a chubby wrist
With love words someone said.

Bound your petticoat with stars,
Clipped blankets from the night.
Built a bassinet of dreams,
Tear-lined with silver-white.

Stitched a lacy robe for you
With threads of my desire.
Wove a lining for your cape
Of my heart's fire . . .

Gladys Ryan Bissett

290

AUTUMN SUNRISE AND FALLING LEAVES

Autumn sunrise and falling leaves
   Through morning shadows of the trees—
      Oh, what a glorious sight to see!

I feel the warmth of summer's breeze
   While leaves are dancing as they please.
      Come—let's join their frivolity!

The winter's cold comes into view—
   A perfect backdrop—a sky of blue—
      The snow-capped trees warm my heart, too!

I see new buds of first spring days
   Brought to life by refreshing rains—
      The sun shines again with brilliant rays!

Autumn sunrise and falling leaves
   Permeate my soul with God's peace.
      May these splendid moments never cease!

Dorothy Derbaum Freehling

THOUGHTS ON LIVING

Like the rustling of leaves by the winds of
   the season, so is our faith—not visible—
   with reason.
Like the ripples in water and the unknown
   world of her depth, thus is a life enchanting
   with every single breath.
Like the peace of a forest after an early, soft rain,
   a heart shall beat for a happiness and forget
   all past pain.
Like the unclouded sky of a warm, serene night,
   is the joy of young love recalled to Mind's
   sight.
Like the recurring newness of summer, autumn,
   winter and spring, we are born in the present,
   by the past, with the future to bring.

Alice Ryan Bacon

MY TREASURE

Something makes me restless here,
   and I can wait no more;
It pulls me from what 'ere I do,
   and takes me toward the shore
Where fog hangs thick; it's hard to see;
   the sand is cold and wet;
It's like this almost every day
   when I come here, and yet
I come and wait and walk the shore
   'till it gets warm and dry;
I love to hear the laughing gulls,
   and watch them in the sky.
When waves come lashing 'gainst the rocks,
   and rolling o'er the sand,
I step aside and watch them glide
   and bubble, oh! it's grand
To see the mighty ocean roll,
   and swell and break away;
And watch the colors of it change
   from blue and green to grey.
I hurry quickly as the waves
   are ebbing to the sea;
To find the oddest trinket that
   it left behind for me.
Shells of curious sizes and,
   some sparkling seaweed then;
The bits and pieces from the deep
   where man has never been
Or dared to venture, so I wait
   until the tide is low;
So I can find the rarest things
   this mighty sea lets go.
Some days I can not find a thing;
   'tho I walk until I'm weak,
But one day soon I'll find it;
   this thing for which I seek.
The day will come, and I'll be there,
   it will be mine to keep
Forever, and I'll cherish it—
   MY TREASURE from the deep.

Lillian Green

COTTAGE CASTLE

My castle has no drawbridge
  No moat, or turrets tall.
It doesn't have a throne room
  Or panelled banquet hall.
It has no gray stone battlements,
  Or gargoyles at the doors.
It doesn't have an iron gate,
  Or polished marble floors.
In fact, I think you'd have to say
  My castle's rather small,
And doesn't seem to have the things
  A castle should, at all.
My castle has a footbridge,
  With a little stream that flows
From summer's sudden showers
  Or melting winter snows.
It has a room with cozy chairs
  To while away the time,
And a little curving stairway
  For a grandson small to climb.
And rugs as bright as jewels
  And lamplight, glowing gold,
And peace, and cheer, and all the love
  Its happy walls can hold.

Clara K. Boyenga

CONSIDER A ROSEBUD

Consider a rosebud laved with dew
  when sunrise paints the skies;
And wonder how long her beauty
  will live,
Until she withers and dies.

One by one her petals unfold
Blood-red in the noonday sun;
The air is filled with a fragrance sweet—
Life's race is nearly run.

Nightfall comes—the sun disappears
The rose must pay her price;
Her petals fall unseen to the ground—
She has made her sacrifice.

Mildred Devere

293

HAPPINESS IS . . .

This has been a very lovely day,
Though why it has is difficult to say.
My husband looked at me with loving eyes
Because I baked his favorite kind of pies.
My daughter liked the party dress I chose
And pirouetted 'round on twinkling toes.
My sons were happy with the baseball score,
And laughed and chatted at the open door.
The setting sun made glory of the sky—
Its beauty seemed to soothe and satisfy.

The time has passed in no spectacular way
Yet, somehow, this has been a lovely day . . .

Berenice M. Gansneder

When I'm sad
I laugh at myself
for being so human
and so much like everyone else
in this massive confusion.

When I worry
I laugh at myself
for making my life
a worse hell than it already is.

When I'm nervous
I laugh at myself
for allowing my body
to be gobbled up in surroundings
that upset me.

But when I'm happy
I laugh at everyone else
because I can own their minds
. . . and their thoughts . . .

MARAT

ASSET OF TIME

Time has no ending,
Won't wait for no-one.
It is a sending,
From the great Some-One.

Has no backward movement,
Always moves fast.
With each precious moment,
A day has gone past.

Used in good measure,
Brings income to gain.
Misused in fool pleasure,
The outcome is vain.

Ain't how many hours,
You have put in the day.
'Tis what's put in the hour,
Gone-bye that pays.

Martha Vetowich

To the Father of my children
And the keeper of my heart.
It's the joy of my lifetime
That we're never far apart.

Tho' the years we've been together
Now have numbered quite a sum,
It's with pleasure that I count them
And I treasure every one.

So here's my toast to Father's Day;
May you have many more
That we together may enjoy
And roam from shore to shore.

Edna Thayer

OUR ANNIVERSARY

Marriages are made in heaven,
We were meant to be.
Sure as Eve was made for Adam,
You were made for me.

Long before the guided tour
We've taken side by side
Our Maker knew that only you
Could answer for a bride.

Ever since I held your hand
And you said you'd be mine
I've seen the hand of God at work
He makes our love divine.

What lies ahead it can be said
Is difficult to tell
But I can say on this, our day,
"My dear, you please me well."

Lawrence Southwick Grennell
1916-1967

A WIFE'S PRAYER

God, give me this day, not for myself, but for
   my husband.
Give me the knowledge to do the things that
   make life happier for him.
God, give me strength to carry my share of the
   burden, to make life easier for him.
God, grant me the courage to face reality, no
   matter how bleak, to make life brighter for him.
God, place in me the responsibility to do the
   things that are to be done to make this house
   a home.
God help me to be a better wife day by day. I
   only want it said of me "She made home happy,
   and filled my life with love."

Judy L. Phillips

WE HURT THOSE WE LOVE

One great truth in life I've found,
While traveling toward the West,
The only folks we really wound,
Are those we love the best.

The man you thoroughly despised,
Can rouse your wrath, 'tis true;
Annoyance in your heart will rise,
At things mere strangers do.

We flatter those we scarcely know,
We please the fleeting guest,
And deal full many a thoughtless blow,
To those we love the best.

Flordia L. Tuggle

WINTER SUNSHINE

The sunshine in the winter
   Seems like a smile from God.
As it sparkles on the snowdrifts
   That hide the dark brown sod.

It seems that God is smiling
   Just to let us know.
That soon the springtime rains will come,
   And melt away the snow.

The sunshine in the winter
   Seems to have a warmer ray.
Because it is God's promise
   That spring is on the way.

Marjorie R. Mercier

WHO?

Who made the stars shine so bright
Who made the sun to give us light,
Who made the beautiful butterfly
Who made the birds fly high in the sky.
Who made the pretty green trees
Who made the stinging bees,
Who made the frosty morning
Who made the dewy evening.
Who made the dancing moon—
'Tis He, who is coming soon,
'Tis He, who made you and me
'Tis in heaven He'll be.

Marsha Ann Perkins

AGEING

A man's life ends as does the tobacco in a pipe—Ashes.
Once the unique blend is put to the flame it slowly
    vanishes.
But before that time it has to be carefully tamped,
Then lit with fire—inspiring fire.
With a little luck it springs to life with the
Aromatic promise of good pleasure.

Then as assuredly as the passage of time,
The embers burn down—like coals just stirred by
    the poker.
Now the fire dies, alive no more,
Only a bowl of gray—dead ashes.

Kenneth R. Reynolds

CAUGHT

only one way of life
for the living now
speaking the same tongue
and occasionally—there are few variations—
drinking the same tea
from the same cup
arguing similar topics and getting
nowhere
doing things that have been done
by people before
and will be done by people after
fighting the same mediocrity
just to land at the beginning
we're stuck my friend like the fly
between the closed window and
the locked screen
in a living death or no life at all.

Paulette Bier

COMPANION

My companion is a phantom
Who walks with me by night.
His voice is often muted,
And fails him in the light.

He beckons me undaunted
Through nights and days of strife.
He follows me unwanted
Through pages of my life.

I only sense his presence,
But once I felt his breath.
My companion is a phantom
Whose name I know as Death.

William R. Minardi

WINTER MAGIC

Snowing all the time,
The weather is fine,
The sun seems to shine
On the tall snow-covered pine.

The tree is as good as a sign,
For under that pine,
There lies an old mine,
Where my Pa stores his bottles of
          WINE!   *Albert Donnay*
                    Age 9

WINTER SECRET

There she stands—all black and white and silent,
A trace of snow on lofty maple arms.
How long she's stood this way and kept her secret!
Will she forever hide her inward charms?

Who knows she bursts with treasured liquid silver
That sun-warm days with frosty nights will loose?
Ask him whose eye has caught the shining shimmer,
Whose tongue has known the sweetness of her juice.

                    Rosa Carter

WINTER SCENE

The silver rails stretched in a ridge
Away in front to cross the bridge.
Along its sides the river sank
With ice bound current, and snow filled bank
Across the field the factory stack
Sent up a tall, thin thread of black,
While hoar frost round the nostrils stood
Of horses, tugging at some wood.

                    Marian Elizabeth Kruse

CALM

To be kissed by a subtle wind,
To be touched by an ocean spray.
To feel that silence is a home-coming,
That's the calm I wish for today.

To see only as far as the eye can see,
To know the world as God meant it to be.
To have complete faith in everyone,
Oh, for that feeling of calm in me.

Joanne Geraci

LEARNING

Let the old speak their words;
From them comes years of experience.
Listen well, for they have learned much.
From them we can learn . . . .

It is for us, the young, to learn
To profit from their experiences
By improving the good
And discarding the bad.

Jerry C. Tate

THE SHEPHERD BOY

Who are you my little one that sits beside the tree?
Who are you? A shepherd boy? What may your tidings be?
Do you think of country wide or do you think of sea?
Or sing your songs of joy and cheer or look up at the
   sky so clear
On this night of Christmas Eve?

Will you adorn the brand new King? Will you offer
   Him your sheep?
And will you go to see Him and watch Him in His
   sleep?

Barbara Lynne Birks
Age 15

301

WHERE'S GRANDMA?

She paints her face and tints her hair,
And wears a "Mini" up to there!
When I suggest she might stay at home,
That at her age, she shouldn't roam,
She gives her false lashes a tiny flick
And inquires sweetly, "Are you sick?"

Where is the Grandma of yesteryear,
Whose image I hold so dear?
Who used to like to sit
And just rock and knit?
On whose capacious lap,
Some grandchild usually took a nap?

Where's Grandma? Well, I just expect,
You'll find her at some discotheque.

Diana M. Moore

I WALK

I walk the lonely ruins of time
In search of shattered dreams
The presence of defeat is here
As proof of dying schemes.

I walk the corridors of life
With unseen chains I'm bound
Desolate in deep despair
For love I've never found!

Linda Mary Gatzka

WINTER

The snowflakes fall from the winter sky
Like little pieces of lace
Some big, some small,
All different
They flutter and fly,
Till slowly they fall to the ground
And melt into nothingness

Christine O'Neill

302

OUR GRANDCHILDREN

Lock doors and drawers and check their catches,
   Up with the clocks and hide all the matches.
Close all the gates and see to their latches—
   Our grandchildren are coming today.

Hide the dog biscuits and watering pan,
   Barricade the stairway and unplug the fan.
Put away the mixer and move the trash can—
   Our grandchildren are coming today.

Aline Ubelhor

THE WAY YOU WALK

You have to walk at the bottom
Before you can walk at the top.
These words—oh, how they haunt me,
And warn me not to stop.

Who labor do not work in vain,
No matter what the task.
So if it's great, or if it's small,
You surely won't be last.

So many who have walked here
And faithful did remain
Are symbols now to you and me.
Let's try to use their lane.

Helen Long Knabe

NOISY SUMMER

Willow trees swaying in the soft summer air.
Clothes dry whitely and flap without care
Children splashing noisily in somebody's pool
And dewdrops in shady spots, shining like jewels
Zinnias and marigolds, sweet peas and moss
Each one to his own, be it velvet or gloss
Fuchias in hanging baskets, purples and reds
Even the daisies, with low hanging heads,
All this is summer, color and riot
But who wants their summer to be lazy and quiet?

Audrey Carter

CLOUDS

The low, white clouds are all
    tired out
With all of heaven in their arms,
They nod and toss and turn
    about,
And drop them on the cherry
    tree.

The pink of morning makes a
    cloud
That feels uncalled to really
    work;
It flits around because it's proud
And lights upon the old peach
    tree.

The dappled pink and white, a
    streak,
Makes just a dainty little puff,
Then swiftly skims along, a
    freak,
That decks the rugged apple tree.

The grey that blends and works
    all day,
As soft and light as pussy's fur,
Moves quickly on its quiet, quaint
    way
To settle on the fine smoke tree.

Anna Younger McPhail

ANNIVERSARY WALTZ

Please—give me the strength to bear it
That black lace—is a total disaster
Then give me the grace to wear it
It was bought by my lord and master.

dede Murphy

304

HOW OFTEN DO I THINK OF THEE?

How often do I see your face?
  As oft as beauty strikes my eye
  and lingers like an angel's sigh
  to stir my soul with heav'nly grace.
  So often do I see your face.

How often do I feel your touch?
  As oft as I am kissed by rain,
  by sun and wind which speak your name.
  Whose gentle, wooing play is such
  to bring the mem'ry of your touch.

How often do I think of thee?
  As oft as I am conscious of
  each day, its sweetness and its love;
  its light, its hope, its constancy.
  As oft I breathe, I think of thee.

Ernestine Kelsey

KINDNESS

Kindness is the oil of life
That lubricates the soul.
And burns away the bitterness,
Within a heart grown cold.

Kindness is the angel's touch,
Upon an old man's brow.
To fan the flame of lasting hope,
Beyond his life of now.

Kindness is the velvet mat,
That softens every tread,
Along the paths of loneliness
Of fear, and doubt, and dread.

Kindness is the golden chain,
That links across the span.
It closes all the doors of hate,
Which man can feel for man.

Evalyne Sheppard

305

NIGHT WATCH

When mystic slumber carries
him away from me,
I remain alert, to listen, to
learn, to understand his every
move, his restless sigh,
his moan, however peaceful, or
sometimes troubled it may be.
When I touch his cheek his breath
comes short; perhaps in that other
world he sees my face—
the one he studied pensively
before he left.
My careful finger traces
gentle lips. A dream pleased
smile is there.
His sleep closed eyes can see
some vale of cherry blossoms,
and lilacs, where I'd love to be.
So I'll wait, and watch, and lie
beside his tired form until
we meet, and romp and play
somewhere away from here,
in other spheres.

Rachel Burke Taaffe

NIGHT TIME PRAYER

God of darkness
God of light
See me safely through this night.

Guide each trembling step I take
Till night time ends
And I awake.

Lee Thompson

THE INTANGIBLE WIND

Courageous wind, breath of the Almighty,
You have built an unseen sanctuary
Where I meditate your diverse ways;
Your peace, your fierceness, and your sudden calm;
    How may I measure your capacity,
    Or reproduce your formless pagentry,
    Your sudden visitations, bold delays,
    That lift the sturdy oak, yet sway the palm.

You swept across the ages of earth's time,
Danced in the hoary caves of yesterday,
Incense cold brine to curl, lash out, declare
Its haughty vehemence to the harmless shore.
    Between bare rocks proclaim your shameless whine,
    Leave glaring havoc of your reckless way,
    You slam a chamber door behind a prayer,
    Creep stealthily along a rustic floor.

You tease the innocent with your caprice,
Evade with mocking glee the outstretched hand,
Goad willing feet to run with you then flee,
Leave no charted path for them to follow.
    Eternal breath, where do your wanderings cease,
    In artful halls of space or burning sand?
    Marshall now your secrets, tell them to me,
    As you told them to the migrant swallow.

Gertrude S. Ward

SO LONG, FRIEND

So long, friend—it's been so nice
To have you here awhile
E'n the rain seemed pleasant
In the sunshine of your smile.

When you're gone, just know you're missed
As you travel on your way
And share a tiny hope that
Our paths may cross again someday.

Carolyn J. Salter

307

THE SEA'S SECRETS

What hidest thou in thy mysterious depths
In hidden caves and cells Suspects
Riches, and beneath some sunken galleons decks
Lies relics of the Ancient Sects.

Thou care not where thy violence or on what shore
Thou wreck, To gather more
Wealth to hide and store
Deep on some dark caverns floor

Had thou been less violent and more serene
Thy secrets could have been seen
In some hall of art or museum
But thou hold fast to thy unworthy claim

But with the morn a new calm is born
And as if thou repent thy harm
Scatter with abandon on some shore of coral
Rainbow colored shells with glistening pearl

James Alexander Murray

HALLOWEEN

Halloween will soon be here,
When witches, and goblins, and ghosts appear.
And children go from door to door,
For candy, and gum, and candy once more.

Some costumes are funny, and others are not,
Gosh, those costumes and masks are hot.
Taffy apples, peanuts, and candy bars, too,
Enough to feed an army or two.

Children all wait for this day to come,
So they can go out and scare someone.
With mothers and fathers they come down the street,
And parents all wonder why there is trick or treat.

Karen Ward

CHILDHOOD NOSTALGIA

The night was cold: snow had fallen thickly.
The stars were out and the sky was dark and bright.
It could almost be Bethlehem:
The shepherds crossing the hills in snow.
The feeling was the same.
The buzz and laughter of voices,
Knowing where you were going,
Yet unsure of the way.
Strength was all around in the night.
Security, and quiet happiness gave warmth
That dispelled the cold of the snow—
What satisfaction, almost sadistic pleasure
To grind the white magic underfoot,
To feel and hear the delightful crunch
As crepe soles left their mark.
The wind was clear and fresh like spring
As it gently blew over the brow of the hill.
This was the hill where, in summer,
The same gentle wind blew, but it was warm,
Deliciously warm, as the fragrant smell of sheep and hay.
The earth and your body soaked up the sun and the pleasure.
The grass short and stubbled,
Brown with so many tramplings of sheep and humans,
Yet it was rich for it held a springiness
That carried you over and beyond on the wings of the wind.
Here you buried your nose in the grass
And felt the warmth and damp.
Here you could be king: away from all civilization:
The dumb creatures merely looked, and chewed,
And looked away again.

Wendy Woodland

THAT SOLID GOLD BELL

The sun is shining and flowers grow.
And man teaches man so that he may know,
   that somewhere there's a heaven and somewhere
   there is hell.
And somewhere there rings for freedom a solid
   gold bell.

J. D. Rotolone

FREEDOM

laughter, like silver slivers of icy crystals of stalagmites
from the caverns of the depths of the earth's womb,
trickles in upon the ears and pleases the listeners
and fills their dusty corners with cool winds.
freedom must be like that open spaced and deep
full of things to do and see.
silence echoes back and in it there lies strengthening
quiet.
behind me lies the dust of ages filling space and
making its eons.
thrilling my creating self with illusion and disillusion.
before me live life's adventures to be challenged and
explored:
first the fields of soft nature's green with flying and
creeping things seen and unseen.
quietly doing sometimes biting, stinging, buzzing,
singing,
mountains and streams man's bridges and his dreams
to cross and conquer and when taken, to conjure up
another.
Blessed be all devices of discovery! for
one day i too will be like the birds and rain and wind
and FREE!

Suzanne

BE PREPARED

A Christian knows within his heart
His life on earth he will depart.
But neither does he have to fear
Because his Savior's always near.
Our life is like a grain of sand.
Compared to all the desert land.
So let us each prepare my friend
As each of us must face the end.
Our life on earth is short, you see.
Compared to all eternity.

Robert Gerald Mitchell

OUR DELINQUENTS

The little hands I held in mine,
Are soiled today with dirt and grime.
Ten little fingers I kept so clean,
Are discolored and stained with nicotine.

Two little ears close to his head,
That heard the prayers we both had said;
Two eyes a grayish blue,
Are bloodshot today from too much brew.

Two ruby lips I taught to talk and speak,
Use words today that are indiscreet;
Two little cheeks, red as a rose,
The tiny freckles across his nose.

Light brown hair that fell in waves,
He seldom combs and he needs to shave.
With his upturned collar, jeans unpressed,
All these bad habits, I detest.

Yet, if we speak, they think we nag,
And on a cigarette they'll drag.
In silence we must sit and shudder,
My heart goes out to a delinquent's mother.

Catherine Ryan

SUSPICION

Small cat feet circled slyly—stalked
    my heart
And pounced with soft and kittenish
    appeal
Your claws were sheathed and harmless
    at the start,
Hypnotic eyes devoted, yet I feel
When winsome, wiley charms have
    gained their goal
I'll glimpse eternal faithless feline
    soul.

Cay Zbonack

THE RACE FOR LIFE

It seems to me that Life today
For us is one big race.
We hurry here, we hurry there,
We go at our fastest pace.

No matter what we have to do
We have to do it fast!
Sometimes I think if we keep on,
The Human Race won't last.

What really is the hurry
In everything we do?
I'm sure it's just a habit
That we can't break, don't you?

So don't you think it's time for us
To slow down just a bit?
And take time out from our mad whirl
To just relax and sit!

For if we don't, I think we'll find
This truth will be a fact,
We'll meet ourselves one day real soon
From somewhere—coming back!

Helen E. Hartley

SANDS OF TYME

I fear that Death sneaks,
   and will sneak up on me.
I don't want to be caught
   unawares,
But . . .
     bolted doors
     and drawn shades
     and heavy covers
   offer no safety;
     only rest
     and comfort.
I fear my time is running out—
   and I'm not ready.
I fear that Death sneaks—
   it sneaks on me.

John C. Lane

SHIP O' DREAMS

I saw a ship a sailing
Sailing on the sea,
And it was filled with treasure
Especially for me.

Slowly it drifted,
Toward the sandy beach
Then suddenly it stopped
Just beyond my reach.

In my mind I saw wonderous things,
Stored within its hold.
There was love, fame and fortune,
Chests all filled with gold.

I tried my best to reach that ship,
But it eluded me.
When I was close enough to climb aboard,
It drifted out to sea.

With it went all my dreams
But I will watch the sea.
Maybe some day the hand of Fate,
Will guide it back to me.

Clover Fields

TODAY IS YOURS

"As ye sow, so shall ye reap,"
And why should you borrow sorrow.
Live today in such a way,
You'll not fear to face tomorrow.

Yesterday is a dream you had,
Tomorrow's a vision bright,
But today is yours, so live it,
Ere it fades into the night.

Each day brings its problems new,
But when you've tried and done your
        best,
Be satisfied, that's all God asks,
And He'll take care of the rest.

Inez Marrs

313

ONE WHO LOVES CHILDREN

I was childless.
For some strange reason I could
    have no children of my own.
But they were all mine
The child in the street,
The child in the stores,
Babies in carriages,
In pictures,
My friends' children,
In school rooms,
Everywhere.
So I dedicated my life to teaching
    other people's children.
I loved them all.
They satisfied my longings in a
    measure
They filled my heart and kept my mind
    busy
So busy I hardly knew it was time to
    retire.
Now that I've finished and I hear
    children's voices at play
I say, "What would the world be
    without their bright spirits?"
Yes, they say I was childless
But they all belonged to me.

Florence Elizábeth Kyle

JESUS LIVES

I know that Jesus lives today
His wonders unfold in every way
A new born child—the thrill of spring
The joy to hear the birds that sing
The strength he gives to those so weak
A peace so true for those who seek
Just walk and talk with Christ today
A heart now full—one kneels to pray
The world is grand—it offers much
Yet the greatest joy—The Master's touch.

Robert E. Quinn

QUIET MAGIC

There is magic in the forest
   if you will only look
The chatter of the squirrel
   and rippling of a brook
The deer, the quail and pheasant
   they all reside there too
The leaves are softly falling
   and skys above are blue
So if you have the time to spare
   and don't know what to do
Just go and see the forest
   quiet magic is there for you

A. J. Craig

MY PILOT

No one understands like Jesus
No one else can help me so;
No one else so kind and gentle
No one else has loved me so.

Oh the sweetness of the moments
When He draws me closer still;
Wraps His loving arms about me
When I'm bent beneath His will.

In Him I find a resting place,
Free from cares that so molest;
In the shelter of His love
I can always rest the best.

Though I walk through the valley,
I shall reach the mountain top;
Since Jesus is my Pilot
And Heaven is His stop.

Goldie A. Jennings

THE PADDLEWHEELER AND RIVERBOAT

The paddlewheeler and riverboat
Up and down Old Man River did float.
The paddlewheel in motion like a small cascade
Momentum of speed did aid.
Proud of possessions of whistle and bell;
The beauty of tone did excel.
The galley graced by French chef connoisseur;
Luxury accomodations for the elite voyageur.
Passengers of plantationers and gamblers
    sometimes held a duel.
Life of the riverman was rough, brawny, tragic
    and cruel.
Music and song skimmed over the waters,
    echoing between the hills and bayou;
It told of legends and spirituals reflecting
    ancestory true.
The paddlewheeler made her last voyage.
Another sign of a passing age.
We miss the riverboat;
No more to see her afloat.
Or the call "Boat's acommin'."
To the water's edge we'd come arunnin'.
No more the joy of paddlewheel and steam on
    the horizon ledge.
Today, wrecked and deserted like a skeleton
    it is beached at the water's edge.

Mildred Moldenhauer

A COMMENT ON HIGH SCHOOLS

Exactly eight hundred twenty-seven
Identical pieces of merchandise
Fell spontaneously from cement cubicles
Back into the conveyor belt
To be automated to the
Next phase of the never-ending
Process of mass production.

Janet Lynne Thomas

THE GOLDEN HOUR

The past pagentry of—
Flags flying, horses prancing—
Trumpets sounding—
Lowered eyes, lifted brows—
A fleeting smile—
Is no more.

The true knight who saluted—
His lady love—
Romances of yesteryear—
That have gone before.

Many years we have—
Only a remembrance of—
Golden days of honor—
And grace.

Their place forever—
In the hearts—
Of all who dream—
What can never be.
Alas! Today has not—
Such precious things—
As chivalry and gallantry.

Sondra Downing

DEARLY BELOVED

You seem to grow much lovelier
much sweeter, and more dear,
You seem to cast a magic spell
On me when you are near,
Dearest, I'll always remember
The day when first we met,
The lovely years we've spent together
Dearly Beloved, I love you yet.
When our sun of life is setting
And its beautiful rays tint the sky,
I'll love you as much then my darling
As I have in the days gone by

Rosa May Hopkins

317

MY HOME

My home's more than a castle
In which to be a king;
My home's a private haven
Where kings don't mean a thing.

My home's where I can come to
Not just to strive for fame,
My home's that cherished one-place
Where I don't need a name.

My home's that longed-for shelter
To shield me from the greed
That keeps men ever seeking
The riches they don't need.

My home is just that—my home—
A paradise on earth
Where simple things are treasured
For all they're truly worth.

Leonard Onos

I was walking in the damp buggy forest
and I watched
leaves shine in the darkness
between moon-rays
I was very lonely
and so I began remembering you
and wishing you were there
to hear me speak

but then I admitted again
that you could never hear
the words
spoken by this minute

Mary Seniuk

'TIS SPRING!

I awoke one wonderful morning,
　　To a world very strange, very new.
My eyes, still clouded with blissful sleep,
　　Turned to the window for a clue.
And there, in all its young beauty,
　　With winter's snow not yet gone;
A tree's first leafy, green buds,
　　Had burst forth with the rosy dawn.

And then, as my eyes lost their dimness,
　　And I no longer thought it a dream;
I rushed to the door of my garden,
　　To feel warmth from the sun's radiant beam.
Suddenly a miracle seemed to appear,
　　From out of the snow patches,
　　Still lingering so near.
A brave little delicate crocus,
　　From its long, cold, winter bed,
Had suddenly risen to greet the sun,
　　To show its lovely yellow head.
　　　　'Tis spring!

Evelyn Elizabeth Searey

Never tell me what you are,
Lest I dare to make you less—
Lest I hold the golden star
To my bosom, and confess
Fire, and dross, and earthliness;
For I know you can not be
Wholly what you mean to me.

Shine behind me, calm and high
Fair to love and far from knowing.
So that, striving to descry
Heaven in you, and slowly growing
Through forgiving and forgoing,
Somehow I may come to be
Worthy your reality.

Joseph M. Bower

319

ODE TO A LITTLE GIRL

An Aquarius by birth, a bit of mirth,
Some silky blond hair, a devil may care,
Big blue eyes, the color of skies,
Her father's joy, feminine wiles employed,
Oh, what a delight to have mothered this sprite.

A soft dandelion, a piggy-bank scion,
Grandma's heart and soul, grandpa's droll,
A mud-pie baker, a kiss taker,
An exasperation, mother's consternation,
What a blessing from above to have her to love.

A magician, politician, and patrician,
A bundle of lace with a dirty face,
A bandaid wearer, an answer to prayer,
An inquirer bold, a three-year-old,
A lifetime is much too short to have an angel of
    this sort!

June Moore Biggio

SNOW BUNNY

When mother nature's white hand gently caresses
Her fields, valleys and countryside,
Strange magic in beauty the snow bunny possesses
Which he proudly displays in his hop-a-long stride.

Untouched or soiled by the wastes of the land,
In silence he appears without a sound,
A friend of the forests, meadows and streams
Has made him more renowned.

His fur changes into a snow-white disguise
To shield him from danger and harm.
Too timid and shy, sometimes not too wise
When he sheds his snow-bunny charm.

Genevieve Klotz Palmas

A MOTHER'S PRAYER

DEAR GOD!
   Don't leave him, as he goes
To fight this war of grief and woes.
   Not long ago, he was so small
He never thought of wars at all.
   And even though he's older grown
He's still so young, much to be known.
   Not long ago, he said to me
"Mom, don't worry, for you see
   It's all God's plan and it must be."
I pray dear God, that plan, you see
   Will bring him safely, back to me.
Go with him God, please hold his hand
   Lead him, guide him, all you can.
He needs you, trusts you, so please stay
   Close at his side, all of the way.
He has no way of knowing, God
   What lies ahead, what road to tread
Please give him wisdom and foresight
   To figure out the way of right
To do his best on foreign ground.
   Return him home both safe and sound.
So, as we put our trust in you
   We pray Thy will, to bring him through
Now, I will rest and feel secure
   In knowing that You will be there.

"Vee" Wright

THE LIVING GOD

In every tree and flower, the face of God I see,
I feel His breath in the strongest wind,
His voice in the roaring sea.

He touches my face in the summer rain and
Smiles in the noonday sun,
He watches me in the moon and stars,
When the end of day is done.

Agnes D. Parker

321

THE ENEMIES

Gyrating circles,
tense in trembling time,
taut and full-pinnacled in precision;
they rotate
on an axis of diplomacy;
swinging, they pull then press
against the certainty
of explosive touch.

Danna Di Bella

TRANSITION
OR
TOO MANYS

Too many pros,
Too many cons,
Too many brunettes
Turning to blondes.

Too many cats,
Playing it cool,
Too many kids
Dropping out of school.

Too many kooks,
Out of their wits;
Too many protesters
Raising their fists.

Too many guys,
Playing at cons;
Too many broads
Putting us on.

Too many fakes.
Too many facts;
Too many parents
Turning their backs.

Too many issues,
Too many dates,
Too many problems
For us to relate.

Not enough love,
Not enough respect;
Not enough time
For us to reflect.

Life isn't money,
Life isn't beer;
We're all in "TRANSITION"
Show that you care.

Patrick Phelan

PEOPLE

And the waves
come up to shore;
Creeping,
then . . .
pouncing.
But I can
get away from them
by running.
I've only been wet
once.

Carol Zanter

ALL HALLOW'S EVE

Unreal is the night
  like the mind at times.
Across the road
  the headstones loom eerily,
Spiritous shadows darting
  in and out,
Seemingly dancing a
  funereal dance!
The wind shrieks in frenzy
  and all is black, black,
Gaunt branches shiver in
  terror,
Suddenly the moon gentle
  and smiling slips in and out
  of the smoky clouds,
Like a ribbon interlacing
  a petticoat.
Oh moon! Like a mother's
  cool hand remembered,
Send forth your astral light
  and cool this fevered earth
  and bring sweet surcease.

Jennifer Camden

PANIC

Like frothy undulations
    of marshland mists,
  the gripping pain
  rolls o'er the heart.

A gray-blue vise
  compresses the spirit
  and exhorts the mind
    to leap
  from stone
    to slippery stone . . .

Then the universe
  slightly shifts awry.
Reality loses perspective
  in a line
    of offset dashes

There follows the realization
  of the Unreal—
    gray blindness
    edged in purple-reds,
A sense of lost control . . . . .

Peggy Becker

323

TEARS

A tear.
    One lone crystal
    Leading a battalion of others in its own path.
    Minute prisms
    To blur and alter, beautify and erase.

Today there are tears of sadness.
Today I have lost one whom I have loved deeply.
Today I feel the weight of a world of sorrow upon
    my all too human body.
Today I am alone.
Sorrow will pass along with today.

One day there will be tears of happiness.
One day I shall find someone who will love me
    deeply.
One day I shall know more joy than I knew
    existed in the entire world.
One day I shall discover security.
I live for my "one day."

Arlene Getchell

CIRCUS OBIT

the fat man is dead.
he's been with the
show for more years
than there are yarns
of his obscene obesity.
the funeral is constrastingly
brief
and fraught (for pallbearers)
with risk of hernia.
approximately unreal
in life,
his death finds him only
randomly
remembered.

Donald Dial

RAINDROPS STOP

Patter—patter
Spatter—spatter
Drops of rain . . . . . .
Scatter—scatter
Little feet
Down the lane . . . . . .
Raindrops stop
Unshod feet
Hippity—hop . . . . . .
Little puddles
Paddle—paddle
Rainbow bright
Broad daylight . . . . . .
Little darts
Pierce my heart . . . . . .

Clare T. Schmitt

Forget the tears,
The things that make you cry,
Pass them by.
Forget them—
Yet, forget me not.

Forget your fears,
The things that make you sad.
Dismiss the bad.
Forget them—
Yet, forget me not.

Forget your hate,
The things that make you depressed,
Let go of the rest,
Forget them—
Yet, forget me not.

Marylyn Newman

he came in the night and remained there until the
    morning
the night was long and I knew him by the rise of
    the sun
while absent from sight, we talked of many things
by morning it was as though an eternity of lifetime
    had passed before us
at first I was afraid of him
but as minutes and years passed
I grew closer to him
I almost touched him before morning.
when the day fulfilled the incompleteness of the
    night
and I finally saw the face of my new found
    companion
I looked upon the image of goodness and life and
    love
I witnessed a refreshing renewal of joy
the joy I knew as a child
the mounted happiness of each awakening day
    found itself within me
and I opened my eyes to see him and all things
    around me.

C. Goodrich

REBIRTH

Today
I stood face to face
With Death,
A grim creature;
The shadow of whose somber wings
Hovered over me an instant,
Her eager fingers snatching
At the temple
In which my soul
Has dwelled these several years.

And then
As though in fitful decision,
The shadow lifted and
Death retreated,
Leaving my soul's dwelling intact
To stay me yet awhile
Upon this earth planet.

Today
I stood face to face
With Death,
A glorious creature
That has often stayed awhile
With me;
With merciful fingers reaching,
She seized the last remnants of self-apart
In which my soul
Has been enshrined these several years.

And then,
As though in gentle benediction,
The shadow lifted and
Death withdrew,
Leaving my soul stripped
Of its encasement
And setting me wholly free
Upon the Path.

Today
I stood face to face
With Life
A radiant creature
Beneath whose shadow I have walked
Ever searching;
Yet whose quiet mysteries
Remained a hidden thing,
A secret substance,
Until today.

And then
Time hesitated
And to me no longer was;
The shadow of Life
Remained, yet
Became to me so transparent
I saw my soul a flame,
And Life a quenchless fire
Consume it.

Olive Chinn

IN MY OLD FASHIONED GARDEN

For rareness of color and beauty,
For fragrance unequalled by man
  Come visit my old fashioned garden
And tarry a while if you can
  To gaze at the foxglove in glory,
The petunias in colors so grand,
  Or the marigold bold in its fragrance,
Where like sentinels hollyhocks stand.
  There you will find the gay colored poppy,
Moss roses and sweet mignonette,
  And the angel-faced bright little pansies,
And sweet peas that we cannot forget.
  With the larkspur, or crow's foot some call it,
And nasturtiums that blaze like the sun,
  Gay zinnias, phlox, and verbeneas,
And,—well, we can't name every one.
  But of all the sweet flowers that bloom there,
Just one is my own special pet—
  The modest, shy, white and gold daisy,
To me the best loved of them yet.

When I walk in my old fashioned garden
With its colors and perfumed air,
I may sit on a seat or the old flag-stoned path
  With its tufts of green grass here and there.
Or I watch while the bee in her toiling
  Makes a quick friendly visit to all,
To find that at some of the quaint little blooms
  The hummingbird making his call.
As I muse, dainty butterfly fairies
  Flit by on their bright velvet wings,
And I dreamingly build my air castles
  While my heart is enraptured and sings.
As I gaze at the sweet happy flowers
  That with smile and a graceful bow speak,
The chivalrous bee leaves her kisses
  And the breezes caress every cheek.
So I sit there and watch and grow jealous,
  Though my thoughts are mixed up sort o' hazy,
And I wish that I might be a breeze or a bee,
  Then I could make love to the daisy.

William J. Jester

NEW LOVE

When nighttime comes the house is dark
And everyone's asleep.
I go into the living room
Quiet I must keep.

I take a little envelope
Out from its hiding place,
I sit and look at all the things
I'm saving "just in case."

The things I'm looking at right now
Are pictures just of you,
Since I can't have you for myself
These pictures just must do.

If only you were here instead
I'd never have to hide,
But since no one knows of our love
I must keep them aside.

I hope someday we can declare
Our true love, how we feel,
This hiding out and sneaking 'round
Just does not have appeal.

If anyone should see me now
I don't know what I'd say,
Until the day when you'll be mine
I'll hide you here this way.

Muriel Haight Tammaro

IMPACT

The impact of a life on time is nil,
    We are born and soon pass away.
The grass that waves upon the hill,
    The child that scampers at his play
Are impermanent until,
    The soul goes home to stay.

Mary A. Loros

I MET A SILLY BLUEJAY

Said I to the bluejay perched on my window sill,
"How dare you try to cheer me up, when I'm trying
   to be ill."
Said he to me (quite rudely, I might add),
"You know I'm going to cheer you up, it isn't good
   to be so sad."

I kept trying to ignore him, but he wouldn't go away.
He sat there with his happy smile and spoke of the
   fine day.
"Did you ever see a flower stretch her petals and
   give a yawn?
Did you fail to hear the bobolink sing his song today
   at dawn?"

"Now, please don't think me nosey, but where were
   you today when the squirrels and all the chipmunks
   gathered here to play?"
Oh, will this chattering little bird never disappear?
He came a few hops closer and said, "Now listen here,
I overheard a secret between the scarecrow and the crow.
There's going to be a cornfield dance, don't you want
   to go?
It's going to be a big affair, with costume, mask and hat.
And they're planning to invite you, what do you say
   to that?"

"There'll be hot dogs, salad, watermelon and the
   lemonade is pink.
It's open house for everyone, all you can eat and drink.
So get out of bed, you sleepy head, stop trying to be
   sick.
Put on your prettiest costume, hurry up now, take
   your pick."
"How can I get any rest, I ask you one and all,
   when such a silly bluejay invites me to a ball."

Arlene J. Hunter

BE CAREFUL WHAT YOU SAY

In speaking of a person's faults,
    Pray don't forget your own;
Remember those with homes of glass
    Should never throw a stone;
If we have nothing else to do
    Than talk of those who sin,
'Tis better to commence at home,
    And from that point begin.

We have no right to judge a man
    Until he's fairly tried;
Should we not like his company,
    We know the world is wide.
Some may have faults—and who has not?
    The old as well as young,
Perhaps we may, for aught we know
    Have fifty to their one.

I'll tell you of a better plan,
    And find it works full well;
To try my own defects to cure
    Ere others' faults I tell;
And though I sometimes hope to be
    No worse than some I know,
My own shortcomings bid me let
    The faults of others go.

Then let us all, when we begin
    To slander friend or foe,
Think of the harm one word may do
    To those we little know.
Remember, curses, sometimes,
    Like our chickens, "roost at home";
Don't speak of others' faults until
    We have none of our own.

Katie Fletcher

TWELVE OAKS REVISITED

The willow weeps; the moss does hang upon
                              the oak,
    In gentle sadness of times gone by.
The columns stand so gaunt but proud,
    Remembering the splendor of their former days.
The great staircase winds upward,
    But not with the joy of former laughter.

Oh to those days:
    When Kings were Kings, and wise men walked
so cautiously upon the Ages.
Alas, the great hall but recalls those days,
    Before the mists of time played mischief
on the lives of men.

James W. Granger

EXECUTION OF THE RIOTERS, MAY 3, 1808
(from a painting by Francisco Goya)

They stand subdued, who never dared to hope,
and weep for dreams that cannot live with death,
nor free a world where fear chokes every breath,
and friends will watch them dangle from a rope.
The city lies asleep behind the slope
down which the blood runs red onto the heath.
Tomorrow they will come and look at death
then wonder what it is that makes men hope.
The soldiers stand in ordered ranks unmoved
while men cry out against the fall of night,
their plea unheard, no tears to ease their pain.
The dice are thrown, the losers' anger soothed,
the dead are stripped, and somewhere out of sight,
a soldier puts a bullet through his brain.

George N. Brotbeck

DAYDREAMS

Today I dreamed of a woodland path,
  It led to fields afar
Out where the daisies nod all day
  Out there the woodchucks are.

The wild rose blooms along the path
  Against the old fence rails,
And scurrying softly along in the grass
  A newly hatched family of quail.

The softest, gentlest coo of a dove,
  The chatter of a noisy jay,
A scolding gray squirrel on a pine tree limb,
  A brook across my way.

Oh, let me live near a woodland path
  Where birds sing sweet all day.
Where flowers grow, and babbling brooks
  Flow merrily on their way.

                              Elayne Thomas

MY FRIENDSHIP ESTATE

Like a lightning flash, with its fatal clash
Came my Beloved's last call, from this earthly hall,
Then fell a gloomy shroud, like a heavy cloud,
Which left in its wake, a loneliness weight.

My treasured Family, dear friends far and near,
Came to the rescue, with words of cheer.
A clasp of the hand, a note in the mail,
A smile when tears flow, in spite of the will,
A word softly spoken, when need is so great,
A hand gently proffered, to steady the gait,
These all add up to my Friendship Estate.

Comes now the calm, a perfect peace,
To know the Oneness, Truth of His word
That my soul will flee as free as a bird
To the One who waits in the Realms above
For the wings of the Dove-Spirit of Love.

                              Omar

DIRGE

Into the room they file
Slow, sad and solemn
Treading down the aisle,
Like a Grecian column
Bodies made from stone
Support the chiseled faces
Of muted grief;
One by one they come alone
Then stare—the last traces
Of humanity—in silent disbelief.

No one can linger
Turning away—relief
The inner sigh,
Then begin to ponder
Life is brief—
They too must die;
Each one suffering
Trying to smile
Only wanting
To stay a short while.

Yet each must console
Those who remain
Try to condole
Or ease the pain,
They murmur their sorrow
And deep regret
Then say goodbye
(They must work tomorrow)
And hope to forget
They too must die.

Michele C. Popovich

THE IMAGE

Man created in the image of God,
Torn, pulled and pried from the sod.
Man the destroyer; this evil of God?
Beast that roams and ravages,
Man, created in the image of God?

Nelson R. Allen

333

IMAGINE

Imagine no stars to twinkle at night
Imagine no sun to make the earth bright
Imagine no one to write you a rhyme
No church bells ever to ring out their chime
Imagine the morning without any dew
No babies to sing a lullaby to
Imagine no birds to sing their song
Imagine not knowing right from wrong
Imagine no one to go to in prayer
No one to help your burdens to share
Imagine not having or being a friend
Imagine no heaven when this life shall end.

Wanda McGaha

WISDOM, PATIENCE, PEACE, LOVE

Oh grant me Thy wisdom, Lord
    To cope with each new day
To understand what kindness is
    And give to all—along the way.

Oh grant me Thy patience, Lord
    To stand with Faith, each day
And take from Thee, the strength I need
    As I go forth along life's way.

Oh let me know Thy peace, Lord
    Within this heart of mine
The peace which comes with understanding
    And brings a joy divine.

Last, but not the least, Thy love, Lord
    Which makes the World go 'round
I would to God, that man one day
    Will know the blessings, I have found.

Jeulettia L. Randee

WISHING FOR COMPANY

I was wishing for company and what should appear
But a little white mouse with tiny pink ears.
His shiny black eyes were jumping with glee,
He was very happy, it was plain to see.

He was on my pillow with one little leap,
Then my features, he began to seek.
He looked at my eyes, my nose, my lips,
Then without warning he cut a small flip.

I was suddenly frightened by his odd little looks
And I wanted to hit him with a near by book.
I kept thinking and thinking and looking around
Just hoping he'd make not one more sound.

He must have sensed my little scheme,
For he became sad or so it seemed.
Suddenly I saw the glisten of a tear
And I could't but help, his wail to hear.

"You wished for company and here I be,
But you're ungrateful for a friend like me.
I meant no harm, I was admiring your looks,
And you wanted to hit me with a book."

"I'm sorry little mouse please share my bed,
It's I who should be hit on the head."
"You're forgiven, you're forgiven, I'm yours to keep,
Just please move over and let's get some sleep."

Crystal Perry

MY PRAYER

Lead Dear LORD the one's who are blind,
Help all people to be gracious and kind.
Guide the footsteps of those who are lame,
Teach all to have honor and bear no shame.
Cleanse all hearts that they may be,
Unselfish and worthy to be more like Thee.

Ann Taylor

THE WOODLAND SOLO

The ascending notes
Of the Hermit Thrush
Are echoing
Through wooded aisles
To knit
The stillness with a song.
A lilting bit
Caresses fir-tipped shade
Of forest hush.
It grips the listening heart
Until replete
With tones of bell-like music
Liquid sweet.
As darkness fades
And dawn is born anew—
I feel the glory
Of delightful things.
Entranced, I listen
As a wild bird sings.

Ada Belle Cogswell

AN AUGUST DAY IN THE CITY

The heat
Of parched high noon
Lies motionless about
The city of inertia
Untouched

By rain
Or cooling air,
The clock counts out the hours
Of humid minutes delaying
The day.

Betty Kennedy Thomae

336

MY ROCKING CHAIR DAYS

All set, for my
   rocking chair days,
Going to have fun in
   so many ways.
Going to travel to
   ports I desire,
Such ventures of joy
   I'll never tire.

But—if—through no
   fault of my own,
I am forced to sit
   in my chair at home,
I will learn to paint
   or play a tune,
I may even learn
   to sit and spoon.
I'll put on paper
   what I'd love to say,
Life will be happy
   I'll make it that way.

Esther B. Lilienthal

IF

If . . . . life for each of us could be
Relived . . . and made the pattern that
Our wiser selves have learned to see,
I wonder just how many "ifs"
Would figure in the looking back,
How many tiny, little "ifs"
We'd find had changed our would-be
   track.

If . . . . life for each of us could be
Relived . . . I greatly fear that we,
Though wise to mis-steps made before,
Would surely make new ones . . . and more!

Zoe Adeline E. Hewitt

OBSERVATIONS—SAINT LOUIS, 1968

Bus Station
   Old grey men, sitting alone;
Napping
   Away from the afternoon heat.
Soldier
   Eyeing the thigh-high skirts,
Baby crying,
   Young mother's soothing whispers.
Sunlight dims
   Clouds, light gray, then darker;
Rolling clouds,
   Wary eyes look up to the sky.
Clouds roll,
   Thunder BOOMS, echoes rebound
Down the canyons of tall buildings
   Wind-swept caverns of the city.
Huge buildings
   Standing beside the muddy river.
People run
   Run for cover, seek shelter;
Summer storm
   A drop
   Then two
   More, hundreds, thousands,
Millions
   Falling faster, heavier
Almost
   A solid sheet of water now,
Water
   Rushing through the littered gutters,
Rivulets,
   A stream, a rushing torrent;
Streets overflowing.
   Suddenly, the shower is over,
The flood slows,
   A few last drops flow down to the drain.
A face appears
   Here, there, people emerge
Faces uplifted
   Into the fresh sweet smell,
Aftermath
   Of a summer storm in the city.

Old men doze,
   Soldier watches, the bold honesty of youth,
A pretty girl
   With thigh-high hem.
Baby sucks contentedly,
   Mother smiles softly,
Gray clouds
   Drift aimlessly above the tourists
Hurrying
   Toward the ARCH
The ARCH
   Proudly reaching for the sky.

D. D. Sherman

FRIENDSHIP

It comes as does a disease.
To the mind it is fatal
But . . .
         only
              if you
                   fear it.

To those of you who are ready
Accept it
But
      only . . .
              if you
                   cherish it.

For to need,
         and want,
                   and love
                           and give

Are the four greatest constructs
Known to man.
But . . .
         only
              if he
                   comprehends
the full impact of a friend.

Sue Golden

339

AUGUST REVERIE

I glanced through the windowpane today,
and thought that things looked somehow changed—
then I became aware of a difference in the trees
and the way all nature seemed arranged.

The August haze hung heavy on the air,
summer's green cloak looked patched and old—
and soon the earth will don a more colorful dress
of flaming red and burnished gold.

All the countryside waits in expectancy,
for the start of another beautiful show—
when Mother Nature wields her artistic brush
and paints the land with autumn's glow.

The air will sparkle with the taste of autumn,
cold and clear as a mountain stream—
and I'll take a walk through fields and woodlands
to sit among the fallen leaves, and dream!

Bill Crider

SUMMER HAS LEFT

The days are growing shorter
And the nights are growing longer
The leaves upon the trees are turning golden brown
And the wind that rustles, and blows them down
Breathes out its icy breath

The season has changed and with it has brought
A world of sparkling whiteness,
A world of chilly coldness

The season has changed and with it has taken away
The birds that sing, the flowers that bloom
And replaced it with a cover of snow

Larry Ballard

340

SPRING

Spring with all its beauty,
And the Happiness it brings,
Birds of gayest colors,
Chirp and sing, "Wake up, 'tis spring."

Flowers of the rarest,
With fragrance so true,
God with his love,
Send all these to you.

The trees with their budding,
Tiny leaves to unfold,
Tell of His love,
For us He'll behold.

Grasses green like velvet,
Kissed with early spring dew,
Just seem to whisper and say—
I gladly welcome you!

Cora B. Robinson

PORTRAIT OF A VERY YOUNG MOTHER

They didn't tell me you were quite so small,
I'm almost scared to handle you at all!
My fingers are so clumsy, and they shake—
I know I'll make some serious mistake.

There now—you're washed and rinsed, and dried as well
And oiled and powdered—why that went just swell!
And now the clothes I made and laid away—
(I used to take a peek at them each day)

At last you're really in them, warm and sweet—
Now let me slip these booties on your feet.
Why—isn't Motherhood the queerest thing—
Here I am crying, when I aught to sing!

Edna Fuchs

341

HOW SMALL AM I

The World so great, and I so small . . .
Beside the timbers strong and tall—
Against the Mountains broad and high . . .
Reaching up toward the sky—
Beside the Ocean deep and wide . . .
With verdant fields on every side—
The fertile plains, the distant sky . . .
Compared to these, how small am I.

Teeming Cities, pleasant towns . . .
Art and Statues of renown.
Country lanes and highways broad . . .
Where wheels have turned and feet have trod.
Ships that sail, and planes that fly . . .
Compared to these, how small am I.

Parks and playgrounds have a place . . .
Shrubs and flowers lend a grace.
Sea and sky and grains of sand . . .
All make up a pleasant land.
And One Divine, Who Creates all . . .
The World so great, and I so small.

Donna Powell

ASTRONAUT

Like an embroyo
cradled in the womb,
he lies imprisoned
in the capsule.
And he is all humanity
stretching against
the umbilical cord
that binds him to the earth
seeking rebirth
in the stars.

Rita S. Zeiss

FROST ARTISTS

The North Wind charges across the land.
    He routs the nymphs and the fairy band
And brings the busy frost sprites down
    To paint each window in the town
With appliques of snowy white
    And snowscapes of the Arctic night.

We wonder at what they've painted there,
    The silver seal and Polar bear,
The rounded top of the cold igloo
    Above the drifts that impede the view,
The frozen sea and the snowy waste,
    And all with frescoes interlaced.

But look! There are flowers and towering trees!
    Now, how could the Frost Sprites know of these?
And there is a brook and a waterfall,
    A bridge, and a border of cat-tails tall,
Frost artists who paint what they've never seen,
    Are the greatest of mysteries, I ween.

                              John V. Troth

LOST BOOTS

Slim pointed boots, black as night
Click down the alley below
Down the dirty, deserted street
In the calm slow eve
Of the loud day that was before—
A quiet little town upon a small laughing hill

Slim pointed boots, black as night
Click down the alley below
And the big golden ball, in the sky
Lights the darkness
And the way
As the boots click click click down the alley below

                      Leslie K. Dolph
                      Age 15

SUMMER HARVEST

O lovely hours I cherish from
  The summer's golden store
For their vibrant, shining beauty
  And countless reasons more.

I hoard them all within my heart
  Then when winter tempests moan
I will not mind, for I shall live
  Again these hours I have known.

I'll see blue skies, smell a scented breeze
  Or know where a curved road lures,
I'll walk by the sea, a river's bend,
  Remember a green hill's contours.

Hours of pleasure, shared joys I've known
  Are a song for the long winter's night;
A melody played on the strings of my heart
  And resung for memory's delight.

Lucile Waer

MY KINSHIP

In this kind of roofless universe, I thank God for
the good treatment of mother earth.

When one door closes another opens, revealing
purpose and hope.

I own a piece of this business, mix and mingle
with these pursuits.

In man's endless search for achievement, this
is my kinship with the people and the land.

Myrtle F. Yomer

SIGNS OF THE TIMES

Dame Nature's wearing green again—
It's time for calves to wean again—
And butterflies are seen again—
It's summer!

Circus posters heralding thrills—
Roller-skaters taking spills—
Handsome chefs at Bar-B-Q grills—
It's summer!

Youngsters so happy they're nearly berserk:
Schoolbooks now they're free to shirk—
Gee whiz! *Must* I go to *work*?
IT'S SUMMER!!

June Johnson

NIGHT MAGIC

The moon is full, round and yellow, riding high.
The clouds, like big moving tufts of black cotton sail
   silently between it and me.

This soft breeze which caresses my cheek; I wonder
   where it has been before reaching me.
From far away, from other shores, it carries
   enchantment in its very mystery.

It is the blackest of nights, and yet the most
   brilliantly lit.
As I gaze upward, I cannot help but be moved by
   the wondrous beauty of it all.
I hold my breath, knowing that this moment in
   eternity will never be again.

Carolyn M. Young

MOURNING

Into the anteroom where night covers day
   and age is heavy,
   the coldness of the world arrives,
with frosty silhouettes and freezing murmers.

Then, with the sweeping of a hand—
The never forgotten quarrels begin once more.

                          David Michaud

SEVEN MOURNERS

The women sat
With their heads bowed:
Their sons had died
Before twenty.

John,
His closed eyelids hiding
The glaze of addiction,
With his needle-punctured arm
Covered by a long-sleeved tunic
Buttoned at the wrist.

Mike,
His body crushed just like
His compact high-powered dragster,
Lay on the slab next to the
Teenage girl whom he'd
Taken with him.

Bob,
The leader of a gang's revenge,
On broken youth codes,
And neighborhood boundaries,
Lay with mortal stab wounds
Under his June
Graduation clothes.

Steve,
With the law's bullet wound
Covered by a tactful patch
At his temple;
A patch that would have matched
His bandit's nylon
Stocking mask.

Tom,
Very still now after
A drunken spree,
After which he drove
His father's car
Smack into a tree;
Now his limbs are as twisted
As the oak
Under his funeral silks.

Bill,
While rioting and looting
In the streets,
Was caught between sniper
And police fire.
An unmarked bullet
Left its mark on him,
Covered by his Sunday best.

The seven women sat,
Six with heads bowed
In shame and sorrow.

The seventh woman's son
Had died before twenty:
Had died in uniform,
In the service of his Country;
His body lay covered by the Flag.

And the six envied the one.

Lillian Baker

SEVEN JOYS

Seeing,
all the wonders of this Earth,
Hearing,
glorious music,
Smelling,
the perfume of the Flowers,
Tasting,
the pure Water from a Stream,
Feeling,
in your Heart, the
Love of Life,
Crying,
for the Joy of it,
Laughing,
with the children
These are the wonderous
things of Life
they make our Lives so dear
So stay awhile
and rest your thoughts
on these few words of cheer.

Rita Pearman

THE BEGGAR

Things are not always what they seem to be
You pity him, but yet you laugh at me.
You pity him because he's blind, you say,
But what of me? I cannot find my way,
A light leads him, although his path is black.
I am the cripple, for it's faith I lack!
With me, it is as Caesar said, "Render me my due,"
I feel perhaps that I deserve a little pity too!

Beryl Brewer

A LOST LOVE

How can I return to myself? I have departed
    for so long.
I know not the way.
I sleep a restless sleep, seen my torn heart
    which I do not know how to mend.
I hear an inner voice, and feel the splash of tears.
Thank God some feeling is still there.

I have become so cold, unfeeling, bitter . . . . .
My love is lost. How long. It seems forever.
    The End.
Perhaps if I have faith and courage I will love
    again,
Eternal love to share with him when we shall
    meet again.

Daisy Scott Brigley

TRUTH

Written in the logs of time
Legends fade on soiled ledgers
Until the words
Can
be
but
vaguely
seen.

Time will tell the tales again
On fresh virgin paper
By men of truth
Who
write
with
lasting
ink.

W. Jerome Taylor

WHY?

Are we all jibbering idiots?
Do none of us comprehend?
Is life that full of comfort and bliss
Or is it merely a hell, waiting for the end?

Are we all completely dazed?
Do we enjoy the never-ending boredom?
Does being enslaved by society fill your needs?
Are you content just to exist—not live—for years
    yet to come?

Is no one honest to his soul?
Must we all wear masks and play roles?
Can no one proclaim, I'm me! An individual?
Or must we conduct ourselves according to popular
    polls?

Is every one afraid and lonely?
Yet we fear ourselves and hate to be alone!
Can none of us face the inner demon—ourselves?
Is that why the restless search to leave unturned
    no stone?

Must we all fear and hate?
Can love find no place in our world?
Or is love a figment of imagination man created?
Some small shimmering gem, where a faint hope
    may swirl?

Man, the most magnificent of all,
Yet with all his ability to disconcert
He's perhaps more muddled than all other creatures,
Because, with the brain, and pondering thought, he
    becomes the most hurt.

Sande Rego

OPUS LUNA

Gently o'er the window beaming
Softly cross the floor in waves
Molten silver flowing drenches
Beds and curtains
Oaken benches
A shining road in silence paved

Across the fields and in the forest
Quietly falling drops of rain
Glistening silver shadows etching
Under trees
Where small pools catching
Mirrored rays of sky's wide plain

Yellow gleams spring off the ocean
Smiling back into the night
Lemon streaks of quivering moonbeams
Lost and swirling
Faint as pipedreams
Now fly up from the depths more bright

Golden visions soon appearing
Liquid globes of luna's glow
Precious spheres of sorrow calling
Love has gone
Let no night falling
Ease the pain that love must know

Spinning thru the velvet darkness
Blinding bright, dimly seen
Silver beauty known as moon
Kisses earth
A sultry tune
A living jewel, most regal queen

William Glessner

351

NEWS REPORT, YEAR ONE

It was cold
I felt the chill
It was so dark
Everything was still
In that Bethlehem stable.

A baby's cry
Broke the still
A mother's love
Warmed the chill
When Jesus Christ was born.

Angels came
From the sky
That glorious song
Sang on high
Glory to the new born king!

Dorothy Byers Barnes

THOUGHTS ON MODERN THEOLOGY

So God is dead!
I scarcely can believe it!
He seemed quite well last night
When I looked at His sky
And thanked Him for the sight.

Who'll do His work?
So many things need care!
How bare will be the land,
And still the air, and sea
Without His loving hand.

So God is dead!
I really don't believe it!
Today a child was born,
A flower bloomed, and I
Can feel no need to mourn.

Dorothy M. Hallsted

THE GRAY-BEARD

the gray-beard sat on the edge of a knotted log
waiting for the tide and his thoughts to turn
glowing embers from his startled fire
flew into his engraved face
his eyes were indistinct in the grinning haze
his magnificence was hidden beneath his disheveled limbs
even Circe and her chorus did not stir him
speechless was he for all his impatience
with the objects of the world
his ears were hypnotized by the soundings of a far
    distant captain's call
which reminded him that his ship had indeed been
    engulfed in the almighty tides
as he alone had been coughed up from the funeral pyre
    of his mates
floating planks continued to mark the location and mask
    his mind
where the wistful wind and his own imaginings had
    gotten the better of him
although he knew not why he should breathe yet
why his yet dizzy head should be baked in a perspiring
    sun
the depths held his secret
a little more bravery and he would not have given
    his gulps
for rescue onto the shore
he would have undoubtedly remained with his crew
which had braided their fate with the wishes of the sea

Esso

ULTIMATE

I span the void of time and space,
Knowing you are standing there,
To clasp hands across universes of foreverness
To galaxies of sunlit gold
And tread interstellar air.
Oh, we'll meet again—if only on the Milky Way.
I promised you Eternity—if only for a day.

Francesca Nainya

CANE BLADES

Cane blades waving in the breezes,
Whisper to my simple heart,
That the Sunlight, Rain and Dew,
Each of these must bear its part
So the sweet exotic juices,
Hidden in the slender stalk,
May be ripened and enriched,
Pleasing tastes of tender folk.

Cane blades waving in the breezes,
Whisper low to me and you,
That in life there must be Sunshine,
Also Rain and sometimes Dew.
That the sweet and gentle graces,
Hidden in the timid breast,
May be strengthened and unfolded,
Gladdening hearts, forever blest.

E. T. Smith

VII

Like a breeze that blows in summer
And ripples through the trees, I
Run to you.
Like a brook that babbles happily and laughs to
All the world, I
Laugh with you.
When all is dark and gray, we'll run
Together hand in hand through fields of flowers
And grass that has yet to be cut.
Like the sun that glows so brightly,
My heart cries and sings to you
That no one on earth is strong enough
To change my love for you.
Like a sea that rushes in to kiss the
Sand upon the shore,
Our hearts will join together
To be one forevermore.

Carol J. Stank

MY RIGHTS

I want the right to be wrong, you know,
Even at times when it doesn't show.

I want the right to be myself
About a car, a book, or a shelf.

I want the right to be tired to death
When it takes great strength to draw a breath.

The precious right to make a mistake
To know when to hurry and when to brake.

The right to make choices should be my own,
What I shall keep, what shall be thrown.

I want the right to be fast or slow.
The right to be less than perfect, you know.

Edith M. Reynolds

NEW ENGLAND STREET SCENE

Storm-clouds are moving,
The sun's coming out—
Snow's slowly melting,
Christmas Spirit's about—
People with packages
Hither and yon!
Red coats, and green coats
To keep them warm.
Some with red mittens—
And red kerchiefs, too,
(Of course, there are those
Who rather wear blue!)
Some in a hurry!
Some not so fast!
But all are aware
'Tis CHRISTMAS—at last!

Emily Glidden Strangman

MONDAY PRAYER

I can be reached here.
"London is calling," the operator says. Or Paris.
The cables are from Belgium, Italy, Japan.
The letters from Denmark and Switzerland.

Contact me here, please
Amid the ringing telephones,
Avalanches of paper work
And red tape tangled in hard knots.

Find me where I am.
I am Monday far from church
And heavy hours from Sunday.
God, find me here.

Mary Ross Welch

YOUR DAY

If you should get up with a terrible grouch
Don't head your body for the nearest couch
Stay on your feet and stick out your chin
Meet the sun with a great big grin
Say to yourself, this is my day to fly
This wonderous day will be yours if you try.

Geneva Jane Ashley

TUNELESS SONG

He was being trained to do the jig
so he watched his teacher closely.
He was being groomed to entertain
and to master his movements perfectly.

But his partner was careless; she stumbled and fell.
She was not a graceful performer.
And the teacher saw this and understood
and stepped on his toes for her.

The teacher laughed and crossed his heart
then he stared into her eyes.
But the pupil wept for the lesson was clear
that his teacher had taught him lies.

The child expelled from his mother's womb
like the toes of the saddened pupil
which were bent from the stomping, weary from travel.
He had wandered from cradle to tomb.

robert h savar

356

JUST BEFORE DAWN

Distant and dark over the land brood the hills.
The valley is shuttered and silent.
The time for the mist to swirl in is not yet.
The dawn's first rosy finger tips still have not appeared.
The farmer turns heavily in the warmth of his bed.
A low moan slipping almost silently from his lips.
As though he realizes altho' still slumbering,
The day's drudgerys are about to begin.
But for now he has gone far away from all this.
And for now he lives, though only a short time,
In a far different place.

Mildred Herrmann

UNREST

Youth stands with lifted head and eager eyes,
Aquiver, waiting for the years to go,
Stretching each nerve to see what lies in store,
Impatient, that the time seems slow.

While old age, forehead bent with silver crown,
Lifts trembling arms, entreating all the while
Swift passing moments that they be less fleet,
Counting each footstep in the hastening mile.

Dorothy Lehman Sumerau

ETCETERA—

Intent upon tomorrow's woes
I oft forget today
And fret and fume and thus it goes
In a rushed sort of way;
But then tomorrow dawns anew
And as I raise my head
I see a day that could have been
A joy but now 'tis dead.
I tell myself each morning fair
Today I'll be content,
But again tomorrow looms ahead,
And today has been spent!

Mildred V. Carroll

357

MARGIE

She is a miracle of God.
A miracle that spreads joy and happiness
    wherever she goes,
A miracle whose beauty comes from the heart
    and soul.
To see her is to know the joy of life,
To know her is to know the grace of God.
To help is her greatest wish,
To give of herself is her greatest joy.
Of life and kindness, she is filled,
Of love, she has mine.

R. Curtis Tugwell

WOOD IN POETRY

Forest,
Thy soothing purity
is vital
ancient and everlasting.

It is rooted so deep
that avoiding its call
will annihilate.

Gusztav S. Antalfy

THE EPITAPH OF THE LONELY

Until the wisps of life have passed
Leaving you content in Death's sweet grasp
You cannot find peace or solitude
For life is only abruptly rude.
Living brings heartaches, sorrow, and fear
You do not find solaces that fools hold dear
The treasure of Death is where I know I'll find
Release from loneliness—yes, peace of mind.
Those who might sorrow when I have passed
Must realize that eternity is vast.
I am happy—cruel life is gone,
Serene Death will go on and on.

Don Wilkerson

COREOPSIS

In the meadow, 'crost the way,
There the coreopsis lay,
Basking in the summer sun,
Calling me from work undone.

Like a field of gleaming gold,
As their sunny heads unfold;
Better than a costlier flower
Holding me within their power.

Oh 'tis there I long to go
When the balmy breezes blow,
Banishing all care and strife
For a happier, healthier life.

Millicent Bliss Paine

WINTER'S NIGHT

A white blanket is woven
And is falling on the ground.
Mother nature's blanket
The loveliest found.
To cover up her children who are
    fast asleep in bed.
To say "sleep well my darlings,
    rest your weary heads."

Joan Elizabeth Hickman

DESERT EVENING

The edge of twilight with its purple fingers
Touches the mountain-top where day still lingers,
A soft breeze murmurs through the green mesquite
Roadrunners seek a place for evening sleep.
The grim contour of desert's daylight face
Is muted now with soft and shadowy grace
The edge of twilight gentles with its hand
Cactus and sun and ever shifting sand.

Margaret Sheridan Paquette

COURAGE OF THE OAK TREE

Like a soldier stands the oak tree,
Upon the ground with no robe of green splendor.
'Twas many years ago this day
When flayed by wind and beat by hail,
All his brothers screamed their anguish,
Tottered, fell around the brave one.
His robe was stripped and left him naked,
But give sway he would not
Till day break and the tempest left him.
Naked and tortured, his brothers dead,
Through five score tempests yet he stood,
Through the wars between the nations,
Through the black nights ever darker,
This tree stands as a warrior.

John Docherty
Age 12

HAIKU

Asleep in the sun
On Lake Winnipesaukee
Lies Echo Island

Albert Donnay
Age 9

IMAGINATION

Fairies and Elves, dancing and dancing.
Skipping, leaping, running, prancing.
Wearing colors of green, red, yellow, blue.
And dancing on the morning dew.
Acting gay, from day to day.
Every month, including May.
Tiny and small,
But never tall.
Hiding, peeking out at you.
But they're timid, so don't say Boo!

Laura Gant
Age 10½

THE MIRROR

Splash! What a horrible sound
As the mirror fell to the floor
Who is that? I shouted
It's I, said an imaginary voice
Come on, see what I've done.
I hurried to the living room
But the mirror was standing still—
What in God's name could it be

I became very angry
And was much frightened too
So I stood beside the cabinet
Wishing to hear the sound once more.
I waited out of patience
But nothing more was heard
Alas! I discovered it was only a dream
Filled with thoughts from imaginations.

William E. Bute

LAMENT

In the air of summer is the expectancy of fall.
The day is wistfully sighing for its crisp,
    metallic loneliness.
The warmth and pulsations of summer are
    winsomely gazing back
And resignedly glancing forward.

Summer is dying. Its death throes are barely
    noticed.
They are feeble and subtle at first. But the
    sensitive can feel the change.
There is that inexpressible expiring of summer and
The growing gestation of winter's fatal veil of sleep.

But for a while, all will be bright and bold.
Nature will go tweedy, in feel and sound.
From the hazy softness of summer to the
Nubby roughness of fall.

Pamela J. Smith

I DON'T LIKE TO FACE

I don't like to face tomorrow
   When I don't know what lies ahead.
I'd rather stay right here and sleep
   Upon my great big bed.

"There's better days a'coming"
   They keep on telling me;
They say, "Things will get better,
   You just wait, you'll see."

They say you have too much time on your hands,
   You've got to find something to do!
Start a hobby, have a party,
   Or go on back to school.

Oh it's easy for them to say
   Get an outside interest and live for today;
'Cause they are happy, their life is content
   While I feel like mine is already spent.

Life I know isn't really that bad;
   It's just days like this
That make me so
         MAD!

Diana Throgmorton

WHY?

Oh why do crickets chirp at dusk
And birds do chirp at morn?
'Tis that they have a word for us,
Or merely glad that they were born?

Perchance we too should be so gay
At early morn and late at dusk.
For these are both best times of day,
Of precious hours thus given us.

Ann Moffatt

WHEN SPRING IS NEAR

When spring is near and soft winds blow,
And grass starts peeping through the snow;
I feel a something in the air
That takes away my every care.

All nature starts then to abound;
There is the throb, there is the pound
In every root and stem and mound;
It's just some thing we can't impound.

Some birds come back and start to sing;
The ducks and geese are on the wing;
The soft wind makes its mournful sound
The daffodils come through the ground.

The mother cow brings forth her calf;
The boys start working on their raft;
The little creek becomes a flood;
Small children then make pies from mud.

The farmer anxiously now must wait
Until the snow and mud abate;
So he can start some early morn
To sow his wheat and oats and corn.

What is this mystery of spring
That wakens plants, all dormant things
With resurrection in its wings?
It must be God from whom life springs.

Gerald H. Smith

TREES

When Joseph and the lad Jesus
Were busy with the wood of trees
Building and making for the living—did
Mary have a foreboding?
Did she sense a rough hewn Cross
From one of these?

Frances Diedimia Sumner

363

NATURE'S WONDER

Nothing is so wonderful,
As a little mountain trail.
Where one can see the tall pine trees,
Or watch a cottontail.

The trail will lead to nowhere,
Or to a lovely mountain stream.
You can see the water running,
And breathe the air of spring.

The little path is narrow,
Just wide enough to see,
And gaze at all the wonders,
That nature has for me.

Oh! The rapture of it all
Is deep inside of me.
The feeling of closeness to God,
Is there for all to see.

The flowers, the birds, the stillness,
There's nothing like it, anywhere.
I had rather travel that mountain trail,
Than to be the richest heir.

Ada M. Anderson

PAIRING

Wrapped in the quilts that built with time,
Made up of patchwork scars from wounds
    forgot—
Without the shed of shields both his and mine
How can our two hiding souls entwine?

The open doors of self cry to be crossed
By one whose being matches mine.
Time, tranquility, and pride may well
    be lost
But pride is false and time cannot be known,
Tranquility: the feeble peace of those
    alone.

Kavel

AN ANIMAL MIND

I am a human with an animal mind.
I no longer think rationally.
Once, intelligent thoughts, now—twisted ideas.
Once, reality, now—a nightmare.
I have hallucinations and horrid dreams.
I emit screams and emotional cries caused by
    sights unbelievable.
I live only in a void of suffering—a mind in
    slavery to my body.

My body craves the substance on which it
    lives from day to day.
My goal is the kick I get from my daily
    subsistence.
I drown in a bottle of escape.
I am an alcoholic—a human with an
    animal mind.

Rose Marie Bullington

DECISIONS

Decisions are so hard. One never knows how
the quest will be answered until the paths of
decisions are pursued.

One cannot tell, nor forsee the answer until
the door to your decision is opened and entered.

As with dark rooms and high walls, one never
knows what lies beyond—but as with love and
hope, one must pursue his dream.

Decisions are the making of all mankind's world.
Of each one's life and happiness. Only decisions
can be made by the maker.

Only the maker—nay, sometimes, not even he
knows how to make the decisions; only time will
tell if he builds a wise truth or a false dream.

Kathleen A. Burhop

A KISS IN THE DARK
OR
WHY YOUR PARENTS
SHOULD TURN ON THE PORCH LIGHT

I went out with a boy last night, I can't remember
    his name.
It doesn't matter who he was; to me, they're all
    the same.
Anyway, he walked me home, he even held my
    hand;
I can't remember who he was but I know that he
    was grand.
As we walked, we neared my house and I suppressed
    a groan:
The light inside our porch was out and there we
    were, alone.
We said goodnight, and then we stood, getting
    awfully cold.
I began to wish that he would leave, for the night
    was growing old.

    For twenty years it seemed we stood,
    And then he bent and kissed me.
    Oh! Too bad the lights were out—
    For in the dark he missed me.

Donna Hanninen

THE POET

    With pen in hand and thought in mind
    The poet writes his lines.
    Inspired by some wide, verdant meadow,
    Or the tactics of a playful kitten,
    He transfers what is in his brain,
    To swaying rhymes and spicy words.
    Writing quickly, the parchment crackles
    Beneath his scratching quill.
    Write quickly, poet, for soon the clouds
    Will scatter and drift away.
    Capture, now, the moment of beauty,
    Before it flies away and leaves no more
    The feeling for a poet's line.

Linda Guyer

SUMMER

Songs of birds
Waken the day,
A distant tractor roars.

Women at words,
Children at play,
And shouts through open doors.

Heat of noon
Has no sound,
A quiet stills the air.

Whispers of dusk,
A squeaking gate,
Soft laughter everywhere.

Dawn of dark,
Sighs of sleep,
A breeze moves from above.

Shadows of crickets,
Music of night,
A lullaby speaks of love.

Edna Earle Harris

TO LEAVE THIS EARTH

When my time comes to leave this earth, I wonder
if to others, I have given all my worth. How many
times did I forget to do my share, or neglected to
show others that I really care.

Did I cherish friendships I have known, and bring
comfort to those who were alone? Did I live up
to the golden rule, or was I too often a selfish fool?

The only way that I will know, is to question my
life, just so. And if I have not done my part, now
is the time I'd better start.

Tonie Jenkins

THE DREAM

I fell asleep one day and dreamed a dream,
And to my senses very strange it seemed:
I saw some children playing happily before my door;
A sight such as I'd never seen before
In all the many years now passed and gone;
It was a sight most beautiful to look upon.
Those children who are members of the colored race
Were playing joyfully in glad embrace,
With my neighbor's children who have skin so white
The contrast is most striking day or night—
The Scriptures say, "to us a child is born";
They do not say if it is black or white.

Blanche G. Lafferty
Age 91

YOU

You are the stars that twinkle at night
You are the sun that shines so bright.
You are the blue sky high above
You are the personification of love
You are the white clouds in the sky
You are the answer to the question why.
You are the moving hands of time
You will someday be mine . . . .

Yvonne I. Arnold

THE WIND THAT DESTROYS

What is the wind: you ask.
Listen, and I shall tell you.
I have not seen the wind but—
I have seen its work many times.
I have watched it blow the limbs of a tree
And raise havoc with the farmers' crops.
I have seen it tear the gentle lilacs apart.
It has snarled and glared down at me
On a cold winter's morning.
I have heard it in the summer shout to the rain,
"Come, my friend, let us ruin this land for good."
It rarely brags and if it does,
It always carries its boastings out.

D. E. Hartley

UP AND BEYOND

God first, others second, SELF last;
   Yesterday is gone, today is soon past.
Keep me TODAY and TOMORROW with Thee, O Lord
   Then from within, my soul has soared.

     My soul then soars to unknown heights
        Above and beyond the day's small blights—
     Soared beyond—outward, upward from "me,"
        Until in retrospect only Thee I see.

Kari C. Day

LAST MOMENTS

    As I sit here in my easy chair
    Surveying my domain
    I think of all the fruitful years
    And days of tears and pain.

       All my triumphs large and small
       I remember clearly as a bell
       And deeds I'd rather not recall
       I remember them as well.

          Those joyous years are over now
          Life's drawing to a close
          We all must go sometime
          To where—God only knows.

             As I sit here reminiscing
             And thinking of my long departed wife
             I pray that I may join her
             In the blessed hereafter life.

                My life is slowly ebbing now
                I feel so deathly tired
                I know before the sun has set
                I will have expired.

Gil Horn

GONE

Gone, gone is his bright and
spirited candle glow, and sleep
and peace have touched his soul.

Shout! out the sorrow and weep in
the corners of your mind, gone.

Robin E. Lee

MEN OF IMPRESSION

Man is a being of impression
For some men long to look at others
And some men long to be looked at
Every man longs for impression
Even if it be to himself.

Some men struggle to impress other men;
Some men struggle to impress only women
For she has previously impressed him.
This impression of man to woman has long lasted
And in this world will last ever on.

A man learned impression by being impressed
And knowing this feeling he presses on.
He searches for the one that he will impress
And the feeling he gains from being the impressioner.
This feeling we know as one's self-pride.

Timothy Burton White

THE IMAGE

Man created in the image of God,
Torn, pulled and pried from the sod.
Man the destroyer; this evil of God?
Beast that roams and ravages:
Man—created in the image of God?

Nelson R. Allen

THE CLOCK OF LIFE

The clock of life is wound but once,
   And no man has the power—
To tell just when the hands will stop—
   At late or early hour.

To lose one's wealth is sad indeed,
   To lose one's health is more,
To lose one's soul is such a loss
   As no man can restore.

Milford Hall, Sr.

TAKE ME TO THE COUNTRY

I love the earth, the good old earth;
Let me to the country go
Where man does work but has not spoiled
The things of nature so.

I love the earth, the good old earth,
That's where I want to be;
And see the things that God has made
To last through eternity.

And feel the peace and sweet release
Of the man-made, hurried world;
Its value is far greater
Than the price of any pearl.

And in the country that I love
There's a church I used to know;
Just bury me there and let me lie
Where the soft, fresh breezes blow.

Flora Rossdeutscher

BLESSING

May there be love and luck
   in all you say and do
And may the joy you bring others
   be richly blessed and returned
   to you.

Rose June Simons

A SMILE

There's something about the smile of a babe,
That turns one's sadness to cheer,
For each little line of that smile represents
God's sunshine to all He holds dear!

Margaret Simmons

OF MYSELF

If I could count the sunsets I have seen
or all the grains of sand washed by the tide,
perhaps I could explain myself to you.

Life is a web woven of many-colored threads
each leading only to another and another,
like the tracks of birds running before a wave.

There is seldom ever time enough, or space enough,
to follow one thread to its conclusion, yet I
would like to follow each of them,
walk in the shoes of everyone, be every leaf
and blade of grass, to know, to experience,
to taste and feel all of life.

But my mind does not have the courage of my heart!
If it did, perhaps even I could make some
contribution to mankind and the universe.
As it is I have far too little to say
and far too many words to use.

Ann Beck

NURSING

To see, to understand another's needs,
To do and search and put at ease,
To comfort those in sorrow and in grief,
Is often overlooked in conquering pain.

To give a smile where there is utter gloom,
To bring up topics which will lift the spirit,
Is very often overlooked by us who should
   bring strength and courage to those
   who suffer pain.

Thea O. Berg

SHOPPING NOTES

I review all the flyers that come thru the mail,
To take good advantage of their weekly sale.

Coupons I clip and exchange by the yard,
At the checkout counters I'm always on guard.

With their minds all a-flutter over some dimpled lad
The girls I find cute, but they just cannot add...

I have to shop wisely for my money to stretch—
If I make a complaint I'm a grouchy old wretch.

They chatter and giggle with the boy who is bagging
While I stand and wait and my patience is sagging...

The canned goods and bleach are *always* on top,
While the pie and the cupcakes I find are a flop.

Then out to my car with my new food supply—
And a new dented fender (I'm ready to cry).

The Manger's sorry, but wearing a frown
As most of his baskets are all over town.

This little story is just a preview
(If it hasn't already happened to you).

                                        Arthur R. Branch

THE FAULTY MIRROR

I look in the mirror and what do I see?
A little old lady, looking at me.

I put on my glasses, the better to see—
Now a much older lady looks back at me.

The mirror is faulty! to this I agree,
For that little old lady just *couldn't* be me!

                            Ruth Kraft Eby

MAY I ALWAYS LOVE

This life has many trials,
Many heartaches, many woes.
Sometimes it seems that all our friends
Are outnumbered by our foes;
And even if we've tried our best
To be each person's friend,
It seems that folks simply delight
In hurting you no end.
They never give a word of praise,
Or thanks for all you've done,
But let our loved ones or ourselves
Do wrong, and watch them run
To neighbors, preachers, anyone
Who'll lend a listening ear,
And soon the whole town's talking,
And your character is smeared.
Throughout my life I've served my Lord
The best way that I could.
I never served Him for man's praise,
Nor because I thought I should.
I love my Saviour. He's my friend;
The one who's always true.
He's always near to hold my hand
When trials make me blue.
Oft times He is the only one
Who sees the tears I shed,
Who knows my heartaches, trials, pain,
And lifts my drooping head.
I hope that I shall never cause
Some other's heart to ache;
But may I be a friend, like Him,
Be true, and not forsake.
And when my life on earth is done,
And I go to live above,
May all I've come in contact with
Say, "She showed me naught but love."

Grace Farlow

374

LOST STITCHES

It's strange how on things of little worth
Memories of other days have a rebirth.
I picked up a pillow, used for years,
And wondered, then, through sudden tears.
Where part of the stitches had gone?

Just where had they dropped along the way
From that far yesteryear until today?
Why had I not, when the space grew bare,
Placed them back with infinite care
And kept the pattern there?

This morning I caught on the radio
The voice of a yodler, soft and low,
Crooning a tune to make me laugh
That I used to play on the phonograph
In other far-off days.

Then I saw a house by the side of the road
Where I once lived in the long ago,
And the sunlight flickered about my feet
As with gentle hands I folded the sheet
Around my baby's crib.

Now there will be moments, as long as life lasts,
When some little thing from out of the past
Will come, as did the yodeling tune,
To remind me again of the days of June,
My summertime of life.

And when the autumn is surely here
There will be much of love and cheer.
A tune will always be changing the scenes,
And where lost stitches were, I shall have dreams,
Just as I have today.

Lora Liming

STAY

Some people think that
The spring comes easily.
The birds don't *sing*; their cries
Pierce their throats as they try
To tell the world.

The rhythms of the earth
Are the sea, tearing from the land,
The heat of the sun from the sky,
The song from the birds.
The rhymes are the sea returning with
    the sea.

Spring doesn't come easily.
It comes like the child in the world,
Forced and drawn from the mother's
    womb.
The cries speak of the joy
And death at moment's being.

Linda Lee Lovell

PLEA FOR PEACE

Uplifted hands with supplication
Speak for surcease from driven strife,
And casts a shadow on the ground
Which echos pleas from a wearied heart.

As long ago upon a lonely mountain top
Punctured hands another shadow cast,
That uplifted hands might ask and so receive
God's blessed peace of single unity.

Jack C. Stewart

TO AN ITALIAN MAIDEN

Shall I tell you
Your hair is more beautiful
Than an orange sunset
Breathing salted air in the winded sea?

Or shall I compare
Your soft skin
To silicon-weathered pebbles
Consuming fire at noon?

Shall I sing to you
Of your brown eyes
Telling me I'm not to go
Or shall I say
I'll love you for an eternity,
Nothing more?

R. J. Petremont, Jr.

LITTLE MOTHER

Just a tiny precious mother
In her brand new rocking chair.
Such a lovely "little" mother
With a lot of love to share.

She is singing to her baby,
As she holds her very tight,
And her voice is so enchanting
For such a tiny mite.

All at once the house is quiet,
No more lullabyes to hear,
For the "little" mother is sleeping
And still holds her baby near.

Some day in the not too distant future,
There'll be another rocking chair
And another "little" mother will be
    sitting there.

Frances Esposito

TEARDROPS

Gentle rain-water of the soul,
Diamond chips of the heart.
They course their way down your cheek
And you wonder how they got their start.
Some rich, full happiness
Or wonderful joy supreme;
A hurt pride or lost love,
Or maybe a shattered dream.

Be happy for those sweet raindrops
That cleanse your very soul,
Let the little diamond chips fall . . .
Use not your self-control!
So as each day comes and goes,
And as the years take their toll . . .
Be happy for those precious chips
And gentle raindrops of the soul!

Rosemary Sharp Vlaisavich

WHY NOT FORGET AND FORGIVE!

Why do we always call to mind . . .
    Some old and hidden hurt . . .
Or worry over little words . . . .
    That sounded somewhat curt? . . .
Why do we make an issue now . . .
    Instead of overlooking it . . .
And burying the past . . .
    Instead of spreading happiness . . .
By turning wrath aside . . .
    And thereby helping other souls . . .
To overcome their pride? . . .
    There is no good in jealousy . . .
Or any vengeful gain . . . .
    And every ounce of selfishness . . .
Is finally in vain . . .
    They only lead to sorrow and . . .
The deepest of regret . . .
    When it is so much better to . . .
Forget and to forgive?

Ronald Lee Hanna

THE STREAM

Down the rugged slopes of mountains
Through the valleys and the towns,
Slowly moving never stopping
Moves the mountain stream along.

By the rich man's castle,
Near the poor man's hut,
It is drawn and it is plenty
And it never seems to stop.

Coming down through heaven's pathways
Going deep into the earth,
Passing through the streets and byways,
And never looking back,
Flows the mountain stream beneath me,
And it never seems to stop.

LAry LOpez

THE GOLDEN YEARS

The years that lie before us
    not so many as behind
We long for fate to take our hand
    and not to be unkind.

Memories we summarize
    fair company to keep
To help us pass the lonely hours
    between the dawn and sleep.

We walk a little slower
    our heads bent somewhat low
Protection from the mighty storm
    and colder winds that blow.

If we could be, but for an hour,
    that child we used to know
What kinder thoughts and loving deeds
    to others would bestow.

Only living makes us wise
    experience through sorrow
The golden years loom sweeter still
    with faith in each tomorrow.

Jacqueline Stilgenbauer

UNKNOWN HEAVEN

Autumn tiptoes in
Like an uninvited guest.
No one actually notices
Until she takes her toll.
Leaves turn to warmer colors
Of yellow, orange and vibrant red,
Only to take a final plunge
Into a heap at the trunk.
Mums spring up to meet
The hazy blue fall sky.
The air has a healthy nip
Which speeds new life to all.
Autumn is a heaven in itself;
The world lies unaware.

Monette Lewallen Krueger

A SPRING SONG

O, if I could wake some fine spring day
And be changed to an elfin sprite at play!

Like a feather I'd float, now here, now there,
Just twirling and sailing in soft warm air.

Like each little shadow I'd flit and hop,
To insect haunts—to the tall tree top,

Take a peek at the robin's eggs of blue,
Then dash to earth for a sip of dew,

Alight on a spider who is planning her web
And find out her secret of needle and thread;

Catch a ride on the cardinal's shiny red wing,
Together we would call and whistle and sing.

On a rippling wave in a babbling stream
I would hop and dance in a spring daydream.
Then as day departs in a glorious blaze
And the sun slips down from its slanting rays,
When breezes sway the jonquil's cup,
I would hop inside and cuddle up
To bask in fragrance in fairy glee
Until morning comes, and I find myself—me!

Eva E. Wollenman

MY BROTHER

Brothers are mean, brothers are fine
Brothers are vicious, brothers are kind
But in all the world there's none like mine

He can be a pain, yet he's always there
He tells me how to act, and what to wear
I know he will always care

Sometimes he's great, sometimes a creep
Sometimes on a pedestal he belongs
Sometimes I wish from a mountain he'd leap

He'll give you a push, he'll give you a shove
There's none below, there's none above
None in this world which more I love.

Jerri Coston

STILL, QUIET BEAUTY

What a beautiful, foggy morning!
As tho' God had dropped an awning.
A dull, grey mist hanging,
Completely shrouding one's being.

A soft quietness over all;
In the sky, the air—a pall,
Resembling a wall.
Man felt quite small.

Awning, mantle, wall—
Whatever one chooses to call;
The effect was one of still, quiet beauty
Refreshing as air from the salty sea.

Kathryn Scott Gooch

IN THE TIME OF CHRIST'S PASSION

A great white snow
  has filled the altars
    with the strangest light
      tonight
and Jesus walks barefoot
    among the mountain flowers
  which grow in blankets
    of white snow
His feet are bare
  (of flesh and blood are made)
  his hands are cold
    holding the frozen world
      between the bones
        and many wounds
The world is sharp-edged
  breaking out in nails
    and bursts of flame
  the pain is sore
My snow
  I gather you
    to my warm eyes
  you melt in artificial tears
    and freeze my skin
The mystery of Jesus, walking,
    again begins
  the baby (rosebud) disappears
    the man is here
      the Word is flesh
        and walking
          with bleeding feet
            into the cut glass
            night
          through the spikey
           relentless air
        to a vague hill
          where crowds will gather
        shout and disappear
      but one tree will stand
        always
          remember
          (He will).

Richard F. Reed

THE FORGOTTEN SOLDIER

Across the great world
Viet Nam is our spot
Where men live out their lives
In a land that God forgot

Here is where we sweat and freeze
It is more than a man can stand
We're not exactly convicts
Earning our meals and pay
Guarding people worth millions
For two and a half a day

Few people know we are here
Fewer give a dam
We're just a bunch of GI's
Who belong to Uncle Sam

We live in our memories
And wait for our gals
Hoping while we're away
They won't marry our pals

But as we pass the pearly gates
We'll hear St. Peter yell
"Fall out you men of Viet Nam
You've served your time in hell."

Sgt. William E. Watson

THE BEAST OF WAR

The horses are on the last lap around
   the track.
The grains of sand that run through
   the narrow neck of the hourglass
   are about depleted.
But this life, this endless struggle for
   survival is not over yet until the
   beast releases me from its grasp.
For my fate could end like the
   towering whitecap in the angry
   sea of life to be cast mercilessly
   against the boulders of some
   huge cliff.

Thomas J. Mapley

383

THE KITE

My nine-year old took sticks and glue
And worked into the night.
He measured everything with care
To get his kite just right.

Then in the early morning
When the chores had to be done,
He said, "Let's go take the kite out
For a special trial run."

But I was far too busy
To do this childish thing,
And so I let him go alone
With kite and ball of string.

As I watched through the window
My heart said, "Foolish One,
One day you won't be asked
To come and share his fun."

So I put down my working tools
And rushed out into the wind.
Oh, it was good to hold the string
And fly the kite with him.

Now he is grown and far away
And this is what he writes
"Remember, Mom, that lovely day,
The day we flew the kite?"

Virginia Keirns

DAISIES

Daisies—one by one in a row.
Black and yellow as they blow.
Wandering, fading in their place.
Bowing, kneeling in her grace.
Sacred, tended day by day
Since September—now it's May.
Stealing heaven from the skies,
And the angel in her eyes.
Each day I pass.
Each day she weeps by daisies
Where her lover sleeps.

Kimberley Smith

EROS

O, love, thou art a mighty gale
A hurricane of feeling
A tempest of emotion.
I taste thy tears upon my cheeks;
I weep for him.
I feel thy breath upon my neck;
I long for him.
I see thy lightning splitting the sky jagged;
Ragged—like my heart.
I hear thy thunder rolling in the clouds;
I ache for him.
The frenzy of the storm beckons me;
I thrill in the glory of God's tantrum.

And after the storm, the calm.
Yon is the rainbow of promise—
I live again.

Pamela Wood

FORGET AND REMEMBER

Forget his name, forget his face,
   Forget his kiss, his warm embrace.
Forget his love that steadily grew,
   Remember now—you're probably through.
Forget the night they played your song,
   Forget how you cried all night long.
Forget how close you two once were,
   Remember now—he's close to her.
Forget the fun you two once shared,
   Forget his love and how he cared.
Forget the times you had together,
   Remember now—he's gone forever.
Forget how you memorized his walk,
   Forget the way he used to talk.
Forget the songs he used to sing,
   Remember now—It's just a dream.
Forget how he was once your world,
   Remember now—you're not his girl.

Jan Klempnauer

```
    i   tic

              you toc

    you toc

              i   tic

              we   tic
              we clock
              the hours
              of today
              tomorrow
              tomorrow
              tomorrow
              tomorrow
              tomorrow
              tomorrow

              we tic—toc.
              the hour and the
              second        hand
              we            stand.
```

Stanley Kapner

AFTERTHOUGHT

Truth has not freed.
It has chained me to reality,
With no escape;
Lashing with the whip of realization
To incognizance of dreams and hope.
Truth betrays liars,
Casting me into a well of heartache,
Filled with tears from the knowledge of deception;
Ever sinking,
Bound to rocks of hate
By the rope of certainty,
Unyielding to dulled shears of hope.

Zandra Lindgren

THE BLESSED FAWN

Gentle child of the forest,
    You abide with flower and tree.
The world is your home of happiness,
    Within you are safe and free.

As I watch you step through the greenwood
    I see wisdom deep in your eyes.
I can tell you know the secret of life
    And concealed in your heart it lies.

Tell me, offspring of nature,
    Where this truth is concealed!
For if I knew the mystery of life
    The joy of living would be revealed.

Is it found in each seed that is planted
    With tender and loving care?
Or in the white daisies that grow on the bank
    So pure and lovely and fair?

Is it sealed in the rich deep soil
    From which all that lives must depend?
This secret of life is a secret of God,
    A thing man cannot comprehend.

God told you all; you are simple and pure.
    The gift of love you possess.
The secret of life is a tender thing,
    And may God always tender things bless.

Wendy E. Holmes
Age 15

I WONDER

Societies banish
As do cultures,
Yet memories remain.
I wonder,
Does Prejudice?

Robert Jusa

INDEX

=A=

=B=

=E=

=F=

=G=

=H=

=I=

=J=

=K=

=L=

=M=

=O=

=P=

=Q=

=R=

=T=

=U=

=V=

=W=

A SPECIAL REMEMBRANCE FOR OUR FRIENDS AT CLEVELAND PARK P.O.

The mail is seldom put out late when the zip code reads "two, three o's, eight."
The box is jammed with varied verse (the editor says we're under a curse!).

Tell me now, my good friend Evans, does it rain down from the heavens?
(Robinson will certify if it drops out of the sky.)

And for the stuff too large to fit, just stand in line and wait for it.

Now on the left is Wiggins wise (she calls the signals with her eyes)
And then there's friendly Mrs. Swett (whose window isn't open yet)...

So four days out of every week, it's Mrs. Douglas' line I seek
And patiently await my turn (because I know they give a *Dern!*)

The Clover Office Boy

COMPLETE LIST OF WINNERS
in the

Clover

COLLECTION

Of

VERSE

1969 INTERNATIONAL POETRY COMPETITION

SPONSORED BY

Clover Publishing Company, Washington, D. C. 20008

CLOVER PUBLISHING COMPANY
WASHINGTON, D. C. 20008

ANNOUNCEMENT OF CONTEST WINNERS—

A monumental task of giving due consideration to entries in this new competition has been finally completed, and it is with great pride that we here announce the winners.

To determine the successful entries, each and every verse submitted was read and graded on a scale from A to F, giving consideration only to the quality of the poem itself. At this stage, all entries were maintained in code number order. In the next stage, the entries were sorted by grade (all A's together, etc.) and re-read, giving each group three categories (good, better, best) within the grade.

The final results showed 102 A's, 1 A+, 1A++ and two A+++. This meant a tie for first place, and that's exactly how it stands. The A++ is second and the A+ is third. All the other A's (102) are fourth prize (Book Award Winners).

The B's are Honorable Mention Award Winners and the C's are Special Mention Award Winners. The D, E and F entries are also-ran.

Our judges were instructed to be very lenient regarding the manner of presentation. Whether typed or handwritten, all were considered equally—barring outright illegibility. But the judges were tough on the quality of the poem itself. As a result, it became a real accomplishment to have an A, B or C entry— and all the Fourth Prize winners were in real contention for the cash prizes.

We hope you are among the winners. If so, you may well be proud of your accomplishment. If not, we hope you will be encouraged to continue your efforts at every opportunity.

The Clover Collection of Verse, Volume III, will contain all the Cash Prize and Book Award winning poems from this competition, plus selected poems from the Honorable Mention and Special Mention entries.

We know you will enjoy Volume III as much as the current and previous Clover Collections, and would like to take this opportunity to thank everyone who has contributed toward making this effort a true and a lasting happiness for so many.

Evelyn Petry   Clinton Browning Petry
Editor   *Publisher*

Statistics

1969 Clover International Poetry Competition

October 15, 1968 to February 14, 1969

Total ENTRIES RECEIVED	7,199
Total CASH PRIZES *(Including Duplicate First Prizes)*	4
Total BOOK AWARDS *(Including 3 Duplicate Prizes)*	102
Total HONORABLE MENTION	768
Total SPECIAL MENTION	685

COMPLETE LIST OF ALL PRIZE AND AWARD WINNERS
1969 CLOVER INTERNATIONAL POETRY COMPETITION

FIRST PRIZE   =TIE=   FIRST PRIZE

$300 $300

Margaret Sheridan Paquette   Floyd Gibson
1403 San Simeon St.,   185 Durant, Apt. 5,
Oceanside, California   Sarnia, Ontario, Canada

SECOND PRIZE   THIRD PRIZE

$150 $50

George E. Wagner   Louise Monahan
403 East North St.,   802 South Orange Drive
Tampa, Florida   Los Angeles, California

FOURTH **BOOK AWARDS** PRIZES

	Code
Anderson, Rebecca L., 12434 S. 33rd St., Omaha, Nebraska	2202
Angus, Bethel A., Cowen, West Virginia	406
Apkarian, Sam S., 3184 Clarence, Melvindale, Michigan	463
Bain, Edna M., 1805 N. Normandie, Los Angeles, California	1146
Barnes, Lakenan, 115 S. Jefferson St., Mexico, Missouri	2423
Barrett, Dolly L., R.D. 1, Martville, New York	2095
Bartelstone, Ada S., 353 St. Johns Ave., Yonkers, New York	411
Baruch, Beth, 950 25th St. N.W., Washington, D.C.	101
Bateman, Sara H., 918 Main Ave., Hagerstown, Maryland	171
Baxter, Mrs. Elizabeth, 190 Clubhouse Rd., King of Prussia, Pennsylvania	1132
Beard, E. C., P.O. Box 567, Wingham, Ontario, Canada	1874
Benson, Valerie A., Rt. 1, Box 391, Warrenville, Illinois	760
Bishop, Thomas E., 455 Pinecrest Dr., Athens, Georgia	1697
Bloksberg, Bertha, 26 Dale Rd., Wanaque, New Jersey	629
Borders, Andrew J., Davisboro, Georgia	636
Borsodi, Marion S., 107 Conduit St., Annapolis, Maryland	241
Brollier, Myrta B., 125 W. Marion St., Mt. Gilead, Ohio	1766
Buell, Stanley, R.D. 4, Corry, Pennsylvania	726
Buschur, Nicholas R., R.R. 1, New Weston, Ohio	371
Campbell-Hardwick, Mrs. Patricia, 42 Oxley St., N.S.W. 2065, Australia	1787
Clark, Mrs. W. Bailey, R. 1, Box 147, Chocowinity, North Carolina	793
Clark, William L., 105 Main St., Black River Falls, Wisconsin	1566
Conroy, Sharon L., 8408 Hopewell Dr., El Paso, Texas	1552
Crider, Bill, 828 N. State St., Greenfield, Indiana	112
D'Alessandro, Terry, 5724 Hollywood Blvd., Hollywood, Florida	638
Dickson, Jean A., 321 W. 24th St., New York, New York	226
Duncan, Janis, Box 627, Fleming Hall, E. Carolina Univ., Greenville, N. Car.	787
Dunn, Mrs. Maude W., 508 S. Buchanan Blvd., Durham, North Carolina	507
Earl, Mrs. Oressa N., 213 Arcadia, Champaign, Illinois	1221
Eckert, Mrs. Vera L., 2723 L.S.U. Ave., San Angelo, Texas	1401
Elsaesser, Louis O., Quarters 111, Aberdeen Proving Grounds, Maryland	305
Flemming, Kay, 7 Altonwood Pl., Yonkers, New York	1798
Gansneder, Berenice M., 7017 38th N.E., Seattle, Washington	1120
Gemeinhardt, Carl J., 3447 N. 115th St., Chicago, Illinois	190
Hansen, Wilbur R., 6606 N. 14th Pl., Phoenix, Arizona	2079
Hart, Mrs. Myra A., 620 E. Pine St., Santa Ana, California	1590
Harter, James L., 3131 Diamond Ave., Allentown, Pennsylvania	1140

Continued

Heath, Olive, 829 Greendale Ave., Needham, Massachusetts 1047
Henderson, Dorothy C., 2975 E. Peakview Ave., Littleton, Colorado 1388
Hill, Martha M., 3330 Eastlawn St., Lorain, Ohio 487
Hopkins, Bruce, 2732½ Lydia St., Jacksonville, Florida 779
Hotch, Madeline, 5473 Newbury Ave., San Bernardino, California 1487
Hudson, Bob, 520 Walker Rd., Hinsdale, Illinois 882
Hulse, Myrtle D., "West Winds," Rt. 2, Box 2206, Port Angeles, Washington 1090
Hunter, Ransdell, 813 Wilford St., Ruston, Louisiana 1439
Hyer, Mrs. Helen von Kolnitz, 15-B Council St., Charleston, South Carolina 1577
Jacobi, Margaret W., 3900 N. Charles St., Apt. 1416, Baltimore, Maryland 633
Johnson, II, Fredric E., 1027 Quebec Ter., Silver Spring, Maryland 2313
Keen, Annetta, 2789 Walker Dr., Yorktown Heights, New York 583
Kerchner, Susan L., Box W005, Bucknell University, Lewisburg, Pennsylvania 796
Kopf, Mrs. L. Joanne, P.O. Box 117, Grandview, Iowa 1285
Lalik, Jeanne D., 361 S. 6th St., Fulton, New York 1152
Landry, Edward J., 11 Central St., Leominster, Massachusetts 1150
Lang, Lillian M., 2006 Rublee St., La Crosse, Wisconsin 1137
LeBaron, Charles E., 362 Main St., Johnson City, New York 1203
Leino, Olga M., 15 Wildwood Gardens, Piedmont, California 683
Litwak, Dan, 7 Bakeman St., Fulton, New York 1407
Makofske, Mary, 1744½ Glendon Ave., West Los Angeles, California 817
Masten, Zelda, 1541 Groton Rd., S.E., East Grand Rapids, Michigan 356
McDonald, Maurene, Box 656, Eden, Texas 906
McGaha, Wanda, Rt. 4, Maryville, Tennessee 1748
McPhail, Anna Y., 319 Clay St., Morocco, Indiana 1781
Metzger, William D., 929 N. Main St., Lima, Ohio 1586
Miller, George H., P.O. Box 286, Thomaston, Georgia 2322
Miskimins, Doris L., 5136 Marathon St., Apt. 104, Hollywood, California 1682
Murphy, Eleanor K., 312 W. Miner St., West Chester, Pennsylvania 819
Nunn, Kem, 408 Sycamore, Claremont, California 175
Owens, Kathryn N., 2125 Bush, San Francisco, California 308
Papademas, Mrs. Maud C., c/o The Embassy of Cyprus, Washington, D.C. 1871
Pearson, Kimberlee D., 8232 Earhart Rd., South Lyon, Michigan 2403
Peck, Earl W., 80 Spring St., Plainville, Massachusetts 1511
Pinque, Dulentino A., P.O. Box 735, Peekskill, New York 1655
Popham, Paul, 1070 Dobbs Ferry Rd., White Plains, New York 1020
Price, Mary P., Rt. 1, Box 367, Lenoir, North Carolina 1306
Radke, M. Elizabeth, R.R. 2, Box 673, Lake Villa, Illinois 1207
Roche, Helen E., 1601 18th St. N.W., Washington, D.C. 2324
Romer, Ann, 4805 Beverly Hills Dr., Cincinnati, Ohio 373
Rowland, Robert B., 1134 W. Brockett, Sherman, Texas 1155
Ryan, Catherine, 6802 Ridge Blvd., Brooklyn, New York 180
Saunders, Lucy B., 1325 Quarrier St., Charleston, West Virginia 392
Schmit, Nancy, 5001 Seminary Rd., Alexandria, Virginia 2357
Schultz, Nell W., 524 W. 4th Ave., Gastonia, North Carolina 1117
Settle, Radell, 1204 9th Ave., Huntington, West Virginia 395
Sher, D. A., 315 57th St. N.W., Albuquerque, New Mexico 813
Smith, Linwood D., D-11 Washington Ter., Raleigh, North Carolina 645
Springer, Karen, Crown Point Rd., Thorofare, New Jersey 135
Swaim, Alice M., Box 426, Dillsburg, Pennsylvania 197
Tozer, Thomas J., 321 S. Range Line Rd., Carmel, Indiana 132
Tramontozzi, Linda P., 664 Washington St., Brighton, Massachusetts 904
Tranbarger, Ossie E., 619 W. Main St., Independence, Kansas 1504
Trask, Jo D., 327 3rd Ave. S.E., Minneapolis, Minnesota 588
Tyler, Eleanor, Box 158, Severy, Kansas 419
Urie, Sherry, Robinson Hall, U.V.M., Burlington, Vermont 369
Vickrey, Mrs. Mack L., Rt. 1, Box 99, Crystal River, Florida 1535
Von Abele, Stephen, 333 S. Glebe Rd., Arlington, Virginia 1834
Wagner, Mrs. Marje, 812 Lincoln Ave. N.E., Fort Payne, Alabama 865
Werling, Mrs. Orvil, R.R. 2, Ossian, Indiana 1581
Whitaker, Maurice, 941 McCallie Ave. at Central, Apt. 4, Chattanooga, Tenn. 2022
Witkowski, Leon, 16 Diamond St., Brooklyn, New York 1447
Wood, Laura H., 1206 Kickapoo, Leavenworth, Kansas 1248
Woodrow, Joseph A., 1732 N. Whitley Ave., Hollywood, California 492
Wright, Margot, 1247 Hawthorne Rd., Grosse Pointe Woods, Michigan 631

End of Book Awards

1969 CLOVER INTERNATIONAL POETRY COMPETITION

=A=

Abuisi, Francis B., 32 Bryant St., North Adams, Mass. HONORABLE MENTION
Acaley, Mrs. Joseph, 90l Fairmount Ave., Pottsville, Pa. Special Mention
Adams, Caroline, 175 West Akers, East Lansing, Mich. Special Mention
Alexander, Sereda G., 370l Eve Circle-A, Mira Loma, Cal. HONORABLE MENTION
Allen, Florence E., 308 Reese St., Emporia, Va. Special Mention
Allen, Nelson R., 408 S. Elmira St., Athens, Pa. HONORABLE MENTION
Allen, Polly, 13326 Cornell Rd., Concord, Mich. HONORABLE MENTION
Allen, Ruth M., 1324 N.E. 7th St., Okla. City, Okla. HONORABLE MENTION
Allen, Mrs. Steven T., R.D. l, Meadville, Pa. HONORABLE MENTION
Allen, Mrs. T. B., 407 S. Williams, Moberly, Mo. Special Mention
Allen, Mrs. T. L., P.O. Box 589, Thomaston, Ga. Special Mention
Anastasi, Charlotte, 829 Great Spring Rd., Rosemont, Pa. Special Mention
Anderson, Claire S., 942 Townsend Blvd., Jacksonville, Fl. Special Mention
Anderson, George, Rt. l, Box B9l, Schaumburg, Ill. Special Mention
Anderson, King E., R.R. 3, Louisville, Ill. Special Mention
Anderson, L. Joyce, 350 50th St., S.E., Wash., D.C. HONORABLE MENTION
Anderson, Margaret E., 705 Chestnut St., Latrobe, Pa. Special Mention
Anderson, Schylar, 60l Sherwood Ave., Waynesboro, Va. HONORABLE MENTION
Anderson, Virginia L., 231 Millersville Rd., Lancaster, Pa. Special Mention
Andrasy, Steve E., 3679 Calumet St., Philadelphia, Pa. Special Mention
Andrews, Margaret, 213 Hampton House, Baltimore, Md. HONORABLE MENTION
Antalfy, Gusztav S., 5920 Skyline Dr., El Sobrante, Cal. Special Mention
Antidormi, Michael F., 127 Matawan Terrace Apts., Matawan, N.J. Special Mention
Antoniadis, Stacy, 237 Hollywood Ave., Bronx, N.Y. HONORABLE MENTION
Aquino, Doris S., 3607 Mississippi Ave., Norfolk, Va. Special Mention
Arancibia, Stella B., 1376 College Ave., Fresno, Cal. HONORABLE MENTION
Arendall, Mrs. Nan B., 4 Kingsway Spg. Hill, Mobile, Ala. HONORABLE MENTION
Arentson, Robert M., P.O. 130 State College, Miss. Special Mention
Arnieri, Mrs. M. E., 8749 Cottage St., Philadelphia, Pa. HONORABLE MENTION
Arricale, Mrs. John J., 32ll Tierney Pl., Bronx, N.Y. HONORABLE MENTION
Arrington, Mrs. Ethel G., Rt. 3, Box 282, Louisbury, N.C. HONORABLE MENTION
Artale, Larry, 30 Olivia St., Port Chester, N.Y. Special Mention
Asbury, Thelma V., 4385 Hazelgreen Rd. N.E., Salem, Ore. Special Mention
Ashley, Mrs. Harlan, No. l b266a, Rittman, Ohio Special Mention
Atlas, Harold, 130 Parsons St., Brighton, Mass. HONORABLE MENTION

=B=

Babcock, Betty L., 314 S. Mill St., Milton Freewater, Ore. Special Mention
Bacharach, Frances R., 8 Mt. Ida St., Newton, Mass. Special Mention
Bailey, Jerry W., 18 Pegram Circle, Ft. Oglethorpe, Ga. HONORABLE MENTION
Bailey, Kathy Jo, 160 Columbia Ave., Astoria, Ore. Special Mention
Bailey, Zerellene, Rt. l, Box 67, Durant, Miss. Special Mention
Baker, Lillian, 15237 Chanera Ave., Gardena, Cal. Special Mention
Baker, Muriel A., 2 Ziegler Pl., Matawan, N.J. HONORABLE MENTION
Baker, Susan F., Rt. l, Chireno, Tex. HONORABLE MENTION
Baker, Twila E., 1416 Plum St., Piqua, Ohio Special Mention
Baker, Virginia M., Lake Pleasant Rd., R.D. 5, Erie, Pa. HONORABLE MENTION
Baldwin, Monterrey F., 2158 N. 5th St., Philadelphia, Pa. Special Mention
Baldwin, Sheila, 306 Oak St., Decorah, Iowa HONORABLE MENTION
Ball, Dorothy, R.R. l, Ft. Jennings, Ohio Special Mention
Ballentine, Lee, 1260 Race St., Denver, Colo. Special Mention
Bangert, Barbara, 5505 Wilsey Way, Carmichael, Cal. HONORABLE MENTION
Banker, Denise, 13717 Allen Rd., Albion, N.Y. HONORABLE MENTION
Banks, Josephine S., Box 235, Gravette, Ark. Special Mention
Barber, Carlene M., 1285 Millville-Shandon Rd., Hamilton, Ohio Special Mention
Bard, Mrs. Jessie, Depoy, Ky. HONORABLE MENTION
Barker, Mrs. Myrl, Coolville Rt. l, Coolville, Ohio Special Mention
Barnes, Kathleen, 92 Campfield St., Irvington, N.J. Special Mention

Barnes, Mrs. Mary I., 117 Hyland Drive, Burkburnett, Tex.	Special Mention
Barnett, Robert, Debden, Sask., Canada	Special Mention
Barnett, Stella B, 2220 B St. N.E., Miama, Okla.	Special Mention
Barnhill, James A., 190 Diamond St., Auburn, Cal.	Special Mention
Barr, Carla M., 16531 S. 88th Ave., Tinley Park, III.	Special Mention
Barra, James, 419 Shelburne St., Burlington, Vt.	Special Mention
Barrett, Dolly L., R.D. I, Martville, N.Y.	HONORABLE MENTION
Barrett, Mary, 231 Almont Ave., W. Seneca, N.Y.	HONORABLE MENTION
Bartelstone, Ada S., 353 St. Johns Ave., Yonkers, N.Y.	HONORABLE MENTION
Bateman, Sara H., 918 Main Ave., Hagerstown, Md.	HONORABLE MENTION
Baumgardt, Wilma J., R.R. I, Box 191-B, Polo, III.	HONORABLE MENTION
Bays, Norman C., 2695 4th Ave., Huntington, W. Va.	HONORABLE MENTION
Bean, Jane A., 506 W. Clark St., Champaign, III.	HONORABLE MENTION
Bear, Mrs. Heywood, 109 Main St., Freeport, Ohio	Special Mention
Beck, JoAnn, Rt. 2, Gray, Ga.	Special Mention
Beck, William, 125-A Beverly Rd., Huntington Sta., N.Y.	Special Mention
Becker, Joy A., 748 Myrna Rd., Paramus, N.J.	Special Mention
Becker, Peggy, 1724 Valley Rd., Champaign, III.	HONORABLE MENTION
Beckman, Lawrence R., Rt. I, Erhard, Minn.	HONORABLE MENTION
Becraft, Carmen S., 405 Noon St., Nogales, Ariz.	HONORABLE MENTION
Bedore, IIa, R.R. 4, Baraboo, Wis.	HONORABLE MENTION
Beebe, Edith E., 4532 Willow Brook, Los Angeles, Cal.	HONORABLE MENTION
Beggs, Linda, 4638 Harrison, Apt. 2S, Kansas City, Mo.	Special Mention
Beinecker, Susan P., 143 Princess Anne Cres., Islington, Ont., Can.	Special Mention
Bell, Beatrice, 79 Sargeant St., Apt. 10, Hartford, Conn.	Special Mention
Beller, Robert J., 18200 Juliana, E. Detroit, Mich.	Special Mention
Bellonzi, Patricia, 28 Rolling Acres Dr., Cumberland, R. I.	Special Mention
Bement, Paula, 312 Cherry St., West Union, Iowa	HONORABLE MENTION
Benamati, Theresa L., I Landor Lane, Cohoes, N.Y.	HONORABLE MENTION
Bench, Jeannie, Rt. 3, Seymour, Tex.	HONORABLE MENTION
Bennett, Mrs. Billy W., Rt. I, Box 115C, Greenville, Miss.	HONORABLE MENTION
Bennett, Bonnie F., Walnut Creek Estates, Goldsboro, N. C.	Special Mention
Bennett, Ida M., 1913 Howard St., Pittsburgh, Pa.	Special Mention
Bennett, Sherry, 3259 N. Knoll Blvd., Wauwatosa, Wis.	HONORABLE MENTION
Bennett, Vivian E., 41 Tomlin St., Waltham, Mass.	HONORABLE MENTION
Bennett, Willie M., Rt. I, Box 153, Lacrosse, Va.	Special Mention
Benoit, Tom, 24 Bower Ave., Brockton, Mass.	Special Mention
Benvenuto, Phyllis, 602 16th St. N., Great Falls, Mont.	HONORABLE MENTION
Bergamini, Yolanda C., P.O. Box 55, Carmichael, Cal.	Special Mention
Berger, Arthur S., 201 Myrtle, No. 9, Iowa City, Iowa	HONORABLE MENTION
Berger, Henry, RPO 0368, Rutgers Univ., New Brunswick, N.J.	Special Mention
Bergeron, Carol E., 16425 George Dr., Oak Forest, III.	Special Mention
Berish, Mrs. Barbara W., 9 Meadowview Rd., Basking Ridge, N.J.	Special Mention
Bernell, Mrs. William, 3619 W. 13th, Wichita, Kan.	HONORABLE MENTION
Beshunsky, Stanley, 700 Elkins Ave., Elkins Park, Pa.	Special Mention
Beswick, Jr., James F., 44A16 Center Grove Rd., Dover, N.J.	Special Mention
Beyerinck, Peter R., 2315 Oak St., Apt. B, Santa Monica, Cal.	Special Mention
Biggs, Donna M., Rt. 2, Box 40, Ottawa, III.	Special Mention
Bilderback, M. J. M., 111 W. State St., Hamel, III.	HONORABLE MENTION
Billings, Mrs. Leslie, 1932 Jeffords St., Clearwater, Fl.	Special Mention
Bish, Suzanne, 9030 West Blvd., Pico Rivera, Cal.	Special Mention
Bixler, Mrs. Donna M., R.D. 3, Newville, Pa.	Special Mention
Bixler, Mrs. Lucy, 1825 Linhart, Dr. 4, Lot 73, Ft. Myers, Fl.	Special Mention
Blackmore, Mrs. Jeanne, 2302 Brilyn Pl., Falls Church, Va.	Special Mention
Blackwell, Dana P., R.R. 2, Eolia, Mo.	Special Mention
Blackwell, Etta M., 211 S. Franklin St., Whiteville, N.C.	HONORABLE MENTION
Blair, Jr., Jimmy, 86 Evac Hosp., Ft. Campbell, Ky.	Special Mention
Blakeman, Grace L., R. 3, Fulton, N.Y.	Special Mention
Blakley, Melva, P.O. Box 234, Highland, Kan.	HONORABLE MENTION
Blanchard, Dorothy F., 23 Hill Ave., Highland Pk., Mich.	HONORABLE MENTION
Bleem, Mrs. John J., C & J's Milky Way, Walsh, III.	HONORABLE MENTION
Blue, Mrs. Audrey, Rt. I, Russell, Iowa	Special Mention
Bluemel, Mary S., Box 60, Granger, Wyo.	HONORABLE MENTION
Bochicchio, Maurice V., 113 E. Grove St., Dunmore, Pa.	HONORABLE MENTION
Boettcher, Evelyn J., 1712 Old Orchard Rd., Rockford, III.	HONORABLE MENTION

Boldon, Mrs. Cecilia R., Box 167, Rt. I, Hillsboro, Wis. HONORABLE MENTION
Bond, Mrs. Charlotte, 1923 18th St., Portsmouth, Ohio Special Mention
Booket, Margaret, 111½ W. 138 St., New York, N.Y. Special Mention
Booz, Kathy L., 2240 Greenleaf St., Allentown, Pa. Special Mention
Borkowski, Sharon M., 29311 Gilbert Dr., Warren, Mich. HONORABLE MENTION
Borsody, Gary, 94 Stone St., New Brunswick, N.J. Special Mention
Boruchoff, Betsy, 3530 Henry Hudson Pkwy., Riverdale, N.Y. Special Mention
Bostick, Charles, P.O. Box 26156, San Francisco, Cal. HONORABLE MENTION
Boswell, Homer, 794 47th Ave., Apt. 2, San Francisco, Cal. Special Mention
Boudreax, Rhonda, 701½ Canal St., Plaquenine, La. Special Mention
Bourne, Mrs. R. L., 4087 Haverhill Dr. N.E., Atlanta, Ga. HONORABLE MENTION
Bower, LuCelia, 324 E. 9th St., Port Angeles, Wash. HONORABLE MENTION
Bowers, Clara D., 100 Clement St., Lafayette, La. HONORABLE MENTION
Bowldes, Joan, 14000 Anglin, Detroit, Mich. HONORABLE MENTION
Bowman, Blanche, 592-C Avenida Majorea, Laguna Hills, Cal. Special Mention
Bowser, Donna G., 106 Whippo Ave., Butler, Pa. Special Mention
Boxer, Howie, 45-50 Springfield Blvd., Bayside, N.Y. Special Mention
Boyd, Patricia, P.O. Box 315, Coconut Grove, Fl. HONORABLE MENTION
Bradford, David A., Cherry Point, N.C. Special Mention
Bradley, Marcia Va., 1605 Floyd St., Lynchburg, Va. HONORABLE MENTION
Bradshaw, Francis C., 505 South Taylor St., Rocky Mount, N.C. Special Mention
Branch, Arthur R., 40 S. Mt. Ave., Cedar Grove, N.J. HONORABLE MENTION
Branch, Lana, 415 West 9th St., Michigan City, Ind. Special Mention
Braun, Raymond H., 805 N. Ottawa Ave., Park Ridge, Ill. HONORABLE MENTION
Bray, Mrs. Dorothy, 3234 So. 9th St., Arlington, Va. HONORABLE MENTION
Breazeale, Alvin, Box 341, Eupora, Miss. Special Mention
Breckling, Aloha, 22½ Shepherd, Raleigh, N.C. HONORABLE MENTION
Brennan, Nelle R., 801 Desert Steppes Dr., Tucson, Ariz. HONORABLE MENTION
Brewer, Beryl, 6753 Clyde, Chicago, Ill. HONORABLE MENTION
Brewer, Nancy E., 2370 Old Oxford Rd., Hamilton, Ohio HONORABLE MENTION
Brice, Julia, 70 Avon Pl., Amytiville, L.I., N.Y. Special Mention
Bridge, Lillian C., 75 Waldron Ave., Staten Island, N.Y. HONORABLE MENTION
Bridwell, Charlotte A., 605 Laramie St., Gillette, Wyo. Special Mention
Briggs, Mildred, 720 11th Ave. S., Naples, Fl. HONORABLE MENTION
Brigley, Daisy S., 6868 Flinn St., Halifax, N.S. Special Mention
Brizendine, Teresa, 1209 Lincoln Ave., Plattsmouth, Neb. Special Mention
Brogan, Mrs. Dorothy, 4481 Dogwood Dr., Batavia, Ohio Special Mention
Bromley, Alma N., 1314 N. Orient, Fairmont, Minn. HONORABLE MENTION
Brooks, Howard N., 2506 Dorrington Dr., Dallas, Tex. HONORABLE MENTION
Brooks, Jeanette B., 1021 Northside Ter., Milan, Tenn. HONORABLE MENTION
Broome, Claudia, 750 Black Ave., Flint, Mich. Special Mention
Brophy, James J., 7007 Preston Rd., Dallas, Tex. HONORABLE MENTION
Brown, Diana L., 3045 West Alice Ave., Phoenix, Ariz. HONORABLE MENTION
Brown, Mrs. Elizabeth, 120 Rose Dr. S.E., Ft. Lauderdale, Fl. Special Mention
Brown, Esther, R.R. I, Winfield, Ill. HONORABLE MENTION
Brown, Judith, Palmer Rd., Monson, Mass. Special Mention
Brown, Lynda M., 157 21st St., Costa Mesa, Cal. HONORABLE MENTION
Brown, Nona H., 193 N. 400 W. St., Cedar City, Utah HONORABLE MENTION
Brown, Sharyl, 11505 2nd Ave. N.W., Seattle, Wash. Special Mention
Brown, Winifred, Allenby Rd., R.R. 3, Duncan, B.C., Can. HONORABLE MENTION
Browning, Donna R., 33 Russell St., Plymouth, N.H. HONORABLE MENTION
Browning, Frances, Rt. I, Box 216, Waterford, Ohio Special Mention
Brownlee, Roxann, Box 205, Adrian, Tex. Special Mention
Brueske, Emily A., 900 Howell Mt. Rd., Augwin, Cal. HONORABLE MENTION
Bryant, Rachel F., Stanley Rd., Winthrop, Me. HONORABLE MENTION
Buckman, Mrs. Caroline, Box 86, Belfield, N.D. Special Mention
Buell, Clarence G., 2716 W. Pierson St., Phoenix, Ariz. HONORABLE MENTION
Buell, Stanley, R.D. 4, Corry, Pa. HONORABLE MENTION
Bulin, Mrs. Beatrice, Box 466, Teague, Tex. HONORABLE MENTION
Bullock, Mary B., 25 4th St., Bangor, Me. HONORABLE MENTION
Bundrock, Sharon E., 820 West Alabama, Houston, Tex. Special Mention
Burd, Lew A., 999 Balmer Rd., Youngstown, N.Y. Special Mention
Burhop, Kathleen A., 141 Concord Rd., Cedarburg, Wis. HONORABLE MENTION
Burt, Bonnie M., 3734 Hilltop Ct. N.E., Grand Rapids, Mich. Special Mention
Burwell, Anna W., 227 N. 2nd St. Pike, Southhampton, Pa. Special Mention

Butcher, Vivian J., 1202 E. 22nd St., Wilmington, Del.   HONORABLE MENTION
Bute, William E., 16 Red Combe Dr., Cartersville, Ga.   Special Mention
Butler, Irene, 195 Smith Lane, Houma, La.   HONORABLE MENTION
Butler, Jannabeth, 827½ Central Ave., Charleston, W.Va.   HONORABLE MENTION
Butner, Joyce, Rt. I, Advance, N.C.   HONORABLE MENTION
Butterworth, Mrs. A., P.O. Box 691, Brookline, Mass.   Special Mention
Byers, Hazel, 125½ E. Main St., Morrison, Ill.   HONORABLE MENTION
Byrne, Rosalie, 900 17th St., Apt. 2, Rock Island, Ill.   HONORABLE MENTION

=C=

Cade, Evelyn, P.O. Box 26, Bingham, Ill.   Special Mention
Cadow, William J., Temple Univ., Philadelphia, Pa.   Special Mention
Camden, Janet, 933 East St., New Britain, Conn.   Special Mention
Campbell, Candice S., 104 N. Oak Tree Dr., Glendora, Ca.   HONORABLE MENTION
Campbell, Ethel, P.O. Box 444, Orange, Tex.   Special Mention
Campbell, Judith, P.O. Box 722, Mims, Fl.   Special Mention
Campbell, Marca J., 201 N.W. End Blvd., Cape Girardeau, Mo.   Special Mention
Campbell, Patrick, 1514 S. 19th St., Birmingham, Ala.   Special Mention
Campone, Francine, 608 E. 82nd St., Brooklyn, N.Y.   HONORABLE MENTION
Cannella, Mrs. Christine, 1732 N. Honore, Chicago, Ill.   Special Mention
Carbone, Francesca C., 10975½ Roebling Ave., W. Los Angeles, Ca.   Special Mention
Carillo, Diane, 146 Schenck Blvd., Floral Park, N.Y.   Special Mention
Carlson, Charlene, 16 Deerbrook Rd., Norwich, Conn.   Special Mention
Carlson, Joyce M., 203 Lore Ave., Hillcrest, Wilm., Del.   HONORABLE MENTION
Carman, Susan, 129 West End Ave., Freeport, L.I., N.Y.   Special Mention
Carr, Leilani, 5709 Oakwood Rd., Alexandria, Va.   HONORABLE MENTION
Carroll, Mildred V., III Dowling Ave., Ozark, Ala.   HONORABLE MENTION
Carson, Brian J., 1110 W. New York St., Aurora, Ill.   HONORABLE MENTION
Carstens, Anna H., P.O. Box 3132, Lafayette, La.   Special Mention
Cartwright, Millie, 1456 San Juan, Stockton, Ca.   HONORABLE MENTION
Carusella, Sandra J., 384 Pearl Harbor St., Bridgeport, Conn.   Special Mention
Casper, Joseph A., 594 54th St., W. New York, N.J.   Special Mention
Caylor, David C., 2000 David Ave., Monterey, Ca.   Special Mention
Cayton, Linda, 2921 Elizabeth Ln., Antioch, Ca.   HONORABLE MENTION
Cerchiaro, Luette, 59 Cozy Corner, Avenel, N.J.   Special Mention
Cevene, Janet S., 719 Parkside Dr., Rockford, Ill.   Special Mention
Chamberlain, Mrs. A. P., 32 Fox Lane, Greenwich, Conn.   HONORABLE MENTION
Champagne, Floris M., Box 529, Luling, La.   Special Mention
Chandler, Rose W., Jefferson Ave., Paintsville, Ky.   Special Mention
Chaney, Clarence, 454 Dodge St., Buffalo, N.Y.   HONORABLE MENTION
Chapel, Mrs. W. L., Box 56, Tombstone, Ariz.   HONORABLE MENTION
Charest, Mrs. Gordon E., 100 N. River Rd., Manchester, N.H.   Special Mention
Christie, Susan, Red Lake Falls, Minn.   HONORABLE MENTION
Chulak, Darlene L., 470 Shelton Rd., Nichols, Conn.   Special Mention
Clabes, Judith G., 709 1st St., Henderson, Ky.   Special Mention
Clark, Alan R., Thiells Mt. Ivy Rd., Pomona, N.Y.   Special Mention
Clark, Barbara, 420 N. Church, Lodi, Ca.   HONORABLE MENTION
Clark, Bonnie J., 3231 S. Meridian St., Indianapolis, Ind.   Special Mention
Clark, Charles R., 755 Tudor Circle, Thousand Oaks, Ca.   HONORABLE MENTION
Clark, Mrs. Dorothy, 5539 Claude Ave., Hammond, Ind.   HONORABLE MENTION
Clark, George N., 510 Wash. Ave., Bremerton, Wash.   HONORABLE MENTION
Clark, William L., 105 Main St., Black River Falls, Wisc.   HONORABLE MENTION
Clarke, Faelynne, 14023 Kingsride Ln., Houston, Tex.   HONORABLE MENTION
Claybaugh, Lorraine, 4637 E. 24th St., Tucson, Ariz.   HONORABLE MENTION
Claypool, Mary E., 1344 N. Dearborn Pkwy., Chicago, Ill.   HONORABLE MENTION
Clayton, Laura E., 950 Rogers Ave., Brooklyn, N.Y.   HONORABLE MENTION
Cochran, Judy, 405 Mound St., Atchison, Kan.   HONORABLE MENTION
Coe, Bethel R., Star Rt. 36, Havre, Mont.   Special Mention
Coffett, Mrs. Janette, 34 Parlin Dr., Grove City, Ohio   Special Mention
Cofield, Mrs. Shirley A., 7011 Racine Ave., Chicago, Ill.   Special Mention
Cogswell, Ada Belle, 7356 Haskell Ave., Van Nuys, Ca.   HONORABLE MENTION
Colby, Mary, R. I, S.R. 66, Piqua, Ohio   Special Mention
Coley, Ellyn, Ben Hur, Ark.   HONORABLE MENTION
Collischan, Judy, 227½ E. Washington, Iowa City, Iowa   Special Mention

Colmenero, Tere, P.O. Box 95, Sierra Blanca, Tex. HONORABLE MENTION
Colna, James M., 406 5th St., Port Carbon, Pa. HONORABLE MENTION
Connell, Linda L., 1602 Connorvale, Houston, Tex. Special Mention
Conner, Viola, 755 N.E. 14th St., Gresham, Ore. HONORABLE MENTION
Connolly, Jack, 536 McLaughlin St., Richmond, Ca. HONORABLE MENTION
Connor, Jane, 227 Orrick Ln., Kirkwood, Mo. Special Mention
Coolen, Virginia S., 2020 Federal Ave. E., Seattle, Wash. HONORABLE MENTION
Cooper, Dorothy F., 503 E. 12th, Winfield, Kan. HONORABLE MENTION
Cooper, Sheri, P.O. Box 3489, Stanford, Ca. HONORABLE MENTION
Cordova, William, 3614 Bartlett Ave., Rosemead, Ca. HONORABLE MENTION
Cornine, Mrs. Virginia, Mt. Bethel Rd., R.D. 2, Hackettstown, N.J. Special Mention
Cornwall, Daniel R., 67 Main St., Wyoming, N.Y. HONORABLE MENTION
Cory, Richard, 216-68 68th Ave., Bayside, N.Y. Special Mention
Cosand, Larry, Box 119, Bentonville, Ark. Special Mention
Cossar, William, P.O. Box 223, Burgeo, Newfoundland HONORABLE MENTION
Cotter, Richard T., 6814 S. Maplewood Ave., Chicago, Ill. Special Mention
Coutcher, Mrs. Dorothy, 914 Kingston Ave., Toledo, Ohio Special Mention
Coutu, Mrs. Wilfred J., Main St., Box 1, Griswoldville, Mass. Special Mention
Cowsert, Patsy S., Rosiclare, Ill. Special Mention
Coyle, Jr., Mrs. Frank A., Rt. 3, Carbondale, Ill. HONORABLE MENTION
Crain, Jenni, 363 Lambeth Ln., Concord, Ca. Special Mention
Criscione, Joanne, 47 3rd St., Westfield, N.Y. HONORABLE MENTION
Crockett, Evelyn, Gen. Delivery, Marlinton, W.Va. Special Mention
Crofut, Rita, 212 New St., Beaufort, S.C. HONORABLE MENTION
Croom, McDonough, 239 Rainier Dr., Fayetteville, N.C. Special Mention
Crooker, M. Elizabeth, 218 Moreland Ave., Mankato, Minn HONORABLE MENTION
Croskey, Francis, R.D. 2, Box 31, Orrville, Ohio HONORABLE MENTION
Crowder, Jerry, Rt. 4, Box 2FF, Portland, Tenn. Special Mention
Crowley, Christian, USS Coral Sea (CVA-43), FPO, San Fran., Ca. Special Mention
Crownover, Mrs. Ruth, 3011 Sherwood Ln., Hopewell, Va. HONORABLE MENTION
Cuedek, Jessie, 62-28 79th St., Middle Village, L.I., N.Y. HONORABLE MENTION
Culbertson, Frank, Rt. 1, Box 333-B, Summerville, S.C. HONORABLE MENTION
Cullinan, Mrs. Virgene, 902 2nd St. S.W., Clarion, Iowa Special Mention
Cumming, Georgia, 2966 Pinellas Pt. Dr., St. Peters., Fl. HONORABLE MENTION
Currence, Nola J., 1111 Quantril Way, Baltimore, Md. HONORABLE MENTION
Curtain, Thorn, USA Medical Records Det., Eur., APO Special Mention
Czernega, Nannette, Fordham Univ., Bronx, N.Y. HONORABLE MENTION

=D=

D'Amico, Mrs. Emil, R. 1, Birchwood, Wisc. Special Mention
Dancy, Martella, 3852 Calumet Ave., Chicago, Ill. Special Mention
Daniel, Martha H., Box 63, Canyon, Tex. Special Mention
Daniel, Sally L., 1210 Longfellow St. N.W., Wash., D.C. HONORABLE MENTION
Danish, Susan E., 236 E. Union Blvd., Bethlehem, Pa. HONORABLE MENTION
Dann, Bernadette, R.D. 1, Rt. 287, Remsen, N.Y. HONORABLE MENTION
Darsie, Bonnie, USAID-METC, APO San Francisco HONORABLE MENTION
Dassaro, Salvatore P., 53-15 32nd Ave., Woodside, N.Y. HONORABLE MENTION
Davis, Angela, 207 Swift Dr., Goodlettsville, Tenn. Special Mention
Davis, Blanche L., 311 Hart St., Dayton, Ohio HONORABLE MENTION
Davis, Debbie, 228 Hayes Ave., Charleston, W.Va. Special Mention
Davis, Elliott H., 1033 W. Nevada St., Philadelphia, Pa. Special Mention
Day, Marian A., Warwick Apts., N.J. Bldg. 2B, Aberdeen, Md. Special Mention
DeAngelis, Mrs. Barbara, 11 Washington St., Belleville, N.J. HONORABLE MENTION
Decker, Frances M., 57 Cayuga St., Seneca Falls, N.Y. HONORABLE MENTION
Deckwa, Jr., William J., 3607 N. Robertson St., New Orleans, La. Special Mention
Deeb, Bula L., 7810 Garland Ave., Takoma Park, Md. HONORABLE MENTION
Demmerle, Barbara, 1403 Gates Ave., Brooklyn, N.Y. HONORABLE MENTION
Denning, Linda E., R. 4, Madison, Ind. Special Mention
Dennis, Doris, 1036 32nd St., Columbus, Ga. Special Mention
Dennis, Julia E., Judy's Mobile Ct., New Buffalo, Mich. Special Mention
Denton, Arthur L, 423 S.E. 22nd Ave., Apt. 3, Portland, Ore. Special Mention
Denton, Mona, 423 S.E. 22nd Ave., Apt. 3, Portland, Ore. Special Mention
DeRamo, Jr., William R., 24 Home Ave., Carnegie, Pa. Special Mention
Devere, Mildred, Golden Age Conval. Home, Baldwin Pk., Ca. Special Mention
Devore, Mrs. Barbara J., 428 5th St. N.W., New Phila., Pa. HONORABLE MENTION

Dial, Donald G., 1314 Sherwood, Baytown, Tex. HONORABLE MENTION
Dickerson, Lynda M., 1205 West Lowell, Shenandoah, Iowa Special Mention
Dickey, Mrs. Evelyn, 146 Longview Rd., Staten Is., N.Y. HONORABLE MENTION
Dietz, Eileen, 14612 S. Kolmar, Midlothian, Ill. HONORABLE MENTION
Dingess, Carolyn, 468 Palmer Ave., Logan, W.Va. HONORABLE MENTION
Doane, Richard M., 1303 S. Main Ave., Sioux Falls, S.D. Special Mention
DoBell, David A., 2003 Clark St., Ames, Iowa HONORABLE MENTION
Dobry, Mrs. Geraldine C., 916 Foxwood Ln., Balt., Md. HONORABLE MENTION
Doddson, Ora, 203 Oak Hill Dr., Carthage, Miss. Special Mention
Dodson, Rebecca, 306 S. Penn., Atoka, Okla. Special Mention
Doering, Mrs. Lester G., R.R. 2, Box 154, Davenport, Iowa Special Mention
Dolph, Leslie K., R.R. 1, Tulip Rd., New Carlisle, Ind. HONORABLE MENTION
Donald, Jenta M., Box 4, Clive, Iowa Special Mention
Donath, Andrea, Box 215, Centenary College, Hackettstown, N.J. Special Mention
Donly, M., 830 N. 2nd St., Reading, Pa. Special Mention
Donovan, Mrs. Judith C., Glen Road, No. Branford, Conn. Special Mention
Donovan, Michael, 506 S. College St., Angola, Ind. Special Mention
Dorr, Scott, 609 W. 7th, Wapato, Wash. HONORABLE MENTION
D'Ottavio, Ray, 607 Westshire Dr., Joliet, Ill. Special Mention
Douglas, Georgia, 2237 Mandeville, Los Angeles, Ca. HONORABLE MENTION
Dowling, James F., Rome-Taberg Rd., R.D., Rome, N.Y. HONORABLE MENTION
Downing, Soncha A., 203 Main St., Worden, Ill. HONORABLE MENTION
Downing, William, 435 8th St., Brooklyn, N.Y. HONORABLE MENTION
Doxtater, Richard, 191 McLeod St., Apt. 1, Ottawa, Ont., Canada Special Mention
Doyle, Myden, 3297 Rocky River Dr., Cleveland, Ohio HONORABLE MENTION
Doyon, Lory, 43 Mary Carroll St., Auburn, Me. HONORABLE MENTION
Drake, Jade, 932-C Louisiana N.E., Albuquerque, N.M. Special Mention
Drew, Lois, P.O. Box 218, Oswego, Ill. Special Mention
DuBois, Mrs. Lillian E., Box 84, New Scotland, N.Y. Special Mention
Duffy, Carol Ann, 2624 Kirkwood Pl., Hyattsville, Md. HONORABLE MENTION
Dugo, Mary Ann, 5704 S. Homan, Chicago, Ill. HONORABLE MENTION
Duncan, Mary, 300 W. Glebe Rd., Alexandria, Va. HONORABLE MENTION
Dungill, Gloria, 1708 Steuben St., Chicago, Ill. Special Mention
Dunham, Florence, Newport, Ark. Special Mention
Dunlap, Charles, 30 Mason, Hammond, Ind. Special Mention
Dunn, Candace K., 104-20 Byrne Ave., CuPertino, Ca. Special Mention
Dunn, Mrs. Maude W., 508 S. Buchanan Blvd., Durhan, N.C. Special Mention
Dunn, Roxann, 17630 42nd Ave. S., Seattle, Wash. Special Mention
Dunn, Jr., William P., 1301 15th St., N.W., Apt. 221, Wash., D.C. Special Mention

=E=

Earl, Oressa N., 213 Arcadia, Champaign, Ill. Special Mention
Early, Beverly, P.O. Box 215, Old Fort, N.C. Special Mention
Eberdt, Mary G., 2422-D Bowen St., Oshkosh, Wis. HONORABLE MENTION
Eckblad, Mrs. Edith B., 5224 Spring St., Racine, Wis. Special Mention
Eckel, Faye A., 172 Huntington Dr., Northfield, Ohio HONORABLE MENTION
Eckels, Mrs. Kay, Rt. 2, Box 148, Aurora, Mo. HONORABLE MENTION
Eckland, Mrs. Ruth, 22 N. 12th St., Keohuk, Iowa Special Mention
Edens, James, 6550 Madison, Hammond, Ind. HONORABLE MENTION
Edmondson, Pearl, 52 W. Evergreen Ave., Youngstown, Ohio Special Mention
Edson, James E., 88 Conway St., Greenfield, Mass. Special Mention
Edwards, Thomas, 491 Green St., Cambridge, Mass. HONORABLE MENTION
Edwerd, Marei E., 28 Grant St., Liberty, N.Y. HONORABLE MENTION
Eldridge, Jessie C., 35 Maple St., Kingston, Mass. Special Mention
Elfers, Viola H., 155 Blake Dr., Skyland, N.C. HONORABLE MENTION
Ellies, Mabel B., 224 N. Hinde St., Wash. Ct. Hse., Ohio HONORABLE MENTION
Ellingwood, Diana J., 7569 Blair Ave., Rohnert Park, Ca. Special Mention
Ellis, Mrs. Coolidge, 714-E Pendleton St., Marion, Va. Special Mention
Ellis, Myra P., 15 Marion Pl., Everett, Mass. HONORABLE MENTION
Elmquist, Evangeline, Rt. 1, Box 75, Hoffman, Minn. HONORABLE MENTION
Elmquist, May, Rt. 1, Box 75, Hoffman, Minn. HONORABLE MENTION
Ely, Nancy, 5366 Lawton Ave., Oakland, Ca. Special Mention
Emerick, Gerard, 222 W. Main St., Boonton, N.J. HONORABLE MENTION
Engstrom, Catherine S., 303 Rosemont Ave., Newfield, N.J. Special Mention
Enlow, Mrs. Margie L., 2276 E. Keys, Springfield, Ill. Special Mention

Erdman, Olive, Box 73, Chester, Ohio — Special Mention
Erickson, Blythe A., 2603 S. 8th, Apt. 551-B, Arlington, Va. — Special Mention
Esch, Anne, 3732 W. 115th St., Chicago, Ill. — HONORABLE MENTION
Evans, Mrs. Yvonne, R.R. I, Brownsville St., Vandalia, Mich. — Special Mention
Everett, Bobbi, 139 W. 6th St., Dover, Ohio — HONORABLE MENTION

=F=

Faber, Frances, 6616 Agnes Ave., North Hollywood, Ca. — Special Mention
Fahey, Ellen A., 55 S. Quaker Ln., W. Hartford, Conn. — HONORABLE MENTION
Fairfield, Frances, 516 W. Grant St., Thorntown, Ind. — HONORABLE MENTION
Faisy, Helen E., 24731 Winlock Dr., Torrance, Ca. — Special Mention
Farber, Joe, 109 E. Gass Ave., Las Vegas, Nev. — HONORABLE MENTION
Farley, Myrtle, 1644 N. 16th Ave., Melrose Pk., Ill. — HONORABLE MENTION
Farlow, Grace A., 315 Cornelia Ave., Lakeland, Fl. — Special Mention
Farlow, Jean B., 3764 Gordinier Hall, MSC, Millersville, Pa. — Special Mention
Farrell, Freida E., 1027 Cresswell St., Pittsburgh, Pa. — Special Mention
Fasciani, Jr., Henry, 2350 Creston Ave., Bronx, N.Y. — Special Mention
Fechner, Jill, Rt. 3, Box 290-N, Springfield, Mo. — Special Mention
Fehskens, Clarice A., 442 Painter Dr., West Haven, Conn. — HONORABLE MENTION
Feld, Ruth, 4240 Olson Memorial Hwy., Golden Valley, Minn. — Special Mention
Feller, Louise, 224-02 Stronghurst Ave., Queens Village, N.Y. — Special Mention
Fellows, Evy S., P.O. Box 1114, Eau Gallie, Fl. — HONORABLE MENTION
Ferrarini, Barbra, 190 N. State St., ABC-TV, Chicago, Ill. — Special Mention
Field, Ruth B., 23 N. Main St., Tray, N.H. — Special Mention
Fierke, Mrs. Oscar, P.O. Box 1723, Yakima, Wash. — HONORABLE MENTION
Figge, Rosalie, 403 Day St., Decorah, Iowa — Special Mention
Filipek, Mrs. Louise, 5738 S. Narragansett, Chicago, Ill. — HONORABLE MENTION
Finch, Donald G., V.A. Hospital, Ward 102-3, Danville, Ill. — HONORABLE MENTION
Fincher, Mrs. Patricia A., 1623 W. 14th St., Texarkana, Tex. — Special Mention
Finnerty, Kathleen, 1069 Gerard Ave., Bronx, N.Y. — HONORABLE MENTION
Fish, Gloria J., 422 Mulberry, Apt. 7, Lake Mills, Wis. — Special Mention
Fitzgerald, Esther J., 57 Parkway Crescent, Milton, Mass. — Special Mention
Fleck, Mrs. Evelyn L., 515 E. National Ave., Indianapolis, Ind. — Special Mention
Flood, Rory A., Windswept, Goldens Bridge, N.Y. — HONORABLE MENTION
Florian, Cecilia, 1257 S. Greenwood, Montebello, Ca. — HONORABLE MENTION
Floyd, Eleanor J., 5562 Fleetwell Ave., Azusa, Ca. — HONORABLE MENTION
Fogell, Louise E., 18426 Poinciana, Detroit, Mich. — HONORABLE MENTION
Foil, Rita M., 324 Baldwin St., Elmira, N.Y. — HONORABLE MENTION
Forbes, Mary E., 2513 Sherborn Rd., Springfield, Ill. — Special Mention
Force, Mrs. Elizabeth W., 4242 3rd Ave. N., St. Petersburg, Fl. — Special Mention
Forrest, Ida M., 3163 Wingate Dr., Murrysville, Pa. — Special Mention
Fortunato, Mrs. Catherine, 55 S. Ridgedale Ave., Hanover, N.J. — Special Mention
Foster, Cecilia, Box 37, Port Royal, S.C. — HONORABLE MENTION
Fountain, M. Sue, 4167 Morro Dr., Woodland Hills, Ca. — HONORABLE MENTION
Fourcaud, L. H. P., 20 Craig Pl., Clifton, N.J. — HONORABLE MENTION
Fowler, Jean C., 915 Greenwood Ave. N.E., Atlanta, Ga. — HONORABLE MENTION
Frank, Karen, 3157 Nilden Ave., Pittsburgh, Pa. — Special Mention
Franklyn, Elizabeth J., 3700 N. 66th St., Birmingham, Ala. — Special Mention
Fraser, Robert B., Scottish Home, N. Riverside, Ill. — HONORABLE MENTION
Frazier, Karen, 1220 Hoover, Great Bend, Kan. — HONORABLE MENTION
Frazier, Larry, 210 Post Ave., Fayetteville, N.C. — HONORABLE MENTION
Fredricks, Arthur J., 801 E. Judd, Greenville, Mich. — Special Mention
Freedman, Gertrude, 22 Fairfield Ave., Danbury, Conn. — HONORABLE MENTION
Freehling, Dorothy D., 1330 Broadview Blvd., Natrona Hghts., Pa. — Special Mention
Frick, Louise, 39-18 223rd St., Bayside, N.Y. — HONORABLE MENTION
Fries, Daisy C., 216½ N. Maple Ave., Martinsburg, W.Va. — Special Mention
Fritz, C. C., 5240 N. Sheridan Rd., Chicago, Ill. — HONORABLE MENTION
Fuchs, Mrs. Edna, R. 2, Sheridan, Ill. — HONORABLE MENTION
Fulton, Mrs. Nyle, Rt. 2, Aitkin, Minn. — HONORABLE MENTION
Furgason, Vickie, 954 Bluff St., Beloit, Wis. — Special Mention

=G=

Gabriele, Joy A., 22 Flanders St., Johnston, R.I. — HONORABLE MENTION

Gaiser, Azalia B., 506 9th Ave., Worthington, Minn.   HONORABLE MENTION
Galiber, Eva L., 841 Estaban Gonzalez, Rio Piedras, P.R.   HONORABLE MENTION
Gallagher, Barbara J., RFD I, Box 238, Gales Ferry, Conn. HONORABLE MENTION
Gallagher, Clare, 12174 Whitehill, Detroit, Mich.   Special Mention
Galea, Patricia A., 332 W. 12th St., Deer Park, N.Y.   Special Mention
Galea, Sylvia, 332 W. 12th St., Deer Park, N.Y.   Special Mention
Gallo, Louise, 431 Kings Hwy., Brooklyn, N.Y.   Special Mention
Gammon, Anne M., 2786 Broadway, North Bend, Ore.   Special Mention
Gant, Patricia A., 3215 Ely Pl. S.E., Wash., D.C.   Special Mention
Garber, Hazel L., R. 7, Box 194, Elkhart, Ind.   Special Mention
Gard, Robert J., 1609 Sicard St., Marysville, Ca.   Special Mention
Garrett, Gertrude M., R.R. I, Hillsboro, Ohio   HONORABLE MENTION
Garrison, Michael L., Rt. I, Box 580, Trussville, Ala.   Special Mention
Garver, Nancy M., 1825 Jackson Ave. N.W., Massillon, Ohio   Special Mention
Gatzka, Linda M., 5298 Proctor, Detroit, Mich.   HONORABLE MENTION
Gatzka, Nancy J., 5298 Proctor, Detroit, Mich.   HONORABLE MENTION
Gatzka, Theresa M., 5298 Proctor, Detroit, Mich.   HONORABLE MENTION
Gavaris, Steven J., 2744 N. Francisco Ave., Chicago, Ill.   Special Mention
Gaylor, G. Avanelle, Box 456, Ellinwood, Kan.   HONORABLE MENTION
Gee, Blanche M., 2233 Muscoday Pass, Ft. Wayne, Ind.   Special Mention
Gentilcore, Rosemary K., 633 Fiot Ave., Bethlehem, Pa.   HONORABLE MENTION
George, Wanda, Rt. 5, Booneville, Miss.   Special Mention
Gerics, Joan, 312 Unqua Rd., Massapequa, L.I., N.Y.   Special Mention
Gerritzen, Mary K., Box 244, Bison, Kan.   HONORABLE MENTION
Gibbs, Bonnie B., 7542 Teasdale Ave., St. Louis, Mo.   HONORABLE MENTION
Gier, Regina E., 20 Melroy St., Lackawanna, N.Y.   HONORABLE MENTION
Gieraltouski, Rita, 4616 N. Sayre, Harwood Heights, Ill.   Special Mention
Giles, Mrs. Lucille H., 9852 Calumet Ave., Chicago, Ill.   HONORABLE MENTION
Gillan, Mary, 4851 S. 24th St., Greenfield, Wis.   HONORABLE MENTION
Gillespie, Geraldine, 2005 Brown St., Wichita Falls, Tex.   Special Mention
Gilley, Geraldine H., Rt. 3, Box 211, Ridgeway, Va.   HONORABLE MENTION
Gilmore, Zelda M., Box 32, Kearsarge, N.H.   Special Mention
Giordano, Dora E., P.O. Box 39, Willow, Alas.   Special Mention
Giordano, Marilyn, P.O. Box 39, Willow, Alas.   HONORABLE MENTION
Gladden, Dorothy F., 49½ Clayton St., Asheville, N.C.   Special Mention
Glaser, Frances M., 3301 W. 58th St., Cleveland, Ohio   Special Mention
Gleason, Olive, 8 McGreevey Way, Roxbury, Mass.   HONORABLE MENTION
Glenn, Alice H., Box 656, Eden, Tex.   HONORABLE MENTION
Gloss, Robert, 2606 7th Ave., East Meadow, N.Y.   Special Mention
Goehring, Paula, 728 Dean St., Kent, Wash.   HONORABLE MENTION
Goff, Mrs. Bernard D., Rt. 3, Box 108, Gainesville, Fl.   Special Mention
Goldberg, Beverly K., 8662 Cromwell Dr., Springfield, Va. HONORABLE MENTION
Golden, Susan R., 115 E. Hellman Ave., Alhambra, Ca.   HONORABLE MENTION
Goldman, Margaret, Old Rt. 17, Rock Hill, N.Y.   Special Mention
Goldy, Nellie, 626 High St., Wabash, Ind.   HONORABLE MENTION
Gonzales, Virginia I., 550 Iris St., Redwood City, Ca.   Special Mention
Goodman, Joan, 4903 N. Hayne Ave., Chicago, Ill.   Special Mention
Goodman, Patsy A., 316-2 Doniphan, Ft. Leavenworth, Kan.   Special Mention
Goodwin, Margaret, 295 N. Garland, Memphis, Tenn.   Special Mention
Goodwine, Alice D., 518 E. Lincoln St., Hoopeston, Ill.   HONORABLE MENTION
Gorse, Marie E., 283 Grove St., Charleston, S.C.   Special Mention
Gourse, Mrs. Alice O., 770 Highview Ave., Somerset, Mass. HONORABLE MENTION
Gower, JoLynn, 1719 N. Neil, Champaign, Ill.   HONORABLE MENTION
Graber, Nat, Rt. 2, Box 101, Broadway, Va.   Special Mention
Graber, William D., 2913 S. 4th St., Springfield, Ill.   Special Mention
Graber, Mrs. William R., 2913 S. 4th St., Springfield, Ill.   Special Mention
Grable, Laurel L., Monticello College, Godfrey, Ill.   Special Mention
Gray, Roberta M., 2086 Walnut Rd., Pontiac, Mich.   Special Mention
Green, Bonita M., 709 Hacienda St., Anaheim, Ca.   HONORABLE MENTION
Green, Gladys, 1014 Market St., Emporia, Kan.   HONORABLE MENTION
Green, Thilbert L., 400 Mitchell, Bryan, Tex.   HONORABLE MENTION
Greene, George L., Rt. I, Box 240, Crawfordville, Fl.   Special Mention
Greene, M. E., 107-10 Shorefront Pkwy., Rockaway Pk., N.Y.   Special Mention
Greenside, Linda, RFD I, Augusta Rd., Vassalboro, Me.   HONORABLE MENTION
Greenwald, Alice, 234 Washington Ave., Cedarhurst, N.Y.   Special Mention

Gregory, Margaret L., 3005 E. Loretta Dr., Tucson, Ariz.   Special Mention
Gregory, Sharon, 71 Campbell Ave., Cuddy, Pa.   HONORABLE MENTION
Grey, Joy, Rt. 2, Box 85, Ronceverte, W.Va.   HONORABLE MENTION
Griffen, Gwen, 1024 Waveland Rd., Lake Forest, Ill.   Special Mention
Griffin, Dorothy M., 3012 Dogwood Dr., Louisville, Ky.   Special Mention
Griffin, Mildred E., 514 Woodside Ave., Bridgeport, Conn. HONERABLE MENTION
Griffith, Nancy, P.O. Box 415, Bentonville, Ark.   Special Mention
Griswold, Bernice P., Box 53, Bonanza, Utah   HONORABLE MENTION
Grove, Marlene J., 328 E. Market St., York, Pa.   HONORABLE MENTION
Grygon, Joseph E., 604 Covington Terrace, Moorestown, N.J.   Special Mention
Guille, Mrs. Helia E., 2325 N.E. Flanders St., Port., Ore.   HONORABLE MENTION
Guinn, Marie Y., 733 N.E. 2nd St., Gainesville, Fl.   HONORABLE MENTION
Guy, George, 7747 18th Ave. N.W., Seattle, Wash.   Special Mention
Guzowski, Leon P., 81 Germain St., Buffalo, N.Y.   Special Mention
Gyenes, Eva, 34 Orchard St., Yonkers, N.Y.   Special Mention

=H=

Hachache, Kathleen, 4109 Ocean Dr., Lauderdale-by-the-Sea, Fl.   Special Mention
Hagedorn, Charlotte L., 1639 Marlowe Ave., Cincin., Ohio HONORABLE MENTION
Hahn, Virginia A., 7475 Kirk Rd., Canfield, Ohio   HONORABLE MENTION
Hairston, Josephine, Rt. 1, Box 347, Martinsville, Va.   Special Mention
Hall, Mrs. Bernice, 3315 Alto Rd., Baltimore, Md.   Special Mention
Hall, Beverly, 907 Adams St., Signal Mtn., Tenn.   HONORABLE MENTION
Hall, J., 1130 Carukin St., Franklin Sq., N.Y.   HONORABLE MENTION
Hall, Sr., Milford, McDowell, Ky.   HONORABLE MENTION
Hall, Natalie R., 3315 Alto Rd., Baltimore, Md.   Special Mentión
Halterman, Lois E., Warrenton, Mo.   Special Mention
Hamilton, Lera B., 320 Calhoun St., West Point, Miss.   HONORABLE MENTION
Hamilton, Phyllis G., 31960 Dolly Madison Dr., Madison Hts., Mich. Special Mention
Hamm, Janet L., Rt. 2, Box 500, Cherryville, N.C.   Special Mention
Hammel, Leslie E., 1517 Wynnewood Rd., Columbia, S.C.   Special Mention
Hammel, Robert J., 1517 Wynnewood Rd., Columbia, S.C.   Special Mention
Hammer, Lillian, 2820 Bronx Pk. E., Bronx, N.Y.   HONORABLE MENTION
Hancock, Jeanette, 5050 N. Sheridan Rd., Chicago, Ill.   HONORABLE MENTION
Handloser, Delma, 824 Rogers Ct., Ashland, Ky.   Special Mention
Handy, Margaret, 1101 Payne St., San Augustine, Tex.   Special Mention
Haney, Jane M., 8959 E. Woodland Rd., Tucson, Ariz.   HONORABLE MENTION
Hankey, Georgiana, 413 Columbus St., Grove City, Ohio   HONORABLE MENTION
Harden, Mrs. Ray, Box M-10, Mendon, Ohio   HONORABLE MENTION
Hardesty, Mrs. Caroline I., 2716 W. Pierson St., Phoenix, Ariz.   Special Mention
Harding, Robert S., 5904 Cranston Rd., Wash., D.C.   HONORABLE MENTION
Harman, Marilyn, 412 N. Broad, Shenandoah, Iowa   Special Mention
Harper, Mrs. Esther, 1307 Washington St., Wilm., Del.   HONORABLE MENTION
Harper, Mrs. Lovetta I., 2103 A Genie Loop S.E., Krtld. AFB, N.M. Special Mention
Harpster, Sandra, 5622 N. 16th St., Omaha, Neb.   Special Mention
Harrington, Jr., J. F., 503 Birmingham Ave., Norfolk, Va. HONORABLE MENTION
Harris, Bill, P.O. Box 155, Elkton, Ky.   HONORABLE MENTION
Harris, Delores E., 3341 Ashley Ln., Indianapolis, Ind.   Special Mention
Harris, Esther E., 730 Augusta Ave., Elgin, Ill.   HONORABLE MENTION
Harrison, Ralph, 2390 Pecan Circle, Memphis, Tenn.   Special Mention
Harrison, Robert C., N. New Mexico State, El Rito, N.M.   Special Mention
Harshman, JoAnn, Box 46, Silver Lake, Ore.   Special Mention
Hart, Esta A., 1107 Wisconsin Ave., Pittsburgh, Pa.   HONORABLE MENTION
Hart, Shirley A., 800 Young's Ln., Nashville, Tenn.   Special Mention
Hartmann, Ruth A., 300 W. 5th St., Marshfield, Wis.   HONORABLE MENTION
Hartwig, Helen M., 2403 Washington Ln., Davenport, Iowa   Special Mention
Harvey, Margie B., 205 Water St., Seagoville, Tex.   HONORABLE MENTION
Harvey, Olga A., 59 Mayo St., Caribou, Me.   HONORABLE MENTION
Hash, Jr., Dr. Cecil J., 250 Iven Ave., St. Davids, Pa.   HONORABLE MENTION
Hash, Judith C., 250 Iven Ave., St. Davids, Pa.   Special Mention
Hatch, Jane, 10543 Cowan Rd., Hanover, Mich.   Special Mention
Hatfield, Myrtle M., 18 Bacon St., Apt. 6, Waltham, Mass.   Special Mention
Haugen, Patrick, 165 15th Ave. W., Babylon, N.Y.   Special Mention
Hauptmann, Mildred, 1060 Lincoln Way, C. D'Alene, Id.   HONORABLE MENTION

Havens, Charlotte, 1205 Elm Ave., West Collingswood, N.J.	Special Mention
Havens, Melline, Rt. I, Enid, Miss.	Special Mention
Hawkins, SuzAnne, Rt. 2, Box 238, New Bern, N.C.	Special Mention
Hayes, Carol M., Robin Hill Rd., Marlboro, Mass.	HONORABLE MENTION
Hayes, Noreen, 809 Hillcrest, DeKalb, Ill.	HONORABLE MENTION
Hayworth, Charles N., 810 B St., Petaluma, Ca.	HONORABLE MENTION
Headapohl, B. R., 655 Columbia Dr., Lima, Ohio	HONORABLE MENTION
Heath, Mrs. Lynn K., P.O. Box 544, Pataskala, Ohio	HONORABLE MENTION
Heath, Olive, 829 Greendale Ave., Needham, Mass.	Special Mention
Hecht, Nina R., 1214 E. 66th, Tacoma, Wash.	Special Mention
Hedges, Mary R., 2518 W. Farmington Rd., Peoria, Ill.	HONORABLE MENTION
Heefner, Mrs. Rodney R., 1036 Harris Dr., Emmaus, Pa.	HONORABLE MENTION
Heibel, Monica C., R.R. I, Dorr, Mich.	Special Mention
Heikkinen, Peggy, 2364 15th Ave. E., North St. Paul, Minn.	Special Mention
Hein, Mrs. Flo, Box 12, Hayden, Colo.	HONORABLE MENTION
Heinrich, June S., 1255 N. Sandburg Ter., Chicago, Ill.	HONORABLE MENTION
Helms, Mrs. Marie, Rt. 7, Box 224A, Chillicothe, Ohio	Special Mention
Hemenway, Mark, R.D. 2, Gouverneur, N.Y.	HONORABLE MENTION
Henderson, Mrs. Jane, 526 Crane St., San Antonio, Tex.	HONORABLE MENTION
Hendricks, Elizabeth A., R.R. I, Sterling, Ill.	Special Mention
Hendrickson, Maryann, Plymouth St. College, Plymouth, N.H.	Special Mention
Herman, Edwin P., 1420 Milner Crscnt., Birmingham, Ala.	Special Mention
Hewitt, Zoe A. E., 2910 Galindo St., Oakland, Ca.	HONORABLE MENTION
Hickman, Deane, 8723 E. Myrtle, Mesa, Ariz.	HONORABLE MENTION
Hickman, Susan E., Box 285, Onset Beach, Mass.	HONORABLE MENTION
Hicks, Ronald E., 5117 Raintree Ave., El Paso, Tex.	HONORABLE MENTION
Higgins, Mrs. Jean C., 2 Roberts Rd., Malvern, Pa.	HONORABLE MENTION
Higgs, Teresa, 15645 Ambaum Blvd. S.W., Seattle, Wash.	Special Mention
Hill, Anne M., II Cottage St., Cambridge, Mass.	Special Mention
Hill, Donald E., Box 14, Guernsey, Wyo.	Special Mention
Hill, Gregory, 6128 N. Kenmore, Chicago, Ill.	Special Mention
Hill, Maurice, P.O. Box 4241, Greensboro, N.C.	Special Mention
Hill, Sr., Valdemar A., P.O. Box 712, St. Thomas, V.I.	HONORABLE MENTION
Hobbs, Christopher R., 20549 Wisteria St., Castro V., Ca.	HONORABLE MENTION
Hodgson, Dean A., 203 May St., Cadillac, Mich.	HONORABLE MENTION
Hoesley, Bonnie J., 377 Washington, Winona, Minn.	HONORABLE MENTION
Hoffmann, Richard C., 3200 5th St. S., Arlington, Va.	Special Mention
Hojara, Mrs. M. E. S., 225 E. Milton St., S. Bend, Ind.	HONORABLE MENTION
Holbrook, V., 4409 Orchard Ln., Obetz, Ohio	Special Mention
Holiman, Ruby L., 512 Glenn St., Scott City, Kan.	HONORABLE MENTION
Hollan, Maureen P., 734 Bridgeman Ter., Towson, Md.	Special Mention
Holland, David O., 441 Vananda, Ajo, Ariz.	Special Mention
Holland, Paula, P.O. Box 255, Cashion, Ariz.	Special Mention
Holmes, Fielda, Box 24, Westfield, Me.	Special Mention
Holve, Shawn, Rt. 5, Box 349, Idaho Falls, Id.	HONORABLE MENTION
Homrich, Mrs. Ronald, R.R. I, Dorr, Mich.	HONORABLE MENTION
Hood, Evelyn, 4541 Houston Ave., Macon, Ga.	HONORABLE MENTION
Hopkins, Bruce, 2732½ Lydia St., Jacksonville, Fl.	HONORABLE MENTION
Hopkins, Edith I., Box 133, Wayland, Ky.	Special Mention
Hopkins, Frances G., Topsides Ln., Newtown, Conn.	Special Mention
Hopkins, Mrs. Rosa M., 2211 Weaver Ln., Baltimore, Md.	HONORABLE MENTION
Hopkins, Smith A., 113 Craig St., Fulton, Ky.	HONORABLE MENTION
Hopkins, Zandra, 247 Easmor Cirl., Palm Springs, Ca.	HONORABLE MENTION
Hopson, Mrs. Gwen A., 825 S. Monroe St., Arlington, Va.	Special Mention
Horner, Daniel, 5310 W. 50th St. Ter., Shawnee Mis., Kan.	HONORABLE MENTION
Hornigold, Mrs. Ellen, 19 Ashford Ave., Teesside, England	Special Mention
Horton, Donna, 1563 Genoa Pl., Columbus, Ohio	Special Mention
Horton, Mary, 74102 Wentworth Ave., Chicago, Ill.	Special Mention
Horvereid, Steve, 3044 Buchanan St. N.E., Minneapolis, Minn.	Special Mention
Houk, Ella L., 783 30th Ave. N., St. Petersburg, Fl.	HONORABLE MENTION
Howell, Violet, Rt. I, Box 75B (Soda Bay), Lake Co., Ca.	HONORABLE MENTION
Howze, Mrs. Patricia, 1530-B Orange Grove Rd., Charleston, S.C.	Special Mention
Hoyt, Jeanette L., 720 Mary Jane St., Lebanon, Ill.	HONORABLE MENTION
Hubbard, Rheid, 2134 Shelby St., Indianapolis, Ind.	Special Mention
Hudnut, Irene, Williamstown, Mo.	HONORABLE MENTION

Huff, L. Gertrude, 227 N. 2nd St. Pike, Southampton, Pa. HONORABLE MENTION
Huffman, Mrs. Laurie A., 1074 Millcreek Way, Salt Lake City, Utah Special Mention
Hughes, Mrs. E. E., R.R. 2, Huntington, Ind.   HONERABLE MENTION
Hughson, Robert S., 34 Caroline St., Albion, N.Y.   Special Mention
Hulen, Catherine L., 1017 E. 19th St., Santa Ana, Ca.   Special Mention
Hulteen, Mae F., 7503 Belle Field Ave., Oxon Hill, Md.   HONORABLE MENTION
Humme, Pamela T., 4 Milford Rd., Newport News, Va.   Special Mention
Humme, Patricia L., 4 Milford Rd., Newport News, Va.   Special Mention
Hunt, Judie R., 712 Ruby St., Jackson, S.C.   HONORABLE MENTION
Hunter, Arlene J., 7986 B Catalina, Millington, Tenn.   Special Mention
Hunter, Mrs. Betty, River Rd., Lyme, N.H.   HONORABLE MENTION
Hurd, Mrs. Virginia, 4406 B Santa Ana, Cudahy, Ca.   Special Mention
Hurrelbrink, Sue, Rt. 5, Box 164, Lawrence, Kan.   Special Mention
Hurst, George S., 45 Dundee St., Buffalo, N.Y.   HONORABLE MENTION
Hutchison, Anita, 762 26th St., Manhattan Beach, Ca.   Special Mention
Hutsenpiller, Connie, Box 5204, Charleston, W.Va.   HONORABLE MENTION
Huttoe, Christopher, Rt. 4, Box 335, Eastman, Ga.   HONORABLE MENTION

=I=

Ingram, Louise, Mountain Rd., Somers, Conn.   Special Mention
Inman, Alta, 111½ S. Locust St., Pana, Ill.   Special Mention
Irwin, Kathy, R.D. 1, Box 77, Jeannette, Pa.   HONORABLE MENTION
Israel, Annie M., 513 S. Cedar Ave., Marshfield, Wis.   Special Mention

=J=

Jackovitch, Mrs. Kathryn, 488 Canova Dr., Akron, Ohio   Special Mention
Jackson, Mrs. Pat, 3101 Market St., Burlington, Iowa   HONORABLE MENTION
Jacobi, Margaret W., 3900 N. Charles St., Baltimore, Md. HONORABLE MENTION
Jacobs, Anna F., Box 77, Ursina, Pa.   Special Mention
Jacobs, M. G., Box K, The Plains, Ohio   HONORABLE MENTION
Jacobson, Dana, 477 Fillmore St., Twin Falls, Id.   HONORABLE MENTION
Jaeger, Ruth B., 1 Hilltop Dr., Roselle, Ill.   Special Mention
James, Craig S., 6810 Alloway St. E., Worthington, Ohio HONORABLE MENTION
James, Gary, 82 Mira Monte Dr., Moraga, Ca.   Special Mention
Jarmow, Betty M., 1027 Cardwell, Garden City, Mich. HONORABLE MENTION
Jarvis, R. E., 1412 W. Chase, Chicago, Ill.   HONORABLE MENTION
Jaynes, Iris, P.O. Box 48, Waynesville, N.C.   Special Mention
Jehle, Dorothy E., 2642 Central Dr., Flossmoor, Ill.   HONORABLE MENTION
Jenkins, A., 541 W. 15th Ave. Sp-22, Escondido, Ca.   Special Mention
Jenkins, Raymond, Hardwicke, N.B., Canada   HONORABLE MENTION
Jenkinson, Jennie S., 315 N. La Grange Rd., La G. Pk., Ill. HONORABLE MENTION
Jennings, Mrs. Goldie A., 353 W. Green St., Scottsburg, Ind.   Special Mention
Jensen, Magny L., 2191 Harbor Blvd., Costa Mesa, Ca.   Special Mention
Jenson, Diane, 109 S. 9th St., River Falls, Wis.   HONORABLE MENTION
Jeremiah, Benjamin A., 1551 W. Fern St., Shamokin, Pa.   Special Mention
Jewell, Linda, 7728 Devon St., Philadelphia, Pa.   Special Mention
Jezek, Joanne, Box 214, Colburn Rd., Staffordvle., Conn. HONORABLE MENTION
Johnson, Albertina G., Box 232, Blaine, Wash.   HONORABLE MENTION
Johnson, Benjamin L., 4545 112th Ave. N.E., Krkld., Wsh. HONORABLE MENTION
Johnson, Brenda, 907 American Ave., Waukesha, Wis.   Special Mention
Johnson, Claire, 341 North St., Woodhand, Ca.   HONORABLE MENTION
Johnson, Debbie, P.O. Box 671, Los Banos, Ca.   Special Mention
Johnson, Mrs. H. E., OK Rt., Gainesville, Mo.   HONORABLE MENTION
Johnson, June, 1490 Pear St., Ann Arbor, Mich.   HONORABLE MENTION
Johnson, Patricia A., Rt. 1, Box 204, Sebeka, Minn.   HONORABLE MENTION
Jones, Mrs. Bruce, R.R. 2, Fairfield, Iowa   HONORABLE MENTION
Jones, Carolyn S., 3561 St. Mary's Rd., Columbus, Ga.   HONORABLE MENTION
Jones, Ellen, 213 1 St. S.E., Wash., D.C.   HONORABLE MENTION
Jones, Mrs. Fred, 178 Main St., Auburn, Me.   Special Mention
Jones, Janet E., H.Q.U.S.E.U.C.O.M., APO N.Y.   HONORABLE MENTION
Jones, Joy B., 529 E. Walnut Ln., Philadelphia, Pa.   HONORABLE MENTION
Jones, Mrs. Melvin, 1977 15th St., Chehalis, Wash.   HONORABLE MENTION
Jones, Wanda Gail, Rt. 2, Box 272, Reidsville, N.C.   Special Mention

Jones, Willie M., 723 Residence St., Moscow, Id.　　HONORABLE MENTION
Jordan, Mrs. Betty L., 1836 Polk St. N.E., Minneapolis, Minn.　　Special Mention
Jordan, Glenwood L., Rt. 5, Box 554, Falmouth, Va.　　Special Mention
Jordan, Gracie M., Rt. 5, Box 590, Falmouth, Va.　　Special Mention
Judge, Kae, 1122 Snyder Ave., Scranton, Pa.　　HONORABLE MENTION
Julian, Don, Cedarland Park, Southbury, Conn.　　HONORABLE MENTION
Julian, Teresa, Rt. 2, Box 518, W. Frankfort, Ill.　　HONORABLE MENTION
Jusa, Robert, 7 C Rolla, Ft. Leonard Wood, Mo.　　HONORABLE MENTION

=K=

Kane, Marjorie A., 2802 Broad Ave., Altoona, Pa.　　HONORABLE MENTION
Kanellis, Ramona T., 1806 7th Ave. S.E., Cedar Rpds., Ia.　　HONORABLE MENTION
Kanowsky, Jeanette M., 4118 Lanterman Ln., La Canada, Ca.　　Special Mention
Kaspin, Mrs. Louis, 4829 N. Lawndale, Chicago, Ill.　　Special Mention
Kavelman, Pam, 228 Mae Smith Tower, Carbondale, Ill.　　HONORABLE MENTION
Kay, Rena, 724 W. 18th St., Chicago, Ill.　　HONORABLE MENTION
Kearns, Virginia V., 6100 Cartwright Ave., N. Hollywd., Ca.　　Special Mention
Keeley, Lillian, 23741 Gulf Ave., Wilmington, Ca.　　Special Mention
Keen, Annetta, 2789 Walker Dr., Yorktown Heights, N.Y.　HONORABLE MENTION
Kehler, David, 19 Hollyhock Ln., Levittown, Pa.　　Special Mention
Keirns, Virginia, 3001 N.W. 174th St., Opa Locka, Fl.　　HONORABLE MENTION
Keiser, Ethelynn, 1697 Hyde Dr., Los Gatos, Ca.　　HONORABLE MENTION
Kellas, Rick, 619 S. 23rd St., Arlington, Va.　　Special Mention
Kelleher, Francis T., Lincoln Ave., Apt. F10, Clementon, N.J.　　Special Mention
Kelley, Brian, 83 Welles Dr., Newington, Conn.　　HONORABLE MENTION
Kelley, Stephanie L., 212 Regent St., Saratoga Spgs., N.Y.　HONORABLE MENTION
Kelley, Zula, N. Main St., Lynn, Ind.　　HONORABLE MENTION
Kelly, May, Box 674, King's Park, L.I., N.Y.　　HONORABLE MENTION
Kelsey, Ernestine, 216 Wakewa Ave., S. Bend, Ind.　　Special Mention
Kennedy, Narvie L., Rt. 2, Box 183, Jefferson, S.C.　　Special Mention
Kervinen, Armi, Stockholmsv 72, Saltsjobaden 13300, Sweden　　Special Mention
Key, Gwendolyn G., Rt. 1, Tallapoosa, Ga.　　Special Mention
Key, Joan, 2310 Stanford, Garland, Tex.　　Special Mention
Keyes, Rodney C., 1835 Old N. Umpqua Hwy., Glide, Ore.　　Special Mention
Kilburg, Cathy, 334 Hetrick Dr., Galion, Ohio　　HONORABLE MENTION
Kilmer, Victoria D., 415 Suburban Pkwy., Norfolk, Va.　　HONORABLE MENTION
Kimmel, Leilani, 833 Kimberley, Apt. 5, DeKalb, Ill.　　HONORABLE MENTION
King, Clare A., 11142 Osage Ave., Lennox, Ca.　　Special Mention
King, James, 1614 S. Michigan Ave., Chicago, Ill.　　Special Mention
King, Linda, 79 Acrebrook Dr., Chicopee Falls, Mass.　　Special Mention
King, Mrs. Sidney E., RFD 1, Box 102, Milford, Va.　　Special Mention
Kingsley, Kathleen, 880 E. 4th St., S. Boston, Mass.　　Special Mention
Kinne, Mrs. Ethel S., 14709 S. Harris Ave., E. Compton, CFA　　Special Mention
Kirchmann, Marjorie, 130 Kirschner Pkwy., Hamburg, N.Y.　　Special Mention
Kitchen, Mrs. George R., Rt. 5, Box 317, Reichard Dr., Mad. H., Va. Special Mention
Kittle, Ronald E., 24 Pandora Dr., Brentwood, N.Y.　　Special Mention
Klimt, Diane L., 3234 S. Villa Circle, West Allis, Wis.　　Special Mention
Kline, Gertrude L., 20 Stanton St., Painted Post, N.Y.　　Special Mention
Klink, Mary L., R.D. 1, Lindy's Lake, Butler P.O., N.J.　　Special Mention
Knapp, Fred S., 36 Twin Oaks Dr., Hampton, Va.　　HONORABLE MENTION
Knepton, Lisa, 6 Canterbury Ct., Savannah, Ga.　　Special Mention
Knight, Sandra J., P.O. Box 169, Lambuth Col., Jksn. Tn.　HONORABLE MENTION
Koctur, Pat, 3116 Backmeyer Rd., Richmond, Ind.　　HONORABLE MENTION
Kohr, Mrs. Robert E., 4 Birch St., Enola, Pa.　　HONORABLE MENTION
Kononchik, Ronald J., 1015 E. 228th St., Bronx, N.Y.　　HONORABLE MENTION
Koopersmith, Adrienne S., 1407 Lakeview Dr. Mendota, Ill.　　Special Mention
Koppler, Vera, Rt. 5, Box 18, Marshall, Ill.　　HONORABLE MENTION
Koski, Mrs. Ida W., 1719 S. Hadley St., Bessemer, Mich.　　Special Mention
Kotowski, Marcia, 206 Russell Ave., Liverpool, N.Y.　　HONORABLE MENTION
Kreglok, Mrs. Beth, Park St., Phelps, N.Y.　　HONORABLE MENTION
Krinsky, Joseph P., 114 Orange Ave., Suffern, N.Y.　　Special Mention
Kronberg, Prudence A., Rt. 2, Highway 150, Neenah, Wis.　　Special Mention
Kropfl, Virginia M., 5421 N.W. 45th St., Okla. City, Okla. HONORABLE MENTION
Krupinski, Mrs. Ruth M., 4609 Hurtt Pl., Oxon Hill, Md.　　Special Mention

Krupkat, DeLois D., Rt. I, Box 50, Tonasket, Wash.   HONORABLE MENTION
Kruse, Marian E., 2922 Calumet Ave., Elkhart, Ind.   HONORABLE MENTION
Kunkel, Pearle T., 8525 S.E. 2lst Ave., Portland, Ore.   HONORABLE MENTION
Kyle, Florence E., 92I Ventura Ave., Chowchilla, Ca.   HONORABLE MENTION

=L=

LaBryer, Nora R., 2529 Clear Lake Way, Sacramento, Ca. HONORABLE MENTION
Lachney, Jr., John, 3307 N. l0th, Terre Haute, Ind.   HONORABLE MENTION
La Duke, Josephine, Box 43, Ebro, Minn.   HONORABLE MENTION
Lakeman, Daniel R., 3105 Yeates Ln., Virginia Beach, Va. HONORABLE MENTION
Lama, Jerry, 2790 Randall Ave., Bronx, N.Y.   HONORABLE MENTION
Landry, Edward J., II Central St., Leominster, Mass.   HONORABLE MENTION
Lane, John C., I00 S. William St., Johnstown, N.Y.   Special Mention
Lange, Sandra, Box 9II, Knox College, Galesburg, Ill.   Special Mention
Langston, Randy E., Rt. 5, Box 46I-H, Kissimmee, Fl.   Special Mention
Langston, Shelia A., Rt. 2, Box I47, Gates, N.C.   Special Mention
Lanier, Barbara, R.R. I, Chambersburg, Ill.   Special Mention
Larson, Vern E., 26I6 Peabody St., Bellingham, Wash.   HONORABLE MENTION
Latta, Richard, 4I0 N. Monroe, Streator, Ill.   HONORABLE MENTION
Latta, Ruth, 8I2 Davis Ave., Uniondale, N.Y.   Special Mention
Lauer, Vivian, I807 Willow Spring Rd., Baltimore, Md.   HONORABLE MENTION
Laufenberg, Ellen, I70 Redwood Ave., Trenton, N.J.   HONORABLE MENTION
Lawson, Katherine R., 207 N. Lovell Ave., Chattanooga, Tenn. Special Mention
Lawson, Peggy A., II37 Florida St., Imperial Beach, Ca.   HONORABLE MENTION
Layton, Helen, 9807 Schiller Blvd., Franklin Park, Ill.   HONORABLE MENTION
LaZerte, Mrs. Hulda, 39 Balmoral Ave. S., Hamilton, Ont., Canada Special Mention
Lear, Barbara, 3I7 Hickory St., Hollidaysburg, Pa.   HONORABLE MENTION
Le Bihan, Alberta I., P.O. Box I82, Glassport, Pa.   HONORABLE MENTION
Lee, Mrs. Doris, 406 Main St., Boonville, N.Y.   Special Mention
Lee, Mary W., 2I8 S. Foster St., Mountain Home, Ark.   HONORABLE MENTION
Lee, Minnie B., 3833 Burwood Ave., Norwood, Ohio   Special Mention
Leeds, Evelyn, 6287 S.W. l2th St., Miami, Fl.   HONORABLE MENTION
Lefever, Nancy L., Box 78, R. I, Nottingham, Pa.   Special Mention
Leftwich, Wayneva, R.R. 2, Burden, Kan.   HONORABLE MENTION
Lehett, Mrs. Nancy, 234 Elm Ave., Sharon, Pa.   Special Mention
Lehman, Helen A., 64I E. Eckman St., South Bend, Ind.   HONORABLE MENTION
Lehmann, Brenda, I6 W. Buchanan, Charleston, Ill.   Special Mention
Lehner, Ann, 745 Lamplight Ln. C.H., Virginia Bch., Va. HONORABLE MENTION
LeMasters, Elaine, 555 Girard Ave., Marion, Ohio   HONORABLE MENTION
Lenk, Mabel R., I070 Beacon St., Brookline, Mass.   HONORABLE MENTION
Leonard, Andrea, Box 353, Osterville, Mass.   HONORABLE MENTION
Lepore, Merry A., 33 Hialeah Ave., Middletown, N.J.   HONORABLE MENTION
Lester, Alice, I8I0 W. Ridgewood Ln., Glenview, Ill.   HONORABLE MENTION
Levy, Mrs. Jessica, I043 W. High St., Haddon Hts., N.J.   HONORABLE MENTION
Lewellen, Ressie L., R.R. 4, Box I9, Fowler, Ind.   HONORABLE MENTION
Lewis, Jeanne C., 2892 Whitney Ave., Hamden, Conn.   HONORABLE MENTION
Lewis, Linda J., I369I Wheeler Pl., Tustin, Ca.   Special Mention
Lewis, Margaret H., 3032 E. Cheltenham Pl., Chic., Ill.   HONORABLE MENTION
Lewis, Ruth, 4I 3rd St., Eastport, Me.   HONORABLE MENTION
Liabenow, Lawrence A., 658 Belton, Garden City, Mich.   Special Mention
Lichty, Mrs. Molly A., 2725 Wendell Lane, Yorktown Hts., N.Y. Special Mention
Lilienthal, Mrs. Esther B., I34 Cedar, Wyandotte, Mich.   HONORABLE MENTION
Liming, Mrs. O. F., 786 Mimosa Dr. S.E., Marietta, Ga.   HONORABLE MENTION
Linden, Alvin, Rt. 2, Box I53, Ogema, Wis.   Special Mention
Linkesh, Mrs. Frances, 4I3 S. Main St., Burgettstown, Pa. HONORABLE MENTION
Little, Mrs. Marjorie A., R.R. I, Box II9, Triangle, Va.   HONORABLE MENTION
Lively, Mary W., I5I3E Eastcrest Dr., Charlotte, N.C.   HONORABLE MENTION
Livingston, Reva, I2422 Elmwood St., Garden Grove, Ca. HONORABLE MENTION
Lock, Suzanne M., 33I2 Ivy Dr., Mesquite, Tex.   HONORABLE MENTION
Loefgren, Lester E., 4307 Village Dr., Marietta, Fl.   HONORABLE MENTION
Logas, Linda A., 832 St. Clair Ave., Sheboygan, Wis.   Special Mention
Lones, Agnes, 2267 Yoakam Rd., Lima, Ohio   Special Mention
Longendyke, Shirley M., R.D. 5, Box 380, Kingston, N.Y. HONORABLE MENTION
Looper, Joanne G., Medical College Hospital, Charleston, S.C. Special Mention

Loros, Mary A., Rt. 2, Watseka, Ill. HONORABLE MENTION
Louder, Mrs. Betty T., 2033 Meadowlake Ct., Norfolk, Va. Special Mention
Love, Sr., Melvin, P.O. Box 302, Alcoa, Tenn. HONORABLE MENTION
Luckenbaugh, Mrs. Ruth M., I09 York St., Hanover, Pa. Special Mention
Ludlow, Clover, C-26 Felton Homes, Macon, Ga. HONORABLE MENTION
Luer, Robert, R.R. 3, Eau Claire, Wis. HONORABLE MENTION
Luna, Florence C., Rt. I, Lewisburg, Tenn. HONORABLE MENTION
Lundgren, Terry R., 3I32 4th Ave., So., Minneapolis, Minn. Special Mention
Lundy, Barbara, 246 Nora Ave., Glenview, Ill. Special Mention
Lutz, Jack, 328 Van Brunt St., Brooklyn, N.Y. HONORABLE MENTION
Lyman, Nancy H., 40I We-Go Trail, Mt. Prospect, Ill. Special Mention

=M=

Maas, Barbara C., Highland Lake, N.Y. HONORABLE MENTION
MacKennik, Mildred V., I00I E. Front St., PInfld., N.J. HONORABLE MENTION
Mac Neill, Diz, I98 Hillside Ave., Leonia, N.J. HONORABLE MENTION
Madary, Millie E., I9048 Stonewood Dr., Riverview, Mich. Special Mention
Maeshiro, Stanley, 25888 Gading Rd., Hayward, Ca. Special Mention
Major, Jr., Sidney M., I420 Huntdale St., Lehigh Acres, Fl.HONORABLE MENTION
Malin, Richard, 440 I0th St. S., Wisconsin Rapids, Wis. Special Mention
Manchester, John, Rt. I, Box 575A, Long Beach, Wash. Special Mention
Mansfield, Bea, 740½ S. Curson Ave., Los Angeles, Ca. HONORABLE MENTION
Marchionda, Luisa M., 5209 Southern Blvd., Youngstown, Ohio Special Mention
Marino, Anne, I806 Corinth Ave., West Los Angeles, Ca. HONORABLE MENTION
Marquardt, Annette, 695 Clear Ave., St. Paul, Minn. HONORABLE MENTION
Marshall, Barbara, I2203 S. Dolan Ave., Downey, Ca. Special Mention
Marshall, Ethel T., 2II6 Park Rd., Charlotte, N.C. HONORABLE MENTION
Marshall, Katherine D., I4 Chimney Rdg. Dr., Mrstn., N.J. HONORABLE MENTION
Marshall, Louise K., P.O. Box 26, Glen Haven, Wis. Special Mention
Marshall, Margo, I4I2 S. Meridian, Tallahassee, Fl. Special Mention
Martello, Fred, 570 Cullan Pl., Franklin Lakes, N.J. Special Mention
Marti, Mrs. Paul R., 23I Clinton Hill Rd., Wolcott, Conn. Special Mention
Martin, Mrs. Elsie, 4I65 Coronation Ave., Salmon Arm, B.C., Can. Special Mention
Martin, Louise, N.N.M. State College, El Rito, N.M. HONORABLE MENTION
Martin, Mitchell L., 9II7 National, Los Angeles, Ca. Special Mention
Martin, Mrs. Patricia, I930 Blue Rdg. Dr., Lancaster, Pa. HONORABLE MENTION
Martins, Rosemarie, 3839 50th St., San Diego, Ca. Special Mention
Martz, Samia, 205 E. Culton, Warrensburg, Mo. HONORABLE MENTION
Massey, Leonard D., P.O. Box 433, Paseagoula, Miss. Special Mention
Matarazzo, Evelyn C., 53-I5 32nd Ave., Woodside, N.Y. HONORABLE MENTION
Mathews, Alexandra, 287 E. Avenida de Los Arboles, Th. Oks., Ca. Special Mention
Mathis, Roberta, Rt. I, Dalzell, S.C. Special Mention
Matta, Henrietta G., 3258 Market St., San Fran., Ca. HONORABLE MENTION
Mauney, Elizabeth N., 5222 Floyd St., Covington, Ga. Special Mention
Maynard, Frances S., 935 Waring Rd., Memphis, Tenn. HONORABLE MENTION
Maziarz, Nancy, 67 School St., Agawam, Mass. HONORABLE MENTION
McCallum, Becky, Rt. I, Honeycreek, Iowa Special Mention
McCallum, Lulu, Pleasant St., North Carver, Mass. Special Mention
McCardell, Mrs. W. R., 4820 N.E. 23rd Ave., Ft. Laud., Fl.HONORABLE MENTION
McCarthy, Margaret A., 6200 Brookville Rd., Indianapolis, Ind. Special Mention
McCollum, Malcolm S., 346 Hervey, Upland, Ca. HONORABLE MENTION
McConnell, Bonnie E., II55I Roxbury, Detroit, Mich. HONORABLE MENTION
McConnell, Gladys L., 7IA Marvin Rd., Melrose, Mass. HONORABLE MENTION
McCorkle, Ruth, I45 N.W. I6th St., Corvallis, Ore. HONORABLE MENTION
McCormick, Alice, Star Rt., Aurora, Mo. HONORABLE MENTION
McCoy, Barbara, 4526 N. 22nd St., Milwaukee, Wis. HONORABLE MENTION
McCrone, Kathleen M., 2505 Roney Dr., Granite City, Ill. Special Mention
McCullough, Robert W., 2025 Walnut St., Phila., Pa. HONORABLE MENTION
McDaniel, David A., 4024 Elizabeth, Texarkana, Tex. Special Mention
McDermott, Patricia, 5834 33rd Pl., Hyattsville, Md. HONORABLE MENTION
McEathron, Mrs. J. M., 2224 Kingston St., Vic., B.C., Canada Special Mention
McGraw, Ida A., East Corinth, Me. HONORABLE MENTION
McLaughlin, Helene A., 5230 Ralston, Indianapolis, Ind. HONORABLE MENTION
McMahon, Jane E., 2I39 Main St., Santa Clara, Ca. HONORABLE MENTION

McMinn, Lena, 301 E. Grant Ave., Altoona, Pa.   HONORABLE MENTION
McWhorter, Bright, Walkersville, W.Va.   Special Mention
Mead, Susan, 183 13th St., Arcata, Ca.   Special Mention
Medallis, Marie E., 2325 Kansas Ave., Santa Monica, Ca.   Special Mention
Medow, Joyce, 540 Briar Pl., Chicago, Ill.   HONORABLE MENTION
Medved, Philip, RVAH-5 Naval Air Sta., Albany, Ga.   Special Mention
Meeg, Herman, 310 Windsor Pl., Brooklyn, N.Y.   Special Mention
Meek, Sally, 113 N. Gold St., Yreka, Ca.   HONORABLE MENTION
Meeker, Fleeta O., P.O. Box 223, Santa Ana, Ca.   HONORABLE MENTION
Meeks, Mrs. Josephine, 2595 W. 9th Ave., Gary, Ind.   Special Mention
Meister, Judy, 9208 S. Monitor, Oak Lawn, Ill.   HONORABLE MENTION
Melcombe, Nancy, Peaceable St., Ridgefield, Conn.   HONORABLE MENTION
Mele, Myrna, 263 Lawrence Rd., Broomall, Pa.   HONORABLE MENTION
Mercier, Marjorie R., 34 Main St., Hope, R.I.   HONORABLE MENTION
Metzger, Jesse W., 10 Center Ln., Bridgeton, N.J.   HONORABLE MENTION
Meurer, Cheryl L., 303 Witherow Ave., N. Troy, N.Y.   Special Mention
Meyerink, Mrs. George, 4576 Washington, St. Jo., Mich.   HONORABLE MENTION
Michel, Sophie I., 9239 Cave Creek Rd., Phoenix, Ariz.   HONORABLE MENTION
Mickle, Hermione, 155 Forest Glen Rd., Woodbridge, Va.   HONORABLE MENTION
Middleton, Sandy, Box 26, Bonanza, Utah   HONORABLE MENTION
Miklas, Becky S., 1709 Beverly Blvd., Montebello, Ca.   HONORABLE MENTION
Milhet, Juliette U., 40 Shore Blvd., Brooklyn, N.Y.   HONORABLE MENTION
Milici, Mrs. Eugene S., Main St., Lakeville, Conn.   HONORABLE MENTION
Miller, Dova A., 3121 Lake Ave., Pueblo, Colo.   HONORABLE MENTION
Miller, Joan, McAuley Residence, 145 Fisk, DeKalb, Ill.   HONORABLE MENTION
Miller, Karen, 128 S. Waller Ave., Chicago, Ill.   Special Mention
Miller, Phyllis, 213 S. 3rd St., Colwyn, Pa.   HONORABLE MENTION
Miller, Ronald R., 5049 Alan Ave., San Jose, Ca.   HONORABLE MENTION
Miller, Sally, 36 Washington Pl., Edwardsville, Ill.   Special Mention
Mills, Peggie, 2013 New Hamp. Ave. N.W., Wash., D.C.   HONORABLE MENTION
Milne, Heather, 346 N. Knox St., Gary, Ind.   Special Mention
Miraj, Mehnaz, 2726 Connecticut Ave. N.W., Wash., D.C.   Special Mention
Mitchell, Mrs. Alexina, 1313 Deep Creek Blvd., Chesapeake, Va.   Special Mention
Mitchell, Robert G., Box 45A Star Rt., Three Spgs., Pa.   HONORABLE MENTION
Moldenhauer, Mildred, 928 S. 76th St., Milwaukee, Wis.   HONORABLE MENTION
Molenaar, Pat, 1208 Greenhills Rd., Sacramento, Ca.   Special Mention
Monilaws, Ora, 54 Humphrey Dr., Syosset, N.Y.   HONORABLE MENTION
Moomaw, Dunbar, Box 232, Dahlgren, Va.   HONORABLE MENTION
Moore, Alice, P.O. Box 891, Beaufort, S.C.   Special Mention
Moore, Mrs. Clarence, Hillsboro, Ind.   HONORABLE MENTION
Moore, Diana M., St. Inigoes, Md.   Special Mention
Moore, James O., 501 Carter's Grove Ct., Hampton, Va.   Special Mention
Moore, Mrs. James O., 501 Carter's Grove Ct., Hptn., Va.   HONORABLE MENTION
Moran, Jr., Mrs. Juanita, 897 Ohio St., W. St. Paul, Minn.   Special Mention
Moretti, Frank A., 326 Winfield Ter., Union, N.J.   HONORABLE MENTION
Morio, Donald, 10-17 47th Ave., L.I., N.Y.   HONORABLE MENTION
Moritz, Dorothy M., 224 Tower Rd., Castle Rock, Wash.   Special Mention
Morris, Miriam A., R.D. 1, Box 955, Linglestown, Pa.   Special Mention
Morris, Richard D., 3101 Mountview Rd., Columbus, Ohio   HONORABLE MENTION
Morrow, Mrs. Marjorie R., 224 W. Jefferson, Dimondl., Mich.   Special Mention
Mosier, Margaret, 1301 Main St., Orange, Tex.   HONORABLE MENTION
Moyer, Pat, Box 44, R.D. 1, The Terrace, Pleasant Mount, Pa.   Special Mention
Moys, Fay C., 620 Kentucky St., Lawrence, Kan.   HONORABLE MENTION
Mucci, John, 57 Maple St., Darien, Conn.   Special Mention
Mullenax, Mrs. Juanita B., Rt. 2, Box 27, Petersbg., W.Va.   HONORABLE MENTION
Murphy, Jr., Mrs. Edward A., 907 Highvw. Ave., Man., Ca.   HONORABLE MENTION
Murray, James A., 820 Rosewood Dr., 101B, Elyria, Ohio   Special Mention
Musgrove, Mrs. Sam, 2152 Stern Dr., Napa, Ca.   HONORABLE MENTION
Myers, Donna K., 1242 Gaylord, Apt. 203, Denver, Colo.   Special Mention
Myers, Kay S., 33263 Vine St., Apt. 15, Eastlake, Ohio   Special Mention
Myers, Marlene M., 328 E. Market St., York, Pa.   Special Mention

=N=

Nagy, Sheri, 5310 8th Rd., S. 4, Arlington, Va.   HONORABLE MENTION

Nance, Norma J., 1840 N. Winona Blvd., L. Angeles, Ca.   HONORABLE MENTION
Napier, Phyllis, Box 23, Lincoln, Ark.   HONORABLE MENTION
Navickis, Janet, 7 N. Auburn Ave., Richmond, Va.   HONORABLE MENTION
Neal, Marian L., 627 W. Calle Medina, Tucson, Ariz.   HONORABLE MENTION
Needs, Mrs. Karen S., R.D. 5, Alliance, Ohio   HONORABLE MENTION
Neighbors, David A., P.O. Box 4491, Boise, Id.   HONORABLE MENTION
Nelson, Cathy, 191 Pascack Ave., Emerson, N.J.   Special Mention
Nelson, Mrs. Helen A., 117 Hayes Ave. S., Rosemt., Minn.   HONORABLE MENTION
Nelson, Jennie V., 3390 E. Beauer Rd., Bay City, Mich.   HONORABLE MENTION
Nelson, Myrna M., Askov, Minn.   Special Mention
Nibbe, Leola, Box 171, Scranton, N.D.   HONORABLE MENTION
Nichols, C. F., 1425 W. Possum Rd., Springfield, Ohio   HONORABLE MENTION
Nichuals, Elizabeth, 344 E. 194th St., Bronx, N.Y.   HONORABLE MENTION
Nickles, Beverly, 1406 Hull Rd., Mansfield, Ohio   HONORABLE MENTION
Niday, Mrs. Edna, Rt. I, Box 8, Gallipolis, Ohio   Special Mention
Nielson, Rose C., 280 E. 7th S., Springville, Utah   HONORABLE MENTION
Nimocks, Jr., Robert E., 2505 Spring Vly. Rd., Fay., N.C. HONORABLE MENTION
Noel, Jennie, 3564 Easy Ave., Long Beach, Ca.   Special Mention
Norby, Sandra, 414 7th Ave. S.W., Sidney, Mont.   Special Mention
Novak, Jerome J., 840 S. Kenwood Ave., Baltimore, Md.   Special Mention
Novack, Sharon, 118 E. 32nd St., Patterson, N.J.   Special Mention
Noyes, Barbara J., R.R. I, Box 453, Escanaba, Mich.   Special Mention

=O=

O'Brien, Melvin, Sinks Grove, W.Va.   HONORABLE MENTION
O'Donnell, Susan E., 2608 Swann Ave., Apt. E, Tampa, Fl.   Special Mention
Oehrtman, Susan, Rt. 2, Box 181, Versailles, Ohio   HONORABLE MENTION
O'Flahavan, John F., 7912 Carey Br. Dr., Oxon Hill, Md.   HONORABLE MENTION
Ohler, Richard, Box 335, Grapeland, Tex.   Special Mention
Olds, Pam, 760 White Rd., Pace, Fl.   Special Mention
Olivares, Olivia M., 2548 Rampart Quarters, Dallas, Tex.   Special Mention
Olsen, Mrs. Wilbur, Ocean Hse. Rd., Cape Elizabeth, Me.   HONORABLE MENTION
O'Neil, Mindy, 5216 W. 110th St., Bloomington, Minn.   Special Mention
Orlowski, Christine, 1217 Strathy Ave., Mississauga, Ont., Canada   Special Mention
Owen, Margaret H., Box 259, Sardis, Ohio   HONORABLE MENTION
Owens, Sallie T., 391 Walnut Rear, Buffalo, N.Y.   Special Mention
Oye, Brian T., 5309 N. Ashland, Chicago, Ill.   HONORABLE MENTION

=P=

Page, Rubye, R. I, Big Rock, Tenn.   HONORABLE MENTION
Pagen, Gerry, R.D. 2, Dunbar, Pa.   HONORABLE MENTION
Paisley, Mrs. Miriam B., 649 N. Paca St., Baltimore, Md.   HONORABLE MENTION
Pancherovich, June E., 209 W. 14th St., Northampton, Pa. HONORABLE MENTION
Panico, Claire, 2515 Wilmette Ave., Wilmette, Ill.   Special Mention
Papa, Beatrice R., Box 536, Chinle, Ariz.   HONORABLE MENTION
Pape, Mrs. Norma A., 23 Harris St., Norwalk, Conn.   Special Mention
Papke, Pamela A., 950 Superior St., Sturgeon Bay, Wis.   HONORABLE MENTION
Pappas, Jimmy, Box 448, Atlanta, Tex.   HONORABLE MENTION
Parent, Elsie, M., 2829 Bosworth Ln., Bowie, Md.   HONORABLE MENTION
Park, Dorothy C., 805 Hawley St., Kalamazoo, Mich.   Special Mention
Parker, Adeline R., 5 Bernhard Ave., El Verano, Ca.   HONORABLE MENTION
Parker, Jr., Eddie, 3020 Vassar Dr., Augusta, Ga.   Special Mention
Parker, Helen R., 27 Newport Ave., Newport News, Va.   Special Mention
Parkinson, Dorothy A., 2300 Hawthorne, Evansville, Ind.   Special Mention
Parks, Jocelyn H., 2732½ Lydia St., Jacksonville, Fl.   HONORABLE MENTION
Parrish, Maudrey A., Northwestern St. Col., Natchitoches, La.   Special Mention
Parson, Lisa, 710 Hickory, New Llano, La.   HONORABLE MENTION
Pasanen, Christine, 3253 Lebanon Ave., El Paso, Tex.   HONORABLE MENTION
Patchen, Nina F., 1901 N. 46th St., Phoenix, Ariz.   Special Mention
Paulson, Mrs. Alma G., 28 Parakeet Hill, Pontiac, Mich.   HONORABLE MENTION
Payne, Sara, Rt. 5, Siloam Springs, Ark.   Special Mention
Peace, George J., 115 Spring St., Reading, Pa.   HONORABLE MENTION
Peacock, Dick, 39 Fuller N.E., Grand Rapids, Mich.   Special Mention

Pearman, Rita, 172 Elena Ave., Atherton, Ca.   HONORABLE MENTION
Pendley, Shelby J., Rt. 2, Box 26, Parrish, Ala.   Special Mention
Pentz, Diana, 1089 E. 13th St., Upland, Ca.   Special Mention
Perry, Crystal, Rt. 2, Campobello, S.C.   HONORABLE MENTION
Perry, Krista M., 177 Paris Rd., New Hartford, N.Y.   HONORABLE MENTION
Perry, Lisa, Box 124, Hot Springs, S.D.   HONORABLE MENTION
Pertlaga, Diane, Box 176, Stewartsville, Ohio   HONORABLE MENTION
Pessah, Noah, Boardwalk & W. 29th St., Brkln., N.Y.   HONORABLE MENTION
Petersen, Barbara, 15229 Evers Ave., Dolton, Ill.   Special Mention
Peterson, Edith, 412 Newton St., Eau Claire, Wis.   HONORABLE MENTION
Peterson, Mrs. Geraldine, 534 Empire Blvd., Brkln., N.Y.   HONORABLE MENTION
Petracek, Ruth E., Box 142, Jennings, Kan.   Special Mention
Phares, Mrs. Mary H., P.O. Box 35, Canal Point, Fl.   HONORABLE MENTION
Phelan, Jr., Patrick J., 136 W. 109th St., N.Y., N.Y.   HONORABLE MENTION
Phelan, Shirley, 208 Hope St., Corning, Ark.   HONORABLE MENTION
Phillips, Floyd E., R.R. 2, Bloomfield, Mo.   Special Mention
Phillips, III, James F., 204 Lafayette St., Salem, Mass.   Special Mention
Picker, Mrs. Norman, 36 Jefferson Ave., Haddonfield, N.J. HONORABLE MENTION
Pieper, Mrs. Florence, 2640 N. Lincoln, Chicago, Ill.   Special Mention
Pierson, Dorothy C., 22638 Gaycrest, Torrance, Ca.   Special Mention
Piro, Georgia A., 1617 Cross Lake Blvd., Shreveport, La.   Special Mention
Pirog, Mrs. Anne, 1152 Hayward St., Manchester, N.H.   HONORABLE MENTION
Pitney, Shirley J., 263 Gardner, Vallejo, Ca.   HONORABLE MENTION
Platts, Frances, 7404 James Ave., Omaha, Neb.   Special Mention
Podruchny, J. C., 46 E. 13th St., Roanoke Rapids, N.C.   HONORABLE MENTION
Poindexter, E. M., Rt. 1, Box 475-A, Dobson, N.C.   HONORABLE MENTION
Poland, Ada K., 2105 4th St., Orange, Tex.   HONORABLE MENTION
Pollard, Vivian E., 1186 N. 26th St., Kalamazoo, Mich.   HONORABLE MENTION
Pollock, Diane M., Univ. of Maryland, College Park, Md.   Special Mention
Pomon, Pam, 30 Mattatuck Rd., Bristol, Conn.   Special Mention
Poncik, Tony L., P.O. Box 1494, Bay City, Tex.   HONORABLE MENTION
Poole, Lorena B., Rt. 1, Horatio, Ark.   HONORABLE MENTION
Popovich, Michele C., 65 Liberty Ave., N. Babylon, N.Y.   HONORABLE MENTION
Porter, Eleanor T., Harrison Nursing Hm., Hrisn., Ark.   HONORABLE MENTION
Potter, Maxeyn S., 1458 Drexel Ave. N.E., Wntr. Hvn., Fl. HONORABLE MENTION
Powel, Rosalie R., 632 Northampton Rd., Nristn., Pa.   HONORABLE MENTION
Powell, Alice M., 2503 1st St., Bradenton, Fl.   HONORABLE MENTION
Powers, Brooks W., 904½ W. Main, Muncie, Ind.   HONORABLE MENTION
Preston, Connie L., 610½ S. 14th St., Lafayette, Ind.   HONORABLE MENTION
Prestwood, Dorothy W., 14747 Quail Grove, Houston, Tex.   Special Mention
Pretty, Graham, 1310 Sedgefield St., Durham, N.C.   HONORABLE MENTION
Prisco, Peter F., 157 Stroud Ave., Staten Island, N.Y.   Special Mention
Pritchard, Donald F., 203 E. Walnut St., Harrisburg, Ill.   Special Mention
Pullen, Norine, 401 Cayuga St., Fulton, N.Y.   Special Mention
Pulliam, Mrs. Norma, 4700 Grayton Rd., Cleveland, Ohio   Special Mention
Purcifull, Virginia M., P.O. Box 155, Dunnigan, Ca.   Special Mention

=Q=

Quackenbush, Gale, 7820 Fostor St., Dist. Hts., Md.   HONORABLE MENTION
Quattrochi, Barbara, 348 E. North Ave., Northlake, Ill.   HONORABLE MENTION
Queen, Fanny, Box 177, Lyman, Wash.   Special Mention
Queen, Thelma J., 7025 Retton Rd., Reynoldsburg, Ohio   Special Mention

=R=

Rabner, Jim, 1232 Marlborough, Inglewood, Ca.   Special Mention
Rader, Frances, 11175 Centerville Rd., Whitehouse, Ohio HONORABLE MENTION
Rader, Phyllis, R.D. 2, Box 330, Beaver Falls, Pa.   HONORABLE MENTION
Radke, M. Elizabeth, R.R. 2, Box 673, Lake Villa, Ill.   HONORABLE MENTION
Radloff, Karen, 445 Mondell St., Thermopolis, Wyo.   HONORABLE MENTION
Radovic, Diana A., 225 Gorrie St., Box 331, Atikokan, Ont., Canada Special Mention
Ragland, Rosetta, 517 Connecticut Ave., Rochester, Pa.   HONORABLE MENTION
Rahorn, Mary E., 307 S. Main, Orangeville, Ill.   Special Mention
Raizk, Christine, 310 Sloan Panhellenic, Mt. Plsnt., Mich. HONORABLE MENTION

Rakers, Albert J., 103 E. 4th St., Trenton, Ill. HONORABLE MENTION
Ramey, Sally G. W., 1408 4th Ave., Seattle, Wash. HONORABLE MENTION
Ramsey, Roberta, 655 Mouse Creek Rd., Cleveld., Tenn. HONORABLE MENTION
Randee, Jeulettia L., 65-18 Parsons Blvd., Flushing, N.Y. HONORABLE MENTION
Randolph, Mrs. Jane M., Rt. 1, Newport, Tenn. HONORABLE MENTION
Ranson, J., 18 Selborne Rd., Littlehampton, Susx., Eng. HONORABLE MENTION
Rapien, Sherry L., 4280 Milaine Dr., Cincinnati, Ohio HONORABLE MENTION
Rasinski, Christine, 5053 W. Parker, Chicago, Ill. HONORABLE MENTION
Rau, Eileen, 99 Willow St., E. Brunswick, N.J. HONORABLE MENTION
Rauckhorst, Beth A., 470 Sandhurst Rd., Akron, Ohio Special Mention
Ray, Pat A., 63 Upper Colorado Dr., Bay City, Tex. HONORABLE MENTION
Rea, Linda, Neff St., Morral, Ohio HONORABLE MENTION
Reaves, Debbie, 10831 Skyline Dr., Santa Ana, Ca. HONORABLE MENTION
Reaves, Mrs. Odell, 2821 Forest Glen Rd., Baltimore, Md. Special Mention
Rector, Mrs. Diane, Glenbush, Sask., Canada Special Mention
Reed, Lissa R., Pyramus Rd., Chester, W.Va. HONORABLE MENTION
Reeder, Mrs. Lillian F., 524 Willow St., Brdntn., N.J. HONORABLE MENTION
Reese, Gayle J., 859 S. Millwood, Wichita, Kan. HONORABLE MENTION
Reeves, Rose H., Lyme, New Hamp. HONORABLE MENTION
Reik, Barbara, 4448 S. Griffin Ave., Milwaukee, Wis. Special Mention
Reinhard, Auguste L., 1301 N.E. Glendale Ave., Peoria, Ill. Special Mention
Relerford, Elsentoria Y., Rt. 1, Box 31, Boley, Okla. Special Mention
Reynolds, Edith M., 420 S. Denwood Ave., Dearborn, Mich. Special Mention
Rhinebeck, Grace, 235 14th St., Buffalo, N.Y. HONORABLE MENTION
Riccitelli, Ellen, 55 Newark St., Providence, R.I. Special Mention
Rice, Ivy, P.O. Box 154, Granby, Colo. Special Mention
Rice, Lily, 10004 Kellogg, El Paso, Tex. Special Mention
Richardson, Edwin A., Star Rt., Box 99, Midkiff, Tex. HONORABLE MENTION
Richardson, Florence A., Box 453, Lyons, Neb. HONORABLE MENTION
Rickenbach, Ruth L., Middle Ave., Waterford Works, N.J. Special Mention
Ridenour, Mrs. Jane, P.O. Box 361, Stony Brook, N.Y. HONORABLE MENTION
Rill, Edith E., 16 Houcksville Ave., Hampstead, Md. HONORABLE MENTION
Rishling, Laura, Box 11, Juliaetta, Id. HONORABLE MENTION
Roberts, Kay, 1319 N.W. 12th Pl., Andrews, Tex. HONORABLE MENTION
Robertson, Maryann B., 1101 W. Spruce St., Oxnard, Ca. HONORABLE MENTION
Robertson, Vesta N., 303 W. 46th Pl. N., Tulsa, Okla. Special Mention
Robichaud, Diane, Box 113, Squantum Rd., Jaffrey, N.H. Special Mention
Robinson, Charlotte M., 738 Longfellow St., N.W., Wash., D.C. Special Mention
Robinson, Cora B., 314 Crawford St., Middletown, Ohio Special Mention
Rochester, Sharon, White Oak Rd., Greenville, S.C. Special Mention
Rodebaugh, Peggy, 410 E. Van Buren, Harlingen, Tex. HONORABLE MENTION
Rodriguez, Mrs. Virginia G., P.O. Box 753, La Feria, Tex. HONORABLE MENTION
Roetcisoender, Christy, Rt. 2, Box 139, Everett, Wash. Special Mention
Roling, Therese, R.R. 2, Dyersville, Iowa HONORABLE MENTION
Romer, Ann, 4805 Beverly Hills Dr., Cincinnati, Ohio HONORABLE MENTION
Rooker, Sandra L., 6616 S. Minerva, Chicago, Ill. HONORABLE MENTION
Rose, Virginia, Rt. 4, Box 181, Coeburn, Va. HONORABLE MENTION
Ross, Carol L., 1102 Union Ave., Apt. 3C, Bronx, N.Y. Special Mention
Ross, Mrs. Merle M., R. 3, Stockport, Ohio HONORABLE MENTION
Rossdeutscher, Flora, 414 E. South St., Richland Center, Wis. Special Mention
Rossi, Leona S., 185 Spring St., Saratoga Springs, N.Y. HONORABLE MENTION
Rossner, Rosemary, 1670 Poplar St., Northampton, Pa. Special Mention
Rotolone, Janice D., 2103 Ramelli Ave., Ventura, Ca. Special Mention
Roup, Mary L., 1412 Church St., Philadelphia, Pa. HONORABLE MENTION
Rowell, Stella, 3714 Columbia Pike, Arlington, Va. Special Mention
Rowland, Robert B., 1134 W. Brockett, Sherman, Tex. Special Mention
Rowon, Jule D., Box 26, Bonanza, Utah Special Mention
Roze, Mrs. Mary A., 4 E. 31st St., Hamilton 53, Ont., Canada Special Mention
Rozen, Mortimer J., 3218 Euclid Hts. Blvd., Cleveland Hts., Ohio Special Mention
Ruatti, Mrs. Lloyd, 1509 Logan Ave., Marinette, Wis. HONORABLE MENTION
Rubinstein, Irene, 1448 Backus St., El Paso, Tex. Special Mention
Rubinstein, Mary L., 1020 N. Quincy St., Apt. 613, Arlington, Va. Special Mention
Rush, Tonda, 7939 Leavenworth Rd., Kansas City, Kan. HONORABLE MENTION
Russ, Roy H., 321 Sunset Ave., Asbury Park, N.J. Special Mention
Russell, Frederick W., 309 Washington, Collinsville, Ill. Special Mention

Russell, Jane H., Stillings Box 994, Durham, N.H.   HONORABLE MENTION
Russell, Willie M., Rt. I, Box 80, Silverton, Tex.   HONORABLE MENTION
Russo, Andrea, 3 Russel Rd., Acton, Mass.   Special Mention
Ryan, Nancy M., 3887 Carman Rd., Schenectady, N.Y.   HONORABLE MENTION

=S=

Sackler, Felicia, 5 Spencer Way, Kings Park, L.I., N.Y.   HONORABLE MENTION
Sadler, W. T., R.R. 3, Kingston, Ont., Canada   HONORABLE MENTION
Salisbury, Bertha, P.O. Box 74I, Farmington, N.M.   HONORABLE MENTION
Salisbury, Bruce, P.O. Box 74I, Farmington, N.M.   HONORABLE MENTION
Salter, Carolyn J., I3806 N.E. 72nd Ave., Vancouver, Wash.   Special Mention
Saltz, Evelyn I., Mt. Zion Rd., R.D. I, W. Pittston, Pa.   HONORABLE MENTION
Sandau, Paul, Rt. I, Box 95, Branch, La.   HONORABLE MENTION
Saunders, Barry W., Box I32, Butner, N.C.   Special Mention
Saville, Priscilla, 223 Seminary Ave., Greensburg, Pa.   HONORABLE MENTION
Scapple, Shari, I425 State St., Eau Claire, Wis.   HONORABLE MENTION
Schaaf, Willa J., Rt. I, Box 540, Durango, Colo.   HONORABLE MENTION
Scheepsma, J. L., 977 Crestview Dr. E., Pine City, N.Y.   HONORABLE MENTION
Schelzi, Robert, II Perry Place, Woburn, Mass.   Special Mention
Schmidt, Clara A., Box 72, Vesta, Minn.   HONORABLE MENTION
Schmidt, Lawrence E., 726 North Bend Rd., Cincinnati, Ohio   Special Mention
Schmidt, Nona, Ogdensburg, Wis.   Special Mention
Schmidt, Ralph, 483 Ottawa St. S., Kitchener, Ont., Can. HONORABLE MENTION
Schmitt, Mrs. Clare, RFD 646, Friday Harbor, Wash.   Special Mention
Schneider, Richard B., Box 34, DePauw Univ., Grncsl., In.HONORABLE MENTION
Schonleber, Gladys M., 435 E. Henrietta, Rochester, N.Y. HONORABLE MENTION
Schorre, Jane A., I3I2 Cambridge, Corpus Christi, Tex.   HONORABLE MENTION
Schroeter, Gina, I7-35 I47th St., Whitestone, N.Y.   HONORABLE MENTION
Schudar, Josephine, Britton, S.D.   HONORABLE MENTION
Schuff, Karen E., I53I0 Windemere, Southgate, Mich.   HONORABLE MENTION
Schuh, Mary, 22I VanSpanje, Michigan City, Ind.   Special Mention
Schultz, Virgiline, P.O. Box 53, Plymouth, Wis.   Special Mention
Schwantes, James, 435 Summit Ave., W. Chicago, Ill.   HONORABLE MENTION
Schwartz, Mrs. Arlene, 32-25 69th St. 2K, Woodside, N.Y.   Special Mention
Schwarz, Patricia, Endicott Jr. College, Beverly, Mass.   HONORABLE MENTION
Schwindamann, Opal A., I7729 I60th, S.E., Monroe, Wash.HONORABLE MENTION
Schwinn, Elaine, I3II2 Marlboro Ave., Alliance, Ohio   HONORABLE MENTION
Schwinn, Mary L., II4I Olive St., Leavenworth, Kan.   HONORABLE MENTION
Sciascia, Susan, I2I Edgecliff Ter., Yonkers, N.Y.   HONORABLE MENTION
Scola, Marie, 855 Union Ave., Memphis, Tenn.   HONORABLE MENTION
Scovel, Myra, 37 Farley Dr., Stony Point, N.Y.   HONORABLE MENTION
Scutt, Elizabeth, 94I McCallie Ave., Chattanooga, Tenn.   HONORABLE MENTION
Sellars, Jim, Box 609, S.S.S., Wahpeton, N.D.   Special Mention
Selway, Mrs. Bessie V., I40I McCurley Ave., Catonsvl., Md.HONORABLE MENTION
Severinson, Mrs. Robert J., Box I76, Climax, Minn.   HONORABLE MENTION
Sexton, Mrs. Marvin, I0II N. 3rd St., Rochelle, Ill.   HONORABLE MENTION
Shaffer, Mabel B., P.O. Box 525, Wharton, Tex.   HONORABLE MENTION
Shaffer, Mrs. Merle, I03 Kirk Ave., Rr. Hse., Mt. Vernon, Ohio   Special Mention
Shane, Tom, 8I0 Pearl St., Martins Ferry, Ohio   HONORABLE MENTION
Shaul, Yvonne L., 4708 Solano Way, Fair Oaks, Ca.   HONORABLE MENTION
Shechtman, Mrs. Phyllis, 8 Wash. Dr., W. Paterson, N.J.   HONORABLE MENTION
Shefcyk, Norma, 23 Brookside Ave., Middletown, Conn.   Special Mention
Sheils, Frances, Box 235, Barboursville, Va.   Special Mention
Shemming, Joan L., 3927 Manitoba Ave., Powl. R., B.C.   HONORABLE MENTION
Shepherd, Elaine, I69 Terry Ave., Charleston, S.C.   Special Mention
Sheppard, Evalyne, 55 Linwood Dr., Marshall, Tex.   Special Mention
Sher, D. A., 3I5 57th St. N.W., Albuquerque, N.M.   HONORABLE MENTION
Sherman, Barbara, 899 Burks Hill, Bedford, Va.   HONORABLE MENTION
Sherman, D. D., I522 Bloomfield, Cape Girardeau, Mo.   HONORABLE MENTION
Sherman, Mrs. Ingrid, I02 Courter Ave., Yonkers, N.Y.   HONORABLE MENTION
Shimp, E. H., 737 W. State St., Newcomerstown, Ohio   Special Mention
Shinall, Linda J., Rt. 2, Cartersville, Ga.   Special Mention
Shinkle, Elsie H., I42 Loop Dr., Moses Lake, Wash.   Special Mention
Shipman, Deborah K., P.O. Box II5, Meridian, N.Y.   HONORABLE MENTION

Shockley, Jane M., 1929 Sansom St., Philadelphia, Pa. Special Mention
Shook, Gertrude G., 1105 Passolt St., Saginaw, Mich. HONORABLE MENTION
Shuff, Gladys M., 19 Bradford St., Charleston, W.Va. Special Mention
Siedzikowski, Stanley, 884 Windemere Ave., Drexel H., Pa. Special Mention
Sieloff, Jean, 9131 Paxton Ave., Chicago, Ill. HONORABLE MENTION
Sill, Shirley, Gen. Delivery, Welfare, Tex. Special Mention
Silvers, Mrs. Vicki, 2951 Ocean Ave., Brooklyn, N.Y. HONORABLE MENTION
Simmons, Melva L., 815 S. 18th St., Arlington, Va. HONORABLE MENTION
Simo, Mrs. Theodore F., 3770 E. Farr Rd., Frtpt., Mich. HONORABLE MENTION
Simones, Pamela S., 230 S. Main St., Winchester, Ind. HONORABLE MENTION
Simpson, Helen, 5916 N.W. Marine Dr., Vancvr., B.C., Can. HONORABLE MENTION
Sims, Mildred, P.O. Box 82, Pascola, Mo. HONORABLE MENTION
Sims, Shirlee P., 966 Leslie Ln., Hanford, Ca. HONORABLE MENTION
Siple, Patricia G., 5002 Holly Ct., Murrysville, Pa. Special Mention
Sirois, Robert, 10676 Bruxelles St., Montreal 459, Que., Canada Special Mention
Skinner, Maxine J., R.R. 1, Irvington, Ky. Special Mention
Skulnik, Sandra S., R.D. 2, Box 18B, Accord, N.Y. HONORABLE MENTION
Slaughter, Mrs. Delia L., 208 East St., Greensboro, Ga. HONORABLE MENTION
Slone, Henry G., 35 Le Blanc, River Rouge, Mich. Special Mention
Sluth, Helen M., 805 St. Barnard Dr., O'Fallon, Mo. HONORABLE MENTION
Smith, Mrs. Carole L., Box 106, Spruce St., Middleborough, Mass. Special Mention
Smith, D. V., 97 Spring Creek Rd., Lockport, Ill. Special Mention
Smith, Delphia F., 202 9th St., Mammoth Spring, Ark. Special Mention
Smith, Elma T., Oban, Rockley, Christ Ch., Barb., W. Ind. HONORABLE MENTION
Smith, Mrs. F. N., 332 E. 5th St., Port Angeles, Wash. HONORABLE MENTION
Smith, Mrs. Inez, 80 Wilkes St., Battle Creek, Mich. Special Mention
Smith, Joan L., 64 Cobble Hill Rd., Lincoln, R.I. HONORABLE MENTION
Smith, Mrs. John T., Rt. 3, Box 198-B, Kilgore, Tex. HONORABLE MENTION
Smith, Kathleen D., 3325 Rocky Point Rd., Bremerton, Wash. Special Mention
Smith, Leo J., R.R. 1, Cedar Valley, Ont., Canada Special Mention
Smith, Linnette, 203 S. Watkins St., Perry, Mich. Special Mention
Smith, Norman, 546 Monticello, Lakeland, Fl. HONORABLE MENTION
Smith, Philip R., 83-20 141st St., Jamaica, N.Y. HONORABLE MENTION
Smith, Mrs. Roberta H., 4936 Hpy. Hllw. Blvd., Omaha, Neb. Special Mention
Smith, Ronald H., 915 Grant St., Newell, W.Va. Special Mention
Smith, Susan M., 3114 W. 113th Pl., Chicago, Ill. HONORABLE MENTION
Smith, Mrs. T. R., 2405 S. Homer, Pittsburg, Kan. HONORABLE MENTION
Smith, Teresa, 1208 S. Crane, Independence, Mo. HONORABLE MENTION
Smith, Tina, 1344 Scenic Hwy., Baton Rouge, La. HONORABLE MENTION
Smith, W. Eugene, 1813-1 Davie Circle, Smyrna, Ga. Special Mention
Smith, Wayne E., Rt. 1, Celina, Tenn. Special Mention
Snyder, Margaret, Sycamore Acres, Ijamsville, Md. Special Mention
Socha, Edward W., 2218 Rio Grande, Austin, Tex. Special Mention
Soffa, George, Preston, Minn. Special Mention
Soifer, Mrs. Maxine R., 4 Leefield Gate, Melville, L.I., N.Y. Special Mention
Solomon, Nancy J., 22311 Frisbee, Detroit, Mich. HONORABLE MENTION
Sorrentino, Deborah, 16 Nightingale Path, Lvrpl., N.Y. HONORABLE MENTION
Sossamon, Sandra, 506 3rd St., Ozark, Ark. HONORABLE MENTION
Southard, Florence, Yaphank Rd., Middle Island, N.Y. Special Mention
Southard, Olga, 1601 Petersen St., San Jose, Ca. Special Mention
Spader, Jeanne C., 62 Silver Spring Rd., Ridgefield, Conn. Special Mention
Spangler, Donna, R.R. 1, New Bloomfield, Pa. HONORABLE MENTION
Speaks, Mrs. Sharon, Rt. 1, Box 49, Pinnacle, N.C. HONORABLE MENTION
Spear, Jay, 709 S. Locust, Greencastle, Ind. Special Mention
Spencer, Bernice, 455 Driver St., Mobile, Ala. Special Mention
Spencer, James, 5808 Durbin Rd., Bethesda, Md. HONORABLE MENTION
Spencer, Katharine C., 1122 W. 37th St., Erie, Pa. Special Mention
Spoor, Dotty, 819 N. 73rd Pl., Scottsdale, Ariz. HONORABLE MENTION
Springer, Karen, Crown Point Rd., Thorofare, N.J. HONORABLE MENTION
Squires, Gloria W., 2 Archer Ct., Middleboro, Mass. Special Mention
Srebro, Mary A., 897 Scott Rd., Dickson City, Pa. HONORABLE MENTION
Stabler, Mrs. Helen, 242 E. Pontiac St., Ft. Wayne, Ind. Special Mention
Stacy, Mrs. Wesley, R.R. 2, Box 53, Hazard, Ky. Special Mention
Stafford, Mrs. June, 4405 Morphens Lane, Sacra., Ca. HONORABLE MENTION
Stamm, D. Ruth, 3168 Cowden, Memphis, Tenn. HONORABLE MENTION

Standish, Mrs. Wm. F., 314 Briarwd. Ln., Battle Ck., Mich. HONORABLE MENTION
Stanfill, Mrs. B. J., 5641 Hibiscus Rd., Pensacola, Fl. Special Mention
Starkey, Cathleen A., Box 99, Centerpoint Rt., W. Union, W.Va. Special Mention
Staton, Mrs. Ida M., 511 Carey St., Dallas, Tex. HONORABLE MENTION
Staudinger, Margaret, 2135 Howe St., Racine, Wis. HONORABLE MENTION
Stebbing, Frank, 600 Nicoll Ave., Baltimore, Md. HONORABLE MENTION
Stechcon, Sherrie, 903 137th St. S.W., Everett, Wash. HONORABLE MENTION
Stefandes, Ann Marie, 220 Cypress St., Rochester, N.Y. HONORABLE MENTION
Steffan, Lana, 1433 Bernard Ave., Findlay, Ohio Special Mention
Steger, Laura, 35 Jonquill Ln., Kings Park, N.Y. Special Mention
Steiger, Art, 7320 Indian Boundary, Gary, Ind. HONORABLE MENTION
Steitz, Joanne M., 29 Brock St., Rochester, N.H. Special Mention
Steller, Glen V., 1420 W. Abingdon Dr., Alexandria, Va. Special Mention
Stelzer, Mrs. Charlotte A., 1121 W. Boulevard, Lewistown, Mont. Special Mention
Stenvall, Mrs. Edith, 6111 S. 124th, Seattle, Wash. HONORABLE MENTION
Stevens, Lee A., 5 Maxfield Ct., Barrington, R.I. Special Mention
Stevenson, Mabel B., 188 W. Raleigh Ave., Mansfield, Ohio Special Mention
Stigall, Sandy, Rt. I, Box 6A, Bracey, Va. Special Mention
Stilgenbauer, Jacqueline, 339 Milford Dr., Corona d. M., Ca. Special Mention
Stilwell, Margaret W., P.O. Box 623, Wendell, N.C. Special Mention
Stinson, Ronald D., Box 359A, Fordham Rd., Sag Harbor, N.Y. Special Mention
Stinson, Virginia E., 8637 S. Lemon Rd., Bancroft, Mich. HONORABLE MENTION
Stockton, Mrs. Philip, 22 Church St., Charleston, S.C. HONORABLE MENTION
Stone, Mrs. Janet, 4617 8th, Ecorse, Mich. Special Mention
Stone, Suzanne, 2194 Barnes Ave., Bronx, N.Y. Special Mention
Stone, Wilburt, 1490 Springbrook Rd., Walnut Creek, Ca. Special Mention
Stonerock, Linda E., 1568 Selkirk Rd., Dayton, Ohio HONORABLE MENTION
Strangman, Mrs. Emily G., 247 Adams St., Milton, Mass. HONORABLE MENTION
Strobel, Mrs. Patricia C., 4205 S. 36th St., Arlington, Va. Special Mention
Strobino, Gaston M., 14642 Keystone Ave., Midlothian, Ill. Special Mention
Stuart, Eugene W., 61 S. 5th St., Fulton, N.Y. HONORABLE MENTION
Stump, Mrs. Loretta, R.R. I, Pierceton, Ind. Special Mention
Sullivan, Blanche, 2200 Harrison Ave., Eureka, Ca. Special Mention
Sullivan, Irma V., 228 Riverside Dr., Canon City, Colo. HONORABLE MENTION
Sullivan, Mrs. Lillian E., Box C320, Miami, Fl. Special Mention
Svinicki, Mary L., Box 35, Stephenson, Mich. HONORABLE MENTION
Swanner, Carol T., 2438 Lauradale Dr., New Orleans, La. HONORABLE MENTION
Sylvia, Davidd, 410 Loftus St., New Bedford, Mass. HONORABLE MENTION
Symms, Peggy, Rt. I, Box 63B, Jasper, Tex. Special Mention

=T=

Tal, Phillip J., 94 Butlertown Rd., Waterford, Conn. Special Mention
Talley, Mrs. M. Lee, 1713 Brentwood, Austin, Tex. Special Mention
Tammaro, Muriel H., P.O. Box 373, Ridgefield, Conn. HONORABLE MENTION
Tarrant, Lucy E., 1423 Hochwalt Ave., Dayton, Ohio HONORABLE MENTION
Tate, Jerry C., 2626 Robertson Dr., Abilene, Tex. HONORABLE MENTION
Tate, Marvin, 5105 N. Gillette, Appleton, Wis. HONORABLE MENTION
Taylor, Ann, 13253 Earl Ave., Baldwin Park, Ca. Special Mention
Taylor, Mrs. Donna, Hamilton, Colo. HONORABLE MENTION
Taylor, Kathy, 11529 Mina Ave., Whittier, Ca. HONORABLE MENTION
Terapak, Mary, 5312 E. Southern Ave., Indianapolis, Ind. HONORABLE MENTION
Terrana, Patricia, 11023 Landseer Dr., St. Louis, Mo. Special Mention
Terry, Mrs. Elouise, 204 Orange St., Oxford, N.C. Special Mention
Terry, Mrs. James, 226 S. Randlett, Hobart, Okla. HONORABLE MENTION
Terry, Roxey P., 1960 W. Broad St., Columbus, Ohio HONORABLE MENTION
Teslevich, John C., 4747 S. Spring, St. Louis, Mo. HONORABLE MENTION
Thayer, Mrs. Edna C., 225 Eason Ave., Detroit, Mich. HONORABLE MENTION
Thayer, Richard C., 111 Franklin, Greenfield, Mass. HONORABLE MENTION
Thomae, Betty K., 635 Wedgewood Dr., Colum., Ohio HONORABLE MENTION
Thomas, Abraham, 1816 Crotona Park E., Bronx, N.Y. Special Mention
Thomas, Elaine, 1314 Carver Rd., Modesto, Ca. HONORABLE MENTION
Thomas, Lillie M., P.O. Box 10003, Station D, 40210 Special Mention
Thomas, Marzetta W., 729 Staunton Ave. N.W., Roanoke, Va. Special Mention
Thomas, Willie, 1212 E. Renfro St., Plant City, Fl. Special Mention

Thompson, Mrs. J. A., Box 514, Vero Beach, Fl.   Special Mention
Thompson, Loretta, 313 B N. Huron St., Cheboygan, Mich.   Special Mention
Thompson, Yolanda K., P.O. Box 97, Springerville, Ariz.   Special Mention
Thornton, Evelyn B., 2438 Lauradale Dr., N. Orl., La.   HONORABLE MENTION
Throgmorton, Diana, R.R. 2, Marion, Ill.   HONORABLE MENTION
Tillery, Judy, 803 Rutland Dr., Dublin, Ga.   Special Mention
Titt, Kenneth W., P.O. Box 412, Van Vleck, Tex.   HONORABLE MENTION
Titus, Carolyn A., 344 Quincy Ave., Bronx, N.Y.   HONORABLE MENTION
Toal, Stanley, 208 Harmony Ln., McComb, Miss.   HONORABLE MENTION
Tochluk, Lena J., 316 W. Baltimore, Las Vegas, Nev.   Special Mention
Toland, Allie R., 1028 Crescent Ln., Wichita Falls, Tex. Special Mention
Toler, Shirley F., 4802 Honeysuckle Ln., Pasadena, Tex.   HONORABLE MENTION
Tomek, Mrs. William, Box 340, R.D. I, Coplay, Pa.   HONORABLE MENTION
Torstrick, Pearl C., 432 W. Stansifer Ave., Clarksville, Ind.   Special Mention
Totten, Mrs. Dan, 400 Harker Ave., Newell, W.Va.   Special Mention
Towich, Thomas N., 543 N. Silk St., Allentown, Pa.   HONORABLE MENTION
Tribble, Mrs. Frances W., 312 Dawnridge Dr., Lynch., Va. HONORABLE MENTION
Trombetta, Mrs. J., 1036 74th St., Brooklyn, N.Y.   HONORABLE MENTION
Troth, Mrs. John V., 209 Monroe Ave., Peoria Hts., Ill.   HONORABLE MENTION
Trowbridge, Mrs. Cecil, R.D. I, Randolph St., Gt. Bd., Pa. HONORABLE MENTION
Tucci, Albert F., 103 Palmer St., Arlington, Mass.   HONORABLE MENTION
Tucker, Ray A., 6218 41st St., Tampa, Fl.   HONORABLE MENTION
Turk, Darlene, 6020 Holly Valley, Toledo, Ohio   HONORABLE MENTION
Turk, Linda L., 6020 Holly Valley, Toledo, Ohio   Special Mention
Turner, Helen, 4812 Pine Tree Dr., Miami Beach, Fl.   Special Mention
Turner, Margo, 618 W. Chesapeake Ave., Towson, Md.   Special Mention
Turner, Veryl K., R. 4, Marshall Woods, Sevierville, Tenn. Special Mention
Tuttle, Leonard G., 814 W. Alma, Milwaukee, Wis.   Special Mention

=U=

Ubelhor, Aline, 7601 Old Boonville Hwy., Evnsvle., Ind.   HONORABLE MENTION
Uhlir, Wesley D., 2417 Gillen St., Racine, Wis.   HONORABLE MENTION
Unangst, Florence B., 88 Church Ave., Brooklyn, N.Y.   Special Mention
Utne, Betty Lou,,Rt. I, Box 292, Prior Lake, Minn.   HONORABLE MENTION

=V=

Valentine, Ralph N., 207 W. Ethel St., Lombard, Ill.   HONORABLE MENTION
Van Alstine, Florence, Rt. I, Dimondale, Mich.   Special Mention
Van Atta, Mrs. Helen M., R.R. I, St. Louisville, Ohio   Special Mention
Van Valkenburg, Eileen, 66 Raiano St., Torring., Conn.   HONORABLE MENTION
Van Wormer, William, 20 Gail Dr., L.I., N.Y.   HONORABLE MENTION
Varner, Neil, Rt. I, Midland, Mich.   Special Mention
Varney, Mrs. Virginia, 513 E. San Juan, Phoenix, Ariz.   HONORABLE MENTION
Vaughn, Gwyn, 1603 Linden Ave., Nashville, Tenn.   HONORABLE MENTION
Vedder, Evea D., 17 Lisa Ln., Kingston, N.Y.   HONORABLE MENTION
Vetowich, Karen, 28735 W. 10 Mile Rd., Farmington, Mich. Special Mention
Vetowich, Mrs. Martha, 28735 W. 10 Mile Rd., Fa., M.   HONORABLE MENTION
Villa, MaryAnn E., 101 Laurel St., Malden, Mass.   Special Mention
Vinch, David A., 343 Caflisch Hall, Meadville, Pa.   HONORABLE MENTION
Vladovich, Violet, 1000 N.W. 21st St., Okla. City, Okla. Special Mention
Voaden, Kathleen M., 4851 S. 24th St., Greenfield, Wis. Special Mention
Vocke, Elizabeth, 2564 Carswell, Omaha, Neb.   HONORABLE MENTION
Volpe, Margie, D., 12 Marhsall St., Irvington, N.J.   HONORABLE MENTION
Von Abele, Barbara, 333 S. Glebe Rd., Arlington, Va.   Special Mention
Von Farra, Mary M., 132 Gullott Dr., Schenectady, N.Y.   Special Mention
Vrabel, Doris, Rt. 2, Box 516, Hartland, Wis.   Special Mention
Vyhnalek, Karen, 12963 Atlantic Rd., Strongsville, Ohio Special Mention
Vyskocil, Mrs. Normajean, 12022 Shady Oak, G. Hts., Ohio Special Mention

= W =

Wagner, Donald W., 4425 Rosemont, Houston, Tex.   HONORABLE MENTION
Wagner, Mrs. Marje, 812 Lincoln Ave., Ft. Payne, Ala.   Special Mention

Wahl, Jo-Ann B., 704 S. Arlington Ave., Harrisburg, Pa. — Special Mention
Walden, Carla R., 5221 Sun Valley Dr., El Paso, Tex. — Special Mention
Walden, Pearl, Box 10, Hutchins, Tex. — Special Mention
Walker, Christopher, DePauw Univ., Greencastle, Ind. — HONORABLE MENTION
Walker, David R., 10 Leeward La., Rochester, N.Y. — HONORABLE MENTION
Walker, Lisa A., 11 Sulgrave Rd., Savannah, Ga. — HONORABLE MENTION
Walker, Orpha, 1980 S. Oak Grove, Springfield, Mo. — HONORABLE MENTION
Walkes, Erica, 211 South View, Oceana, Ill. — Special Mention
Wall, Isabelle M., 6817 Newell St., Huntington Park, Ca. — HONORABLE MENTION
Wallace, Alice M., 937 Sunflower Rd., Rochester, Pa. — Special Mention
Wallace, Mrs. Josephine L., P.O. Box 252, Pine Mt., Ga. — HONORABLE MENTION
Wallerstein, Sheila, 117B Minebrook Rd., Edison, N.J. — HONORABLE MENTION
Waltner, Alta R., Box 1644, Taos, N.M. — HONORABLE MENTION
Wardish, Mrs. Anna, P.O. Box 1065, Sunnyvale, Ca. — Special Mention
Wardrobe, John, 406 Linden St., Reno, Nev. — HONORABLE MENTION
Warshauer, Larry, 279 E. 203rd St., Bronx, N.Y. — HONORABLE MENTION
Wartt, Grace E., 709 Milan St., New Orleans, La. — HONORABLE MENTION
Waters, Gloria F., 317 Alta Vista Ter., Creve Coeur, Ill. — Special Mention
Watson, Judy C., Box 36, Pasadena College, Pasadena, Ca. — HONORABLE MENTION
Watson, Theresa, 4036 Gilman Ave., Louisville, Ky. — HONORABLE MENTION
Wayne, Mrs. George H., 18207 Stewart Ave., Homwd., Ill. — HONORABLE MENTION
Weber, Mrs. Lela K., 1733 Louis Ln., Bogalusa, La. — HONORABLE MENTION
Weidacher, Clare M., RFD 1, Lancaster, N.H. — Special Mention
Weigner, Marsha, 9 Oswego Ave., White Meadow Lake, Rock., N.J. — Special Mention
Weiner, Laurie, 1940 N.E. 186th Dr., N. Miami Bch., Fl. — HONORABLE MENTION
Weisser, Paula, 265 Hobson St., Newark, N.J. — HONORABLE MENTION
Welch, Mrs. Mary, 1687 175th St., Hammond, Ind. — HONORABLE MENTION
Welke, Susan, Rt. 2, Menomonie, Wis. — Special Mention
Weller, Jessie E., 11645 S.W. Pac. Hwy., Tigard, Ore. — Special Mention
Wells, Sharon, P.O. Box 69, Frisco, Tex. — HONORABLE MENTION
Wenzel, Mrs. Bertha, Rt. A-2, Box 317, Dunnellon, Fl. — Special Mention
Wenzel, Susan H., 1306 Broad St., Oshkosh, Wis. — Special Mention
Werling, Mrs. Orvil, R.R. 2, Ossian, Ind. — HONORABLE MENTION
Wertz, Betty, Warfordsburg, Pa. — HONORABLE MENTION
West, James M., 54 Aspen Dr., Jackson, Tenn. — HONORABLE MENTION
Westhoven, Vincent P., St. Martin's Chapel, Ft. Bel., Va. — HONORABLE MENTION
Westover, Mrs. Janice, 3851 Highview S.W., Canton, Ohio — Special Mention
Westrick, Mrs. Elsie, 15769 Imlay Cty. Rd., Capac, Mich. — HONORABLE MENTION
Wetzel, Sandra R., 1327 14th St., Bismarck, N.D. — HONORABLE MENTION
Whaley, Anna J., 250 S. Main St., Freeport, N.Y. — Special Mention
Wheeler, Eunice, Rt. 1, Box 22A, Alum Creek, W.Va. — Special Mention
Wheeler, Everlene, 23 W. Hunter St., Sumter, S.C. — Special Mention
Wheeler, W. Blaine, 2135 E. Skelly, Apt. 115, Tulsa, Okla. — HONORABLE MENTION
White, Madeleine, 885 Jefferson Ave., Memphis, Tenn. — HONORABLE MENTION
White, Marion G., P.O. Box 1847, Odessa, Tex. — HONORABLE MENTION
White, Raymond V. I., 8553 S. Drexel Ave., Chicago, Ill. — HONORABLE MENTION
White, Timothy B., 1304 N. Rock Island, Angleton, Tex. — HONORABLE MENTION
Whitehouse, Mrs. Elsie, 82 3rd Ave., Newark, N.J. — Special Mention
Whitfield, Laura, 4406 S. Oakenwald, Chicago, Ill. — Special Mention
Whitman, Patricia, Richville, Minn. — HONORABLE MENTION
Whitney, Dorothy E., 20 Dorchester Ave., Asheville, N.C. — Special Mention
Whitten, Roberta, 2308 Fulton St., Aurora, Colo. — HONORABLE MENTION
Wier, Susan G., 410 10th N.W., Ardmore, Okla. — Special Mention
Wigby, Signe, 3440 Fulton Ave., Sacramento, Ca. — HONORABLE MENTION
Wimpy, Vivian, 1516 Southern Heights, Norman, Okla. — Special Mention
Wilcox, Mrs. Fred, North Branch, Minn. — HONORABLE MENTION
Wilcox, Ida E., 39574 Grand Ave., Beaumont, Ca. — HONORABLE MENTION
Wilkes, Rose M., 13345 N.W. 22nd Ave., Miami, Fl. — Special Mention
Williams, Bernice, 30604 W. Sullivan Rd., Gustine, Ca. — Special Mention
Williams, Cynthia, 5000 O'Neil Blvd., Lorain, Ohio — HONORABLE MENTION
Williams, Dorothy, 557 E. Tower, Fresno, Ca. — HONORABLE MENTION
Williams, George M., MCAS, Beaufort, S.C. — HONORABLE MENTION
Williams, Mrs. Martha, P.O. Box 283, Seneca, Pa. — HONORABLE MENTION
Williams, Mary L., 178 Victoria St., St. John, N.B., Canada — Special Mention
Williams, Teeny, 413 W. 7th St., Florence, Kan. — Special Mention

Williams, William E., 13030 W. 99th St., Lenexa, Kan.   Special Mention
Williamson, Fredrica, 1116 Pacific, Osawatomie, Kan.   HONORABLE MENTION
Willoughby, Myrtle, 1216 S. 12th, Parsons, Kan.   HONORABLE MENTION
Wilmoth, Sondra K., 1510 Newman Ave., Lakewood, Ohio HONORABLE MENTION
Wilson, Mrs. Donna, 195 S. G St., Porterville, Ca.   HONORABLE MENTION
Wilson, Elaine, 9-1111 Apple Dr., Mechanicsburg, Pa.   HONORABLE MENTION
Wilson, Irene, 343 Williston Rd., Sagamore Beach, Mass.   HONORABLE MENTION
Wilson, Nan, 45 W. 70th St., Apt. B, N.Y., N.Y.   HONORABLE MENTION
Windisch, Eva P., 289 5th St. N.W., Barberton, Ohio   HONORABLE MENTION
Winter, Robert H., 502 Patterson Rd., Bethel Park, Pa.   HONORABLE MENTION
Wise, Howard L., Box 531, Davis, W.Va.   Special Mention
Wise, John H., 241 Noble Ave., Montgomery, Ala.   HONORABLE MENTION
Withers, James, 39 Hester St., Piermont, N.Y.   Special Mention
Witt, Allen A., P.O. Box 75, Lake City, Fl.   HONORABLE MENTION
Wohnson, II, Fredric E., 1027 Quebec Ter., Sil. Sprg., Md. HONORABLE MENTION
Wolbrink, Marthe A., Box 507, Wellsburg, Iowa   Special Mention
Wolfskill, Edna M., 1108 N. Monterey St., Alhambra, Ca.   Special Mention
Womer, Victoria, Box 58, Planting Fields, Oyster Bay, L.I., N.Y.   Special Mention
Wood, Mrs. Jean, 2 Stone Villa, Burlington, N.J.   HONORABLE MENTION
Woodland, Wendy A., 3917 76th St., Urbandale, Des Moines, Iowa Special Mention
Woolsey, Jeanne, 8609 Flower Ave., Takoma Park, Md.   Special Mention
Wootten, Gary, 1607 Smead St., Logansport, Ind.   HONORABLE MENTION
Wright, Don, 733 E. 29th St., Erie, Pa.   Special Mention
Wright, Genevieve, Cordelia Dr., N. Little Rock, Ark.   HONORABLE MENTION
Wright, Mildred E., 550 School St., Cloverdale, Ca.   HONORABLE MENTION
Wynn, Barbara, 1142 34th Street, Newport News, Va.   Special Mention

=Y=

Yarbrough, Janet A., 490 Waldemere, Bridgeport, Conn.   HONORABLE MENTION
Yeomans, Hazel M., Box 414, Mancos, Colo.   HONORABLE MENTION
Yoke, Thomas W., P.O. Box 3, Dellslow, W.Va.   HONORABLE MENTION
Yomer, Mrs. Myrtle F., 427 Prospect Ave., Horsham, Pa. HONORABLE MENTION
Young, Ann, 1128 Bayshore Ave., Bayshore, N.Y.   Special Mention
Young, Irene, Box 11192, W. Ga. College, Carrollton, Ga.   Special Mention
Young, III, James A., 998 Bockman Rd., San Lorenzo, Ca.HONORABLE MENTION
Young, LaVerne M., Box 933, Torrington, Wy.   HONORABLE MENTION
Young, Nancy D., 20801 S. Woodward Ave., Manteca, Ca.   Special Mention
Young, Patricia J., 2918 8th Ave., Huntington, W.Va.   HONORABLE MENTION
Young, Mrs. Pearl, 315 W. Belle Mead, Meade, Kan.   Special Mention
Yount, Mrs. Larue, 100 Arthur St., Kittanning, Pa.   HONORABLE MENTION

=Z=

Zammetti, Diane M., 38 Kennedy Ave., N. Babylon, N.Y.   Special Mention
Zeiss, Rita S., 680 Fairway Dr., Union, N.J.   HONORABLE MENTION
Zelnick, Barbara, 267 Pringle St., Kingston, Pa.   HONORABLE MENTION
Zewan, Dean, 707 Beaver Hall, Pa. St. Univ., Un. Pk., Pa. HONORABLE MENTION
Zimmerman, Janet, Box 125, Geneva, Ind.   Special Mention
Zimmerman, Richard, 18-15 215th St., Bayside, N.Y.   HONORABLE MENTION
Zoladz, Ken, 59 N. Wisconsin St., Hobart, Ind.   Special Mention

End of Awards

The 1969 International Poetry Competition was sponsored by
CLOVER PUBLISHING COMPANY
WASHINGTON, D. C. 20008
October 15, 1968 to February 14, 1969

–POETS–

In making verse we are employed–
        –Underpaid but overjoyed!
                                Aspira